NATIONALISM AND THE RULE OF LAW

The relationship between nationalism and the rule of law has been largely neglected by scholars despite the fact that, separately, they have often captured public discourse and emerged as critical concepts for the social sciences. This book provides the first systematic account of this relationship. The book develops an analytical framework for understanding the interactions of nationalism and the rule of law by focusing on the domains of citizenship, transitional justice, and international justice, and engages these insights further in a detailed empirical analysis of three case studies from the former Yugoslavia. The author argues that although the tensions and contradictions between nationalism and the rule of law have become more apparent in the post–Cold War era, they can also be harnessed for productive purposes. In exploring the role of law in managing and transforming nationalism, the book emphasizes the deliberative character of legal processes and offers an original perspective on the power of international law to reshape public discourse, politics, and legal orders.

Iavor Rangelov is Global Security Research Fellow at the London School of Economics and Political Science and Co-Chair of the London Transitional Justice Network.

Nationalism and the Rule of Law

LESSONS FROM THE BALKANS AND BEYOND

Iavor Rangelov

London School of Economics and Political Science

CAMBRIDGE
UNIVERSITY PRESS

CAMBRIDGE
UNIVERSITY PRESS

32 Avenue of the Americas, New York, NY 10013-2473, USA

Cambridge University Press is part of the University of Cambridge.

It furthers the University's mission by disseminating knowledge in the pursuit of
education, learning, and research at the highest international levels of excellence.

www.cambridge.org
Information on this title: www.cambridge.org/9781107012196

© Iavor Rangelov 2014

First published 2014

Printed in the United States of America

A catalog record for this publication is available from the British Library.

Library of Congress Cataloging in Publication data
Rangelov, Iavor, 1977–
Nationalism and the rule of law : lessons from the Balkans and beyond / Iavor Rangelov,
London School of Economics and Political Science.
   pages   cm
Includes bibliographical references and index.
ISBN 978-1-107-01219-6 (hardback)
1. Rule of law – Europe.   2. Transitional justice – Europe.   3. Nationalism –
Europe.   4. International criminal law – Europe   5. Yugoslav War, 1991–1995 – Law and
legislation.   6. Transitional justice – Former Yugolsav republics.   I. Title.
KJC4426.R36   2013
342.08'3–dc23   2013018458

ISBN 978-1-107-01219-6 Hardback

For my parents

CONTENTS

ACKNOWLEDGMENTS

I am deeply grateful to a number of colleagues, friends, and institutions for making this book possible. Mary Kaldor first encouraged me to pursue doctoral studies at the London School of Economics and Political Science (LSE) nearly a decade ago and ever since, working with her on this and other projects has been a fascinating journey of intellectual exploration and discovery. Nataša Kandić generously shared her unique insight into the issues I was grappling with in the Balkans; in the end, our collaboration enabled me to become a participant in many of the processes in the region I was studying. Nicola Lacey encouraged me to engage with law and lawyers and gave me the reassurance and support I needed to cross disciplinary boundaries. I have accumulated enormous debts of gratitude to all of them in the course of writing this book and thank them warmly.

My research on the Balkans was shaped by countless conversations and interactions across the region, some of which have developed into great friendships. The Humanitarian Law Center in Belgrade and its dedicated staff provided a most hospitable base for conducting my field research in Serbia and extending it throughout the region. Jelka Zorn helped me secure key contacts and materials in Slovenia and spent long hours discussing my ideas in the cafés of Ljubljana. Tvrtko Jakovina was incredibly generous with his time and connections in Zagreb and enriched my research with his insightful reflections on the history of Yugoslavia. The Fellows of the Faculty Development in South East Europe Programme at the LSE were always available to meet with me and discuss the issues I had on my mind whenever they were in London or I was in the region. I am grateful to them and everyone else in the Balkans who engaged with me formally and informally, and often repeatedly, in the course of conducting my research.

Many friends and colleagues provided critical feedback on different parts and versions of the material presented in the book. They are in no way responsible for any lapses in judgment or knowledge. For their advice and comments I am grateful to Amélie Barras, Steve Bell, Saša Drezgić, Mohanad Hage-Ali, David Held, Rob Howse, Milanka Šaponja-Hadžić, Gerry Simpson, Jelena Stevančević, Marika Theros, and Kristian Ulrichsen. At the LSE, I have benefited from endless discussions in the Nationalism seminars run by John Breuilly and John Hutchinson, and with colleagues in the departments of Government and International Development and the Centre for the Study of Global Governance. I would like to express my appreciation for the enthusiastic support of my editor, John Berger. The book owes a great deal to his faith in the project and expert guidance in seeing it through. Pippa Bore provided invaluable assistance at the final stages of producing the book, for which I thank her warmly.

I have been fortunate to present my ideas to diverse audiences over the years and these engagements shaped my evolving thinking and enriched my work immensely. I am grateful to the organizations and institutions that invited me to participate in conferences, seminars, and workshops: Association for the Study of Ethnicity and Nationalism at the LSE; Association for the Study of Nationalities at Columbia University; Cambridge University; European Policy Centre; Humanitarian Law Center, Belgrade; Institute for European Studies, FU Brussels; Instituto Affari Internazionali; International Studies Association; Inter-University Center, Dubrovnik; King's College London; Lund University; Minerva Center for Human Rights, Hebrew University; Osteuropa-Institut, FU Berlin; Oxford University; Renner Institute; Südosteuropa-Gesellschaft; University of Gothenburg; University of Ljubljana; University of Sarajevo; and University of Zagreb. My students at the LSE and the University of Sarajevo have often been my most stimulating and challenging critics over the years. I thank them for shaping the ideas in this book and I am sure they will recognize their influence.

I gratefully acknowledge the generous financial support for my doctoral studies provided by the Department of Government at the

LSE and the Open Society Institute. My field research in Slovenia was funded by the Central Research Fund of the University of London. In Croatia and Serbia, field research conducted for a related project and funded by the Charles Stuart Mott Foundation was crucial for advancing my work on the book. I am also grateful to the research and training program European Foreign & Security Policy Studies, funded by Riksbankens Jubileumsfond, Compagnia di San Paolo, and VolkswagenStiftung, which supported my postdoctoral research and visiting fellowships at the European Policy Centre in Brussels, EU Institute for Security Studies in Paris, Institut Barcelona d'Estudis Internacionals, and T.M.C. Asser Instituut in The Hague.

I owe the greatest debt of all to my parents, Elena and Percho, to whom this book is dedicated.

INTRODUCTION

The idea for this book was born nearly a decade ago in Belgrade. I was monitoring the trial of Saša Cvjetan at Belgrade District Court, the first serious attempt by the Serbian judiciary to confront the legacy of war crimes from the Kosovo crisis. The defendant was prosecuted for his role in a massacre in Podujevo, which involved the killing of eighteen ethnic Albanian civilians by members of the Scorpions, a notorious irregular unit implicated in some of the worst atrocities of the Balkan wars in the 1990s. The proceedings were highly dramatic and their outcome remained uncertain until the very end. The courtroom was packed with Cvjetan's fellow Scorpions, who looked like thugs but acted like national heroes, confident that they had the Serbian state and public on their side. The presiding judge was subjected to various forms of intimidation throughout the trial, including anonymous death threats. A local human rights group managed to convince several Albanian witnesses to come to Belgrade to testify, some of them children who had survived the massacre and subsequently relocated to the United Kingdom, and worked closely with the police to ensure protection for the key insider witness – a former member of the Scorpions, who provided a shocking account of the massacre.

On 17 March 2004, the defendant was convicted and sentenced to twenty years in prison. The decision was significant, not only as a step toward strengthening the rule of law in Serbia but also as a statement that challenged the accepted narratives of Serbian nationalism, which often portrayed the Kosovo campaign as an antiterrorist operation and emphasized war crimes committed on the Albanian side of the conflict. That same day, however, the local media were preoccupied

1

with another story and had little time to ponder the significance of the judgment. Rumors blaming Serbs for the drowning of two Albanian children in the Ibar River had sparked violent unrest across Kosovo. In the course of the next couple of days, large Albanian crowds attacked Serbs and other minorities in more than thirty locations in Kosovo, causing several deaths, extensive property destruction, and a wave of expulsions. The riots soon spread to the streets of Serbian cities; in one incident I witnessed, an angry mob of several hundred set fire to the historic Bajrakli Mosque in the old quarters of Belgrade.

These events were unfolding five years after the end of the war over Kosovo. At a time when the rule of law seemed to provide an answer to the excesses of nationalism, the resurgence of nationalist passions and ethnic violence posed the most significant challenge to law and order since the end of the war. Understanding such contradictory developments presented an intellectual puzzle and raised a set of questions that have preoccupied me ever since, prompting and guiding the investigation that informed this book. What is the relationship between nationalism and the rule of law? Are they mutually reinforcing or conflicting? What conditions may favor one outcome over another? Are there fundamental tensions that are inherent in their interrelationship? How are such tensions managed and negotiated in practice and could they be harnessed for any productive purposes? Answering these questions requires a broader framework, which emphasizes the "deliberative" character of legal processes and takes seriously the role of law as a vehicle for public debate.

THE LACUNA IN THE LITERATURE

The relationship between nationalism and the rule of law has been largely neglected by scholars despite the fact that separately, they have often captured public discourse and political imagination in recent decades and have emerged as critical concepts for the social sciences. Since the end of the Cold War, nationalism has been invoked to reconfigure the political map of large parts of the world and has become implicated in pressing global problems, from the resurgence of ethnic conflict to the growing pressures on citizenship in an era of intensified migration and pervasive identity politics. At the same time, the rule of law has emerged as perhaps the only universally shared political ideal and a cornerstone of domestic and international policy in promoting peace, democracy, and development. The study of nationalism has developed into a well-established, multidisciplinary field, equipped with its own academic journals, international associations, and annual conventions. The rule of law literature has moved well beyond its traditional base in legal and political theory, reflecting the growing preoccupation of social scientists with rule of law issues and the emergence of an entire "industry" that seeks to promote, rebuild, and reform the rule of law around the world. And yet, a sustained examination of the relationship between nationalism and the rule of law has remained outside the scholarly lens. Comprehensive discussions of the history, theory, and politics of nationalism barely mention the rule of law, whereas similar explorations of the rule of law often completely ignore the semantics of nations and nationalism.[1] Thinking about possible explanations for the gap in the literature is an appropriate starting point for an investigation that seeks to address it.

One problem with the literature is the "methodological nationalism" that can be detected in much of the scholarship on the rule of law – the tendency to treat the nation-state as the natural unit of analysis and to assume that "nation" and "state" are in fact congruent. This tendency can be explained in part by the influence of a long tradition of the rule of law ideal that goes back to its classic origins in Greek and Roman thought, which has been concerned first and foremost with restraining state tyranny (Tamanaha 2004). The rule of law is preoccupied with the relationship between state and society to the extent that law imposes limits on the exercise of power by sovereigns and government officials, rather than with the relationship between cultural and political units. That such units are coextensive is assumed in accounts that emphasize the formal or procedural aspects of the rule of law but also in substantive conceptions, which often depend on the existence of a moral community to justify claims that the rule of law expresses certain moral and political principles inherent in the community. Nations

---

[1] See, for example, Smith (2001) and Tamanaha (2004). For a rare exception, see some of the essays in Fitzpatrick (1995).

are the main contenders for the role of such moral communities in the modern era, but they are also a source of moral pluralism, which nationalism both expresses and seeks to overcome. Thus, nations and nationalism potentially create as many problems for rule of law theory as they may be able to solve. Margaret Canovan (1996) argues that many political theorists tacitly assume an existing nation-state while rejecting nationhood on principle; theorists of the rule of law often presuppose an existing nation-state while avoiding the issues raised by nations and nationalism altogether.

Another challenge is the current division of labor in the literature on nationalism. As Anthony Smith (1998: 225) points out, "the study of nations and nationalism is rent with deep schisms." The field has been contested by modernist, ethno-symbolist, and critical approaches and theories of nationalism for several decades, which continue to animate much of the scholarly debate. Another schism, however, may be more important for grasping the lack of sustained examination of the relationship between nationalism and the rule of law in the literature: the distinction between analytical and normative approaches to nationalism. The tendency to segregate scholarly work by keeping norms and analysis separate in the study of nationalism discourages engagement with concepts like the rule of law, which is a political ideal and requires grappling with normative claims as well as social processes and practices.

The study of nationalism struggles to navigate the interface of norms and analysis and often conflates them in ways that cannot withstand critical scrutiny. This can be observed, for example, in debates over classification. The opposition between "civic" and "ethnic" nationalism is pervasive in the literature and has been rearticulated in a number of related typologies, such as "political" and "cultural" or "voluntarist" and "organicist" understandings of nationalism. An early version of the debate goes back to the 1882 lecture of Ernest Renan, who famously challenged the ethnolinguistic conception of nationhood: "A nation's existence is, if you will pardon the metaphor, a daily plebiscite, just as the individual's existence is a perpetual affirmation of life" (Renan 1990: 12). The opposition of civic and ethnic nationalism was developed by Hans Kohn (1944) and embedded in his account of Western and Eastern versions of modernity, taken up by

Anthony Smith (1986) in his discussion of "territorial" and "ethnic" conceptions of the nation, and later revived in the work of Michael Ignatieff (1994). And yet, as critics have pointed out, the civic-ethnic distinction is ridden with analytical and normative ambiguity. Rogers Brubaker (2004a), for example, notes that if "ethnic" is taken to denote "descent," ethnic nationalism would be defined out of existence, but if it denotes "culture," it would incorporate virtually all nationalisms. He argues that the distinction is overdrawn but also normatively loaded, and detects an attempt to legitimate certain (Western) nationalisms as liberal and inclusive while dismissing others as illiberal and exclusive.[2]

The normative aspects of nationalism are confronted head on by political theorists. Such accounts often strive to reconcile the claims of nationalism with the requirements of liberal democracy. Theorists of liberal nationalism reinterpret the relationship between culture and politics by aligning cultural communities horizontally in an overarching political framework (Tamir 1993), or positing an overarching identity that binds together culturally diverse groups in the polity (Miller 1995). Multiculturalists, on the other hand, point out that the "civic" nationalism of liberal states does not prevent them from privileging the culture of dominant majorities and diffusing it as a national culture. Some advocate supplementing liberal frameworks with group-specific rights and self-government for national minorities with a distinct "societal culture" (Kymlicka 1995), whereas others favor a "multiculturally constituted" culture that emerges from the pervasive encounters and interactions of different cultures in society (Parekh 2000). Such normative accounts, however, are always embedded in empirical analysis of the conditions that prevail in particular states and the dilemmas that confront their citizens. The liberal nationalism of David Miller (1995) reflects the circumstances of the contemporary United States, while the account of Yael Tamir (1993) is informed by the dilemmas faced by Israel; the multiculturalism of Will Kymlicka (1995) is preoccupied with Quebec and pulls in a different direction from Bhikhu Parekh's (2000) concerns with Britain.

All these approaches bear out the difficulties of managing the normative-analytical interface in the study of nations and nationalism, and

---

[2] See also the discussion of Kohn's original distinction in Calhoun (2007: 117–146).

suggest that there is no easy answer for resolving the underlying tensions. An inquiry into the relationship of nationalism and the rule of law inevitably encounters these challenges, perhaps even more so given the inherent normativity of the rule of law ideal itself. My approach is to acknowledge such challenges as much as possible without allowing them to stifle the investigation. Throughout the book, an effort is made to recognize the normativity of the issues at stake and to integrate it into the analysis. One way of doing this involves highlighting the role of nationalism and the rule of law in the legitimation of political order, and treating legitimacy as a critical concept that helps illuminate the complex interrelationship between nationalism and the rule of law.

NATIONALISM, LEGITIMACY, AND THE RULE OF LAW

Although the study of nationalism and the rule of law literature have not been engaged in a productive dialogue, there are interesting parallels in the way they regard the significance of their respective subjects of study. In one of the classic surveys of nationalism, Anthony Smith describes nationalism as the dominant principle of legitimation of the state and the international order in the second half of the twentieth century, and underscores the "near universal acceptance of 'nationalist' propositions as the sole grounds for the exercise of state power" (Smith 2001: 120). In his seminal study on the rule of law, Brian Tamanaha argues that the idea of adherence to the rule of law has universal appeal and the rule of law stands as "*the* preeminent legitimating political ideal in the world today" (Tamanaha 2004: 4; emphasis in the original). There is more in these assertions than a self-referential bias about the importance of one's own subject of study. By emphasizing the legitimating functions of nationalism and the rule of law, such claims draw attention to the importance of legitimacy as a central dynamic that needs to be examined in seeking to understand their interrelationship.

Investigating the interactions of nationalism and the rule of law through the prism of legitimacy requires some conceptual clarifications. My approach to nationalism is aligned with scholars who acknowledge that the multiplicity of nationalist ideologies, movements, and projects cannot be comprehended and done justice to in treating "nationalism" as a single phenomenon, but nevertheless emphasize the significance of a common rhetoric that holds this multiplicity together in the "discourse of nationalism" (Calhoun 1997: 21–22; Özkirimli 2000: 228–230). All forms of nationalism share a certain way of seeing the world and constructing social reality, and make normative claims about the primacy of nationalist interests and values and the moral significance of the opposition between "us" and "them" through which nations work as categories of practice. Seen in this way, nationalism represents a form of discourse premised on a particular theory of legitimation of state power, one that "regards the nation as the only source of legitimacy" (Özkirimli 2000: 230).

There is also no one "rule of law" that can be authoritatively defined from the outset and employed throughout the inquiry. Theorists have put forward a range of understandings that invoke two core meanings of the rule of law ideal: formal conceptions that are concerned with the sources and form of legality, and substantive conceptions that are also interested in the content of law (Tamanaha 2004: 91–92; Craig 1997). Formal theories of the rule of law start from the proposition that laws must be general, prospective, clear, and stable, and elaborate additional requirements such as access to justice and restraints on discretion (Raz 1979), congruence between official action and declared rule (Fuller 1969), avoidance of arbitrary distinctions between groups of citizens (Hayek 1960), and adherence to democratic procedures in determining the content of law (Habermas 1996). Substantive theories of the rule of law build on formal legality but go further by specifying requirements also for the content of law, such as the primacy of human rights (Dworkin 1978) and equal citizenship (Allan 2001). The two branches of the rule of law represent a continuum, as formal versions have substantive implications whereas substantive versions incorporate the formal ones. More importantly for the purposes of this book, all these formulations can be reinterpreted as principles of political legitimation. The dominant conceptions of the rule of law elaborate a set of attributes that can also be understood as principles underpinning the legitimacy of political order, some of them concerned with legal form and procedure, others with substantive issues such as individual rights. Approached in this way, the rule of law designates a spectrum of understandings, all of which are closely bound up with legitimacy.

As social phenomena and sources of political legitimacy, nationalism and the rule of law interact in complex and often contradictory ways. On the one hand, nationalism and the rule of law coexist and reinforce each other, and may be seen as not only compatible but mutually constitutive. The rise and spread of nationalism since the nineteenth century has often unfolded in parallel with the strengthening of the rule of law in the modern state, as nations have furnished structures in which the rule of law ideal can take root. The integrative and legitimating work done by nations and nationalism can serve as a catalyst for the development of the rule of law by encouraging the emergence of unifying solidarities, promoting ideas of self-government, and facilitating the extension of individual rights and citizenship. These dynamics are implicit in many of the modernist and ethno-symbolist "grand narratives" in the study of nationalism, which often emphasize factors such as the extension of citizenship rights (e.g., Breuilly 1993; Smith 1991). The nation-state, which binds together cultural and political units, has so far provided the most favorable framework for advancing the rule of law ideal. As Craig Calhoun puts it, the nation-state is "basic to the rule of law, not only because most law remains a domestic matter of nation-states but because most international law is literally that: structured by agreements among nation-states" (Calhoun 2007: 4).

On the other hand, the relationship between nationalism and the rule of law is marked by deep tensions and contradictions: nationalism often appears incompatible with the rule of law and signals its retreat. Nations work as structures of integration but also of exclusion: their bounded character cannot be easily reconciled with the notion of equality before the law. The rule of law is called into question whenever national loyalties and fidelity to law come into conflict, whether law itself is employed or subverted in the pursuit of particular nationalist projects and purposes. Some of the challenges for the rule of law may arise from subtle forms of discrimination and bias in the everyday administration of justice; others are more serious and may amount to maintaining regimes of differentiated citizenship. At the extreme, the pursuit of the nationalist principle precipitates the breakdown of the rule of law: as Ernest Gellner has pointed out, cultural and political boundaries can only be made to coincide if the national group "either kills, expels, or assimilates all non-nationals" (Gellner 1983: 2).

The tensions between nationalism and the rule of law are particularly acute when the state itself is harnessed by nationalists, thus limiting the ability of law and legal institutions to absorb and mediate social conflict and to underwrite the legitimacy of the existing order. When states are challenged by nationalist movements, the outcome often hinges on the commitment of the state and its agents to uphold the principles of the rule of law and harness their legitimating power. In both scenarios, nationalism and the rule of law are associated with competing political agendas and sources of legitimacy.

At the current juncture, the tensions between nationalism and the rule of law have become more important in a variety of contexts. This could be explained in part by contemporary developments affecting the character of nationalism and of the rule of law that shape their evolving relationship. Some of these changes are internal to nationalism and reflect its remarkable success in organizing the modern polity. The forces that have been driving the alignment of cultural and political units in the nation-state are also working to pull them apart. Anthony Smith (1995) points out that the national state is far from retreating, despite global trends that may be limiting its power in economic and military matters.[3] In fact, the penetration of the state in the cultural and social domains has been further augmented, for example in public education and cultural policy. Smith identifies an "internal" crisis of legitimacy of the nation-state that derives precisely from this unprecedented penetration in the cultural field, which prompts recent immigrants and long-standing minorities to call into question the national articulation of identity and culture. Their claims for cultural expression and autonomy, in turn, elicit a backlash, because they are seen as threatening the nation: "And these perceptions are grounded in a social transformation wrought by the very expansion and penetration of the national state, and by its project of national acculturation and homogenization" (Smith 1995: 95). Smith believes that the contradictions will be eventually resolved as new nation-states are constructed

---

[3] The main thrust of the debate over nationalism and globalization concerns the questions of whether or not nationalism is on the retreat, and how it is transformed and reconstructed, in a global era. See Hobsbawm (1990); Smith (1995); Kaldor (2004); Calhoun (2007).

and the nationalist principle is reaffirmed. A more likely outcome, however, is the entrenchment of such contradictions in existing states, continuously reproducing the conditions that engender crises of legitimacy and disrupt political and legal orders.

Another important issue concerns the changing role of war in shaping collective identities. Nation-states were often forged in the experience of war with other states and colonial powers, and nations depended on contests with external enemies for their mythologies, political claims, and emotive power. Waging such wars often involved bargains between states and citizens that encouraged the development of the rule of law domestically, for example through the extension of citizenship rights in exchange for conscription and taxation. In this sense, nationalism and the rule of law were mutually constitutive. The dramatic decline of interstate war in recent decades has important implications for the ability of states to shape collective identities, which are yet to be fully understood. In most contemporary wars, nationalism is mobilized against internal "others" and disrupts the rule of law; in fact, it both encourages and feeds off the spread of lawlessness and insecurity. Zygmunt Bauman notes that such wars give rise to group solidarity based on active complicity in atrocities, as communities "need enemies that threaten their extinction and enemies to be collectively persecuted, tortured and mutilated, in order to make every member of the community into an accessory" (Bauman 2001: 22). The violence produces communities of accomplices where extremist political ideologies and projects can thrive, and rebuilding the rule of law in the aftermath of war becomes a daunting task.

Similar dynamics can be observed in the West, where the discourse of nationalism is more likely today to take the form of xenophobia than jingoism, and the favorite targets of nationalists are immigration and Islam. But whether it is driven by far-right political movements in established democracies or campaigns for ethnic cleansing in collapsing states, this "new nationalism" (Delanty 2000; Kaldor 2004) presents serious challenges for the rule of law in every society where it takes root. It promotes social exclusion and hinders integration, eroding the legitimacy of political and legal orders without being able to provide any viable alternatives. As Gerard Delanty (2000: 96) notes, "Whatever form it takes, [the new nationalism] cannot easily be harnessed for the purpose of the legitimation of state power." In an increasingly globalized world, the boundaries between the inside and the outside are blurring, and even when nationalism is supposed to be mobilized against external enemies, as in the War on Terror after 9/11, its disruptive effects on the rule of law are also felt domestically through growing abuse of power, erosion of legal rights and protections, and targeting of minorities. The liberal state is not immune to the problems raised by nations and nationalism, and it is a mistake to take for granted the resilience of its legal institutions.

It could be argued that the tensions between nationalism and the rule of law have always been deeply embedded in the nation-state, but in the current period they have become more apparent and destabilizing. In some sense, this is a question of shifting emphasis and framing, of changing sensibilities and expectations that shape our ways of seeing and interpreting the world. Although traditionally the rule of law has directed attention to the relations between power holders and subjects or citizens framed as a collective, its application has always been uneven and reflected pervasive inequalities based on class, gender, race, and ethnicity. The fiction of the "nation" as a shorthand for the "people" that underpins the rule of law ideal quickly unravels as one takes into account the role of capitalism, patriarchy, empire, and dominant ethnicity in structuring power relations and the role of law in supporting the underlying inequalities.

The vestiges of such historic inequalities and their contemporary manifestations are more visible today because social actors choose to mobilize around these issues and frame them differently, as breaches of the principle of non-discrimination or human rights violations that are seen as incompatible with the rule of law. The rule of law itself is also changing to reflect the organizing logic of "global" assemblages of territory, authority, and rights (Sassen 2006), and the emergence of international legal regimes that go beyond the nation-state to engage other subjects and sources of legitimacy (Teitel 2011). The tensions between nationalism and the rule of law come to the fore in these structural transformations and the work of a multiplicity of social actors, who take up the discourse of the rule of law and seek to reframe and redeploy it for their own projects and purposes. Inevitably, the more we read into and expect from the rule of law, the stronger becomes the perception of its disruption and decline.

The main focus of the book is to illuminate some of these tensions and contradictions and explore some of the ways in which they become expressed and negotiated in specific empirical contexts. But I treat the outcome of the tensions between nationalism and the rule of law as open, rather than predetermined. I am intrigued by the question of whether such tensions can be harnessed for any productive purposes, and the idea of "productive conflict" leads me to investigate the role of nationalism in disrupting the rule of law but also the potential of the rule of law to manage and transform nationalism. Another central concern of the book is to consider how the underlying tensions are reframed by the development of international legal norms and structures that are conceived as responses to nationalism, which seek to suppress and criminalize some of its manifestations. In areas of international law such as accountability for international crimes and human rights, nationalism plays a constitutive role in the articulation of the international rule of law in this reactive sense, and these developments in turn have important implications for the ability of nationalism to reinforce the legitimacy of the state and international order.

A ROAD MAP

The first part of the book develops an analytical framework for studying nationalism and the rule of law, which seeks to comprehend their complex and contradictory relationship by leaving room for plural understandings and clarifying some of the key concepts that frame the investigation. With this intention in mind, I employ a broad analytical lens that goes beyond the legal domain to capture the interactions of law, politics, and public discourse, and draw on evidence from a range of contexts and cases that are seen as useful in elaborating the argument. In the second part of the book, the focus shifts to the Balkans. The influence of the disintegration of Yugoslavia and ensuing developments in the region is palpable in many of the academic discussions that inform the book. I treat the Balkans not so much as a paradigm but rather as an opportunity to engage in fine-grained empirical investigation. Part I sets out the analytical framework in three chapters that focus on citizenship, transitional justice, and international justice. Part II includes three case studies from the former Yugoslavia, each chapter illustrating and taking further different aspects of the argument.

One of the objectives is to understand how nationalism works to disrupt and subvert the rule of law. Chapter 1 explores this question in the domain of citizenship, where nationalism and the rule of law interact in tangible ways and many of the underlying issues – such as identity, membership, and rights – are in play. I develop the concept of "ethnic citizenship" to capture a particular form of differentiated membership defined in ethnic terms and enshrined in law, and distinguish between strategies of incorporation and exclusion that nation-states employ in promoting this type of citizenship. Nationalism and the rule of law provide competing objectives of state policy and principles of political legitimacy, engendering deep tensions that promote instability, but the legal articulation of the ethnic citizenship construct also leaves room for adaptation and transformation. The final section considers the analytical traction of ethnic citizenship as a lens into the changing character of citizenship in a global era, drawing attention to the contradictory dynamics of denationalization and renationalization of citizenship that we are witnessing and highlighting the revaluation of citizenship as a symbolic resource for the nation-state in shaping collective identities.

A detailed analysis of the construction and maintenance of a regime of ethnic citizenship is provided in Chapter 4, which examines the case of Slovenia. I am particularly interested in one aspect of ethnic citizenship in that context: the "erasure" of more than 1 percent of Slovenia's population from the Registry of Permanent Residents at the time of declaring independence from the former Yugoslavia, which amounted to their denaturalization. I locate the emergence of ethnic citizenship in Slovenia in three narratives of transition that trace the country's uneven processes of democratization, economic liberalization, and Europeanization over the past three decades. The Slovenian case demonstrates how the pursuit of ethnic citizenship can precipitate the decline and breakdown of the rule of law, but it also draws attention to the flexible character of citizenship and highlights opportunities for its realignment with shifting conceptions of nationhood.

If Chapter 1 is about the potential of nationalism to undermine the rule of law, then Chapter 2 can be viewed as the reverse of that relationship because it concerns the potential of the rule of law to manage and transform nationalism. I explore these possibilities in the field of transitional justice, which provides a focal point for a range of responses to legacies of human rights abuse in the aftermath of armed conflict and repressive rule. I theorize a "deliberative" understanding of transitional justice, emphasizing the ability of judicial processes to serve as a vehicle for public debate and contestation. Such processes afford opportunities to interrogate nationalism by exposing its "dark side" and submitting it to public scrutiny and reassessment. I treat the late trials in France for crimes against humanity from the Vichy era as a paradigm of the deliberative conception of justice, and contrast it with the dynamics of "transition without justice," illustrated with the case of Turkey. If transitional justice processes have the potential to open up and renegotiate questions of national identity and state legitimacy, transitions without justice may create a legitimacy dilemma for the state and encourage nationalist mobilization and radicalization.

Chapter 5 draws on this analytical framework to examine the public discourse of war crimes in Croatia since the 1980s and introduces some new elements into the discussion. The unaddressed legacies of mass atrocity from the Second World War came back to haunt Yugoslavia after the death of Tito, paving the way for the resurgence of nationalism and disintegration of the state. Law and nationalism became closely intertwined in Croatia during the 1990s, when the breakdown of the rule of law was associated not only with the war itself, but also with the tendency of the judiciary to pursue wartime policies and purposes with judicial means. Since the turn of the new century, the relationship between nationalism and the rule of law has shifted once again and the initiation of transitional justice processes has raised the question of war crimes in new ways in the public domain. The chapter demonstrates how the public conversation about mass atrocity interacts with the legal response of the state and reflects the struggle over nationalism, illuminating both the promise and limits of deliberative transitional justice.

In the end, this book is as much about the relationship between nationalism and the rule of law as it is about the transformation of that relationship. Chapter 3 explores this theme a bit further by tracing the constitutive role of nationalism in the articulation of the rule of law beyond the state, focusing on the development of international criminal justice as one branch of international law that illuminates these dynamics. I interpret the historical trajectory of international justice from the Nuremberg and Tokyo Trials to the ad hoc tribunals for Yugoslavia and Rwanda as a shift from crimes against peace to crimes against humanity in the articulation of the international rule of law, which reflects the particular forms of nationalism and war that are selected for criminalization and suppression at the international level. The chapter also examines the impact of international justice in the Balkans, seeking to approach from a different direction the relationship between nationalism and the rule of law beyond the state. I identify as most significant the role of international justice in encouraging "pluralization" of public discourse, politics, and law in the region, and interpret these pluralized spaces as sites where the tensions between nationalism and the rule of law become expressed and negotiated.

International justice, however, has also encountered significant opposition in the countries of the former Yugoslavia. Chapter 6 examines such opposition in the case of Serbia, where international justice has been particularly contentious, and locates its sources in deeply entrenched and more pervasive politics of resistance to dealing with the past. Beyond the rhetoric, I recover a set of vested interests and power structures that developed during the 1990s, which are implicated not only in the wars and war crimes but also in the progressive capture and criminalization of the Serbian state. The continuing resistance to dealing with the past in Serbia reveals the multiple roles that nationalism can play in undermining the rule of law: mobilizing for war and justifying state repression; providing a cover for atrocities and abuse of power; and serving to legitimate a discourse of resistance to any form of reckoning with these interconnected legacies of abuse. The politics of resistance to dealing with the past is the context for understanding both the continuing opposition to international justice in Serbia and the ways in which international justice has encouraged pluralization of law, politics, and public discourse.

The book closes with an elaboration of some of the more concrete and practical lessons that can be taken away from the investigation.

Drawing such lessons from academic research always risks simplifying and generalizing in ways that betray the complexity of the issues at stake. Nevertheless, the exercise is worthwhile if it opens the conversation to diverse audiences and interlocutors – not only those of us who study nationalism and the rule of law but also the social actors whose work shapes our subjects of study, nationalists and lawyers (and nationalists trained in law, who are part of a long tradition going back to Bismarck and Mazzini), as well as the civil society actors and policymakers who grapple with some of the problems discussed in the following pages in a variety of different contexts. In writing the book, my intention is to encourage such conversations and offer a set of starting points for discussion.

PART I   NATIONALISM AND THE RULE OF LAW

1 ETHNIC CITIZENSHIP

In his reflections on nationalism in contemporary America, Rogers Brubaker (2004b) criticizes the tendency of liberal academia to dismiss nationalism out of hand. Scholars should treat nationhood, he argues, not as an ethnocultural fact but rather as a political claim – a claim on people's loyalties that seeks to mobilize them. Approached in this way, the interesting questions for students of nationalism concern the uses of "nation" to include and exclude in specific contexts – the various ways in which "nation" works as a category of practice. Firstly, when nationalist movements make a claim to nationhood, what they demand is an autonomous polity for the putative nation, and they primarily address the members of that nation. Secondly, in what is usually referred to as "nation-building," "nation" is invoked in order to create a sense of national unity for a given state and to foster an inclusive national identity that transcends ethnic differences. Finally, "nation" can also be used in an internally exclusive way in seeking to "assert 'ownership' of the polity on behalf of a 'core' ethnocultural 'nation' distinct from the citizenry of the state as a whole, and thereby to define and redefine the state as the state *of* and *for* the core nation" (Brubaker 2004b: 117).

Leaving aside for the moment the issues around groups and identities that may be marginalized or suppressed in notionally inclusive projects of nation-building (Kymlicka 2000; Young 1990), in this chapter I investigate how "nation" works in that last sense described by Brubaker and with what implications for the rule of law, taking my cues in the American context from the racial legislation that defined the limits of membership in the political community well into the twentieth century.

In particular, my analysis seeks to illuminate how states employ law in order to construct citizenship frameworks that produce forms of dominance and exclusion of those (citizens or residents) who do not belong to the "core nation" exercising ownership of the state, such as ethnic minorities, indigenous peoples, or migrants.[1] I elaborate the concept of ethnic citizenship to help theorize such nationalist uses of constitutional law, citizenship law, and a variety of other legislative and executive instruments. Most of the discussion is limited to the post-Cold War era, which has witnessed a remarkable revival of scholarly interest in questions of citizenship and multiple reinterpretations of the concept, reflecting important changes in its objective conditions and subjective dimensions (see, e.g., Sassen 2006). My purpose is to examine key characteristics of the model of ethnic citizenship as a lens into the framing question of this book about the relationship between nationalism and the rule of law.

Law plays a distinctive and rather ambivalent role in the ethnic citizenship construct, and my analysis bears that out: it serves as an instrument of formalization and codification of membership tied to particular projects of the nation-state and, at the same time, it also provides a potential arena for contestation and transformation of citizenship along the lines of alternative logics and normativities. The power of the law may be harnessed to promote and entrench ethnic citizenship in the nation-state but it may also become subversive and destabilizing, for instance, when aligned with human rights norms and international legal instruments that impinge on, and may even be applied within, the authority of the state. In the final section of the chapter, I discuss some of the broader questions that ethnic citizenship raises for current debates over citizenship, which often emphasize the uneven impact of global processes and transformations that are both external and internal to citizenship as a formal institution. I seek to recover from these

---

[1] The concept of citizenship has become increasingly contested in recent decades, not least by the proliferation of terminology that reflects diverse meanings and understandings of citizenship, from well-established concepts such as "social citizenship" to more recent notions of "cultural citizenship" and "environmental citizenship." See Marshall (1992); Vega and van Hensbroek (2010); Dobson and Bell (2006). I use citizenship here in the narrow sense to denote formal membership in a polity, and unless specified otherwise, I take that polity to be the national state.

explorations the significance of salient dynamics of denationalization and renationalization of citizenship in a global era and to understand the role of law in the negotiation of the underlying tensions.

ETHNIC CITIZENSHIP

The Nuremberg Laws of 1935 represent the most elaborate articulation of a system of ethnic citizenship in twentieth-century Europe. The Law for the Protection of German Blood and Honour recast racial purity as essential for the survival of the German nation and, inter alia, criminalized marriage and sexual intercourse between Jews and citizens of "German or kindred blood." The Reich Citizenship Law effectively stripped Jews of political rights, confining them to the status of second-class citizens, and paved the way for further exclusions from educational and professional opportunities reserved for full citizens. Implementing the legislation required an official and authoritative definition of "Jew," which was elaborated in the First Regulation to the Reich Citizenship Law of November 1935, and specific provisions were put in place to define and regulate the status of individuals of "mixed Jewish Blood" or *Mischlinge* (Miller, R.L. 1995; Hilberg 2003).

The Nuremberg Laws represent an extreme example of a wider set of practices of nation-states employing law in order to restrict citizenship and limit its full benefits, such as legal rights and equality before the law, to members of a titular nation. Such state-driven projects tend to define "nation" in ethnocultural terms, emphasizing markers such as descent, language, or religion, and use it as a quasi-legal category in constructing citizenship regimes that formalize, to varying degrees, social hierarchies and dynamics of discrimination and exclusion. I examine such projects as examples of *ethnic citizenship*, by which I mean a particular form of differentiated membership defined in ethnic terms and enshrined in law. To maintain my focus on such uses of the law, I limit the discussion in ways that circumvent much of the scholarship that has applied a citizenship lens to diverse forms of exclusion and discrimination that may be less formalized but are equally important. For instance, advocates of multiculturalism have persuasively challenged the notion that states with liberal democratic laws and institutions are ethnoculturally neutral, suggesting that all states, liberal and illiberal, in one way or another seek to diffuse the culture of the dominant majority as a single societal culture, with more or less repressive implications for minorities.[2] This apparent "illiberal under-side" of the liberal citizenship construct raises a different set of questions from ethnic citizenship understood in a narrow sense, although I examine some of the possible linkages in the final section.

The concept of ethnic citizenship, as defined here, is useful because it draws attention to a specific intersection of law and nationhood, one that highlights how law can be aligned with particular nationalist projects and purposes, serving as a device for inclusion and exclusion. The legal articulation of ethnic citizenship is recovered from a variety of sources that include constitutional law and traditions of interpretations, citizenship law, immigration law, and other types of legislation, but also executive decrees that are particularly important in the case of ethnic citizenship in Slovenia, examined later in the book.[3] In theorizing ethnic citizenship, I highlight two types of strategies commonly used by nation-states in activating the inclusion/exclusion function of the law. For analytical purposes, these can be usefully distinguished as *strategies of incorporation*, which produce differentiated frameworks of first- and second-class citizens; and *strategies of exclusion*, aimed at restricting access to citizenship or revoking the citizenship status and rights of particular groups. Despite significant differences in the nature and implementation of these strategies, all forms of ethnic citizenship create a gap between those included in the titular nation and those citizens and residents in the state whose identities are expressed as subordinate or alien. In historical and contemporary polities this gap has been occupied by diverse groups: from indigenous populations and long-standing ethnic minorities to more recent migrants.

Two accounts of constitutional nationalism provide a useful starting point for the inquiry. James Tully (1995) identifies nationalism as one of the dominant traditions of modern constitutionalism, alongside traditions associated with the liberal and communitarian schools

---

[2] Another example is the literature on cultural citizenship, which is preoccupied with issues of cultural and social dominance rather than lack of formal rights. See, e.g., Kymlicka (2000); Vega and van Hensbroek (2010).

[3] See Chapter 4, § "The Erased."

of thought. On his account, in the era of the nation-state, constitutional nationalism has been manifested in pervasive recognition of one culture to the exclusion or assimilation of other cultures prevalent in a particular society. A more embedded conception of constitutional nationalism is advanced by Robert Hayden (1992) in his reflections on the construction of new nation-states in the wake of the Cold War. His analysis of the disintegration of Yugoslavia in the 1990s focuses on the tendency of the newly established successor states to enshrine in their constitutions an ethnically framed conception of the nation and to privilege its members in relation to other citizens. These two understandings of constitutional *nationalism* should not be confused with the idea of constitutional *patriotism* advanced by Jürgen Habermas (1998), which pulls in the opposite direction by vesting loyalties in the constitution itself.[4]

Tully offers a compelling account of the core features of modern constitutionalism as a shared horizon for understanding nationalist, communitarian, and liberal traditions. He argues that "nation" has played a central role in these constructs by providing the source of sovereignty; only liberals have defined it as a nation of sovereign individuals with rights, whereas nationalists and communitarians have framed it as a collective. Approached in this way, liberal constitutions are seen as employing culture-blind language in order to mask the dominance of one "imperial" culture. Nevertheless, the nationalist use of constitutional law remains distinctive in how it defines the nation and its relationship to the state. Unlike liberal constitutionalism, in the nationalist tradition one culture is openly recognized at the expense of all others: "This widespread constitutional nationalism comes in a variety of types and has been recommended by writers as different as the authors of *The federalist papers* in the 1780s, Johann Gottlieb Fichte in the *Address to the German nation* in 1807–8 and Sir John Seeley, in *The expansion of England* in the 1880s" (Tully 1995: 85).

Analyzing a more limited set of cases, Hayden defines constitutional nationalism as a "constitutional and legal structure that privileges the

---

[4] Constitutional patriotism can be understood as a reaction to the rise of extreme nationalism in the twentieth century, in particular National Socialism and the Holocaust. For a critical discussion of constitutional patriotism, see Calhoun (2002).

members of one ethnically defined nation over other residents in a particular state" (Hayden 1992: 655). He discerns a shared constitutional vision emerging at the republican level at the time of the breakup of Yugoslavia and advanced by the new states that emerged from it, which posits that sovereignty resides only in the nation defined in ethnic terms and only members of that nation are entitled to decide on questions of state and identity. Analyzing a series of constitutional texts adopted in Croatia (1990), Slovenia (1989 and 1991), Macedonia (1991), and Serbia (1990), Hayden concludes that in the post–Yugoslav state, constitutional nationalism "establishes and attempts to protect the construction of a nation as a bounded unit: a sovereign being with its own defining language, culture, and perhaps 'biological essence,' the uniqueness of which must be defended at any cost" (ibid. 663).

What is the relationship between such projects of constitutional nationalism and the model of ethnic citizenship? Constitutional nationalism in its contemporary incarnations often turns on how nonmembers of a titular nation are incorporated in the constitutional association, what status they are assigned in the constitutional order, rather than how they may be excluded or assimilated through the law. In the case of most countries that emerged from the disintegration of Yugoslavia, for example, such constitutional texts authoritatively define "nation" and "minorities" and extend citizenship rights to both, but on different terms. The result is neither a straightforward exclusion of minorities, which is barred by the extension of formal citizenship rights and status, nor a possibility for their assimilation, which is precluded by the reliance on an ascriptive conception of ethnicity that emphasizes and stabilizes cultural difference.

In other words, constitutional nationalism of this kind does not neglect, marginalize, or seek to assimilate cultural difference; instead, it tends to reify it by adopting a monolithic, billiard-ball understanding of culture and paves the way for the incorporation of minorities in a constitutional association of unequal status and power relations.[5] The implications of this mode of incorporation cannot be grasped in the vocabulary of formal equality, individual and group rights; indeed,

---

[5] There is a parallel here – despite the very different context – with critical and postcolonial explorations of the uses of culture for incorporation in hegemonic structures of power. See, for example, Mamdani 1996.

these may be codified and guaranteed in the actual text of the constitution. What must be taken into account in this respect is how culture (ethnicity) is employed to enshrine in law a hierarchical system of differentiated citizenship. Constitutional law is invoked here to perform two functions: to distinguish between members and nonmembers of the nation; and to incorporate them in a framework of first- and second-class citizenship.

There is a rich empirical literature that applies a citizenship lens to make legible the implications of various forms of constitutional nationalism. Hayden, for instance, notes that as long as the nation is defined in ethnic terms and minorities are seen as "foreign to the bodies politic and social," establishing equal citizenship in the countries of the former Yugoslavia is not possible (Hayden 1992: 673). Examining the operation of constitutional nationalism in Slovakia, Nadya Nedelsky (2003) relates how in that particular framework only members of the "sovereign nation" enjoy an integral relationship to the state, whereas the citizenship of minorities is deflated because the state is seen to express neither their sovereignty nor their self-determination.

If strategies of incorporation serve to stratify citizenship, which is often experienced as a form of cultural and social dominance, strategies of exclusion may have more radical implications for those affected. Such strategies are often employed in pursuing state-driven projects to align the boundaries of the nation and citizenry or to maintain their presumed congruence. I focus on two dynamics in this regard: policies of denaturalization of citizens who are members of ethnic and national minorities; and instances of particularly strict naturalization laws that effectively bar access to citizenship for long-term immigrants and their descendents. As it will become clear, both of these strategies make some use of the law to ascribe citizenship on the basis of descent (jus sanguinis) but often preclude the moderating influence of territorial principles (jus soli) in determining who qualifies for membership.[6] In recent decades, the first set of strategies have been important primarily in the context of newly independent and transitional states, whereas the second type have also been pursued in well-established polities.

---

[6] Most states regulate access to citizenship by relying on some sort of combination of jus sanguinis and jus soli. See also the discussion of the normative issues raised by ascriptive birthright membership in Shachar 2002.

My discussion focuses on denaturalization policies pursued in the period since the end of the Cold War; such policies, however, have targeted members of different minorities throughout the twentieth century. In Europe, large-scale denaturalization of Germans took place after the Second World War; in the postcolonial world it has affected groups such as the Indian Tamils in Sri Lanka. In the 1980s, the communist regime in Bulgaria pursued a national Revival Process targeting the Turkish minority in the country, which involved launching a large-scale campaign to forcibly change their names and de facto denaturalizing 300,000 citizens, who fled to Turkey in an exodus known as the Big Excursion (Bojkov 2004). In a sense, the plight of Bulgaria's Turkish minority prefigured the resurgence of ethnic cleansing and the reappearance of denaturalization policies in the 1990s, often pursued by what Brubaker calls the "nationalizing nationalisms" of newly independent states:

> Nationalizing nationalisms involve claims made in the name of a "core nation" or nationality, defined in ethnocultural terms, and sharply distinguished from the citizenry as a whole. The core nation is understood as the "owner" of the state, which is conceived as the state *of* and *for* the core nation. Despite having "its own" state, however, the core nation is conceived as being in a situation of weak cultural, economic, or demographic position within the state. This weak position – seen as a legacy of discrimination against the nation before it attained independence – is held to justify the "remedial" or "compensatory" project of using state power to promote the specific (and previously inadequately served) interests of the core nation. (Brubaker 1996: 5)

Shortly after gaining independence from the Soviet Union, Estonia and Latvia introduced citizenship policies and legislation that amounted to large-scale denaturalization of ethnic Russians who had been long-term and often lifelong residents of the two republics (Orentlicher 1998; Barrington 2000). Observers have noted the emergence of three distinct discourses of "homeland" in the Baltic countries around the time of independence. A "core nation" discourse asserting that citizenship in the newly independent state should be granted only to citizens of the interwar (i.e., pre–Soviet occupation) state and their descendents; a "multiculturalist" discourse advocating automatic citizenship for all residents at the time of independence; and, finally, a nostalgic "neo-Soviet" discourse claiming Russia as an ethnic patron for Russian minorities in these countries (Smith et al. 1998). The "core nation" discourse prevailed in Latvia and Estonia and was accompanied by the adoption of citizenship laws that granted automatic citizenship only to interwar citizens and their descendents.[7] In principle, members of the Russian settler communities could acquire citizenship through naturalization, but in practice the strict conditions specified (residency requirements, language competence, naturalization quotas, nonaffiliation with the occupying Soviet forces) served to discourage and preclude the extension of citizenship to many members of these communities. As one study put it, the status of Russian minorities was effectively "demoted from that of citizens to that of denizens, in which certain privileges not accorded to 'foreigners' exist, but in which those rights enjoyed by the national majority are denied" (ibid. 94).

Denaturalization policies in Latvia and Estonia ended up affecting up to a third of their population (Smith 1996: 27). In other countries, such as the Czech Republic, restrictive citizenship policies have affected in a similar fashion a smaller number of people (Orentlicher 1998: 302–303). These policies were generally visible and attracted scrutiny and criticism from a variety of international actors, reactions to which I return later. The case of Slovenia, however, is particularly interesting because the pursuit of de facto denaturalization in the post–Yugoslav period was shrouded in secrecy. Slovenia declared independence in 1991, granted automatic citizenship to ethnic Slovenes, and allowed most of its permanent residents from ethnic minorities originating in other former Yugoslav republics to acquire citizenship ex lege. In February 1992, however, the authorities erased from the Registry of Permanent Residents those who had either failed to apply for citizenship or whose applications had been rejected. As a result, more than 1 percent of the population of Slovenia at the time, including many individuals who had moved to the republic mostly in the 1960s and 1970s as internal migrants within Yugoslavia, became denaturalized ex officio without even being informed of the measure.[8]

---

[7] The third Baltic state, Lithuania, granted automatic citizenship to all residents in the state at the time of declaring independence. See Popovski (1996).

[8] See Chapter 4, § "The Erased."

When the construction of ethnic citizenship is associated with such strategies of exclusion, minorities with legitimate claims to citizenship are transformed into denizens and may even become stateless persons, with harsh consequences for those affected. Viewed more abstractly, such nation-building strategies often reflect a vision in which ethnicity, nationhood, and citizenship become increasingly conflated and tightly intertwined concepts. Newly independent and transitional states have pursued such strategies by coupling jus sanguinis with restrictive rules for determining what historical periods and polities count as authoritative sources of citizenship claims. But states with established liberal democratic identities have also relied on a combination of jus sanguinis and restrictive naturalization rules to maintain some form of ethnic citizenship. Japan is a frequently cited example in this respect. A system of second-class citizenship for indigenous populations and persistent exclusion of immigrants have been maintained in the Japanese context alongside a liberal constitutional order and, more recently, a limited move toward multiculturalism. The ambivalent role of law in this context can be observed in the coexistence of the liberal post-war constitution of 1946 and the Ainu Cultural Promotion Act of 1997 with elements of ethnic citizenship, and the pervasive sense that in Japan, as one observer puts it, "citizenship is conceived of as membership of an ethno-cultural nation" (Clammer 2007: 33).

The legal articulation of ethnic citizenship in Japan is complex and multilayered, combining a variety of strategies of incorporation and exclusion, reflecting significant historical continuities and an ongoing process of adaptation. Constructing this complex constellation has involved adopting policies effectively disenfranchising and denaturalizing ethnic minorities, which go back to the post-war period; legislating in ways that preclude immigrants and their descendents from acquiring Japanese citizenship; and extending some recognition to the indigenous Ainu but without the requisite rights that may allow them to challenge their historical status as second-class citizens of the Japanese state.

Contrary to the widespread myth of Japan's ethnic homogeneity, Japanese society is ethnically diverse and includes long-standing migrant communities and more recent arrivals, as well as indigenous populations. Koreans represent the largest ethnic minority in Japan, and their treatment in the post-war era conveys the range of policies and legal instruments that the state has employed in order to restrict access to citizenship for those residents who are seen as nonmembers of the nation:

> Today's resident Koreans comprise former colonial subjects and their descendents and are estimated at 950,000: 640,000 are registered foreigners, the rest are either naturalized Japanese citizens or children of intermarriage between Koreans and Japanese. At the end of World War II, there were two million Koreans in Japan, the majority returning to the Korean Peninsula. Without offering these residents the opportunity to choose between Korean and Japanese nationalities, the Japanese government denied their status as nationals through several legal measures: first depriving them of voting rights; second forcing them to register under the Alien Registration Ordinance; and finally by unilaterally abrogating the Japanese nationality of former colonial subjects in 1952. Thus, the Koreans in Japan had to struggle to acquire rights on a par with those of Japanese citizenship.(Kibe 2006: 40–41)

More recent waves of immigrants, reflecting permanent labor shortages, have also encountered serious obstacles in regulating their legal status or securing any status at all. In fact, the restrictive immigration and citizenship policies of the Japanese state have been analyzed by scholars as elements of a system of "ethnic hegemony" (Yamanaka 2004). Another, less-known aspect of ethnic hegemony in Japan can be recovered from the experience of the indigenous Ainu people from the island of Hokkaido. The imperial state moved to nationalize Ainu lands in the nineteenth century, and enshrined its "native policy" for the Ainu in the Hokkaido Former Natives Protection Act of 1899. As in other places, "protection" of the native population became a euphemism for a set of practices that involved social and cultural exclusion and discrimination. Richard Siddle (2003) describes the trajectory of the Ainu in the post-war era as a transition from second-class subjects to second-class citizens, further complicated by persistent disadvantage and discrimination. Since the 1970s, however, Ainu mobilization has intensified and increasingly challenged the state to recognize their status as an indigenous people and extend groups rights as a precondition for full citizenship.

The Japanese state finally retreated from the official narrative of mono-ethnicity with the adoption of the Ainu Cultural Promotion Act in 1997. Commentators have pointed out that although the legislation extended recognition and protection to Ainu culture, it did little to empower the Ainu or reverse their long-standing marginalization in Japanese politics and society. Indeed, the special legislation for the Ainu may have served to circumscribe and reify an "authentic" minority culture, while ultimately deflecting Ainu demands for recognition as an indigenous people:

> The official protection of Ainu culture, albeit a state-defined, fossilized complex of "traditional" practices, is a limited first step towards cultural rights. But Japan is still a long way from embracing any meaningful form of multiculturalism. The state approves of Ainu culture as a commodity to be enjoyed by all Japanese, but is not prepared to grant the Ainu, as a disadvantaged group, any meaningful political or economic rights or mechanisms to overcome the legacies of their material and ideological marginalization as indigenous people.... Citizenship in Japan remains mono-ethnic in both its intent and symbolism.(Siddle 2003: 460)

In terms of my analysis of ethnic citizenship, the Ainu example suggests how law can be used to (re)incorporate certain minority groups in the framework of ethnic citizenship on more favorable terms without challenging the framework itself or redressing harms incurred in the past. The logic of ethnic citizenship, however, may also be challenged in more decisive ways. Citizenship is a dynamic, flexible institution that responds to a variety of pressures and changing conditions. Nationhood and national identity are themselves shifting constructs that have to be continuously produced and reproduced. There is a debate in the literature between those scholars who maintain that citizenship is shaped by long-standing conceptions of nationhood (Brubaker 1992) and those who argue that there is no necessary association between the two (Joppke 2003, 2007b). Nevertheless, even when the relationship between citizenship and nationhood is important, it still remains open to the possibility of change and transformation in a variety of ways, including by moving away from the pursuit of the sort of nationalist projects that are associated with the model of ethnic citizenship.

Historical continuities that shape models of citizenship may become diluted and suspended under the influence of new forces, or reactivated but endowed with new meanings and purposes that reflect the changing conditions in which they play out. These dynamics are borne out in debates over citizenship and nationhood in Germany, long considered a paradigm for understanding the ethnic model of citizenship. In his seminal study of citizenship and nationhood published in the early nineties, Brubaker (1992) discerns precisely such continuities in German citizenship law, sustained by an ethnocultural framing of German nationalism and effectively excluding long-term immigrants and their descendents. In Germany, he argues, "naturalization is perceived as involving not only a change in legal status, but a change in nature, a change in political and cultural identity, a social transubstantiation that immigrants have difficulty imagining, let alone desiring" (Brubaker 1992: 78). Since Germany's unification, both the discourse and practice of citizenship have been opened up and contested in a variety of ways: the legal regime has been liberalized and naturalization has become easier; and some of the old tensions have become expressed and negotiated in new ways in debates over dual nationality and norms of non-discrimination (Joppke 2007b; Faist 2006; Kastoryano 2006; Levy and Weiss 2002). It is precisely because the model of ethnic citizenship depends on a legal framework for its articulation that it is also open, at least potentially, to ongoing change and transformation.

INCORPORATION, EXCLUSION, AND THE RULE OF LAW

The framework of ethnic citizenship and the range of practices associated with it raise profound dilemmas for the rule of law. At a fundamental level, they challenge the basic principle of equality before the law and the norms of non-discrimination that substantiate its application in diverse legal fora. The forms of incorporation and exclusion that are engendered by the model of ethnic citizenship serve to undermine the principle of equality and pave the way for discrimination by giving it legal expression and justification. In the specific empirical cases discussed in this chapter, the effort to construct and maintain systems of ethnic citizenship often compromises the requirements of formal legality that laws must be general, prospective, and stable, and challenges substantive principles of the rule of law such as the primacy of human rights and equal citizenship.[9] Moreover, the inherent ambivalence of the model of ethnic citizenship regarding "membership" in the state and "ownership" of the state open up the possibility for abuse of power and unrestrained exercise of discretion in the interactions of the state with those who are subject to its authority and jurisdiction but do not enjoy the privileged status reserved for members of the titular nation. In this sense, ethnic citizenship encourages precisely the sort of arbitrariness in the exercise of state power that the rule of law ideal seeks to limit and prevent.

At a more abstract level of analysis, the tensions and contradictions between ethnic citizenship and the rule of law can be seen as expressing an underlying legitimation problem. The ability of law and legal institutions to underwrite the legitimacy of the state is undermined both from above and from below. For the state and its agents, ethnic citizenship and the rule of law become entangled with alternative sources of legitimacy and objectives of state policy; when they are seen as competing and conflicting, maintaining the model of ethnic citizenship entails compromising the rule of law. For individuals and communities whose identities are suppressed in the framework of ethnic citizenship and who confront various forms of exclusion and discrimination in their daily lives, the legitimacy of the political and legal order is inherently problematic, and their allegiance cannot be assumed.[10]

There are a number of contexts that could be relevant here to illustrate these dynamics. Writing at the time of the Arab Awakening suggests an obvious choice. The political upheaval in large parts of the Middle East and North Africa has revived the importance of many questions raised in previous "waves of democratization" (Huntington 1991). The spectre of ethnic, tribal, and sectarian conflict, both real and imagined, has been repeatedly invoked in the West to justify caution

---

[9] See Introduction, § "Nationalism, Legitimacy, and the Rule of Law."

[10] Such loss of legitimacy, combined with insecurity and uncertainty about the future, proved to be a potent source of nationalist mobilization in the former Yugoslavia, where many citizens of the disintegrating state were transformed overnight into minorities in the new nation-states. See, for example, Hayden (1992) and Mann (2005).

in extending support to certain democratic struggles and movements in the region, as in the case of Syria. Some of these arguments have been dismissed as selective and dishonest, given the role of the West in regime change in Libya, which was accomplished only after months of air strikes and other forms of support for the rebels. But there are also genuine concerns for majority-minority and interfaith relations in these societies, often expressed within the region itself. In countries embarking on an uncertain transition, such as Egypt, questions of national identity and citizenship (in the dual sense of membership in and ownership of the state) are debated both by citizens and the elites that are supposed to deliver constitutional change and promote the rule of law.

Two regime types are often expected to emerge as a result of ongoing processes of democratization in the region. Observers suggest that countries such as Egypt and Tunisia are likely to combine some elements of Western-style democratic governance with specific cultural and religious understandings of legitimate political authority that may have particular traction in these societies. Libya, on the other hand, is expected to take on some of the features of the Gulf states, where oil wealth and related dynamics play a prominent role. Although elements of the ethnic citizenship model can be detected across the region, I take Israel and Kuwait as two examples roughly approximating these generalized regime types, which are helpful in illustrating how the tension between ethnic citizenship and the rule of law may play out in specific empirical contexts. In both cases, scholars tend to use the "ethnic" qualifier to convey the specificity of their political systems and citizenship regimes. For instance, Israel has been analyzed as an archetype of "ethnic democracy" (Smooha 1997) with a form of "ethnic citizenship" (Levy and Weiss 2002), whereas Kuwait has been described as neither democracy nor autocracy but "ethnocracy" (Longva 2005).

The work of Yoev Peled (2005, 2008) is particularly illuminating here because it conveys the complexities of citizenship in Israel in a way that is sensitive both to issues of identity and the challenges for the rule of law. His approach highlights three discourses of citizenship that are invoked at different junctures to delineate the boundaries between the major groups constituting Israeli society:

> An ethno-nationalist discourse of inclusion and exclusion, a republican discourse of community goals and civic virtue, and a liberal, Marshallian discourse of civil, political and social rights. Thus, the differential allocation of entitlements, obligations and domination has proceeded in a number of stages. First, the liberal idea of citizenship functions to separate the citizen Jews and Palestinians from the non-citizen Palestinians in the occupied territories. Then the ethno-nationalist discourse is invoked to discriminate between Jewish and Palestinian citizens within the sovereign State of Israel. Last, the republican discourse is used to legitimate the different positions occupied by the major Jewish social groups: *ashkenazim* vs. *mizrachim*, males vs. females, secular vs. religiously orthodox.(Peled 2008: 336)

Peled's analysis brings out the dynamic interaction of these three discourses while also highlighting the instability of the rule of law and the tension between ethno-nationalist and liberal forms of legitimation at specific junctures. At the time when the state was established, the integrative capacity of a uniform rule of law was harnessed by granting Israeli citizenship to all residents – Jewish and Palestinian. Between 1948 and 1966, Palestinian citizens were subjected to military law and administration and de facto excluded from the benefits and protections afforded by full citizenship; following the abolition of military administration, the liberal framework of rights was extended to them once again. The 1985 amendment to the Basic Law opened up the possibility to exclude political parties contesting Israel's self-definition as a Jewish state, but also parties challenging Israel's self-definition as a democratic state or inciting to racism. The law advanced both the nationalist and liberal projects of the state, limiting the scope for political participation of Israel's Palestinian citizens but entrenching their rights in other domains. The 2003 Citizenship and Entry into Israel Law barred Palestinians from the occupied territories from acquiring Israeli citizenship or residency, even if their spouses, parents, or children were Israeli citizens. As Peled notes, "The new citizenship law established, for the first time, an explicit, if only consequential, distinction between the citizenship rights of Jewish and Palestinian citizens, because only Palestinian citizens are likely to marry non-citizen Palestinians from the occupied territories" (Peled 2008: 36).

This uneven trajectory captures in a microcosm the legitimation problems inherent in the model of ethnic citizenship. It suggests how on certain occasions, the Israeli state prioritizes the requirements of ethnic citizenship over principles of the rule of law when the two are seen as conflicting. In such instances, the legitimacy of public policy and law is framed in an ethno-nationalist discourse addressing the titular nation and neglecting (or constructing as a threat) Israel's Arab citizens. Employing a citizenship lens, Peled (2005) also sheds light on issues implicating law enforcement, for instance the excessive use of force by the Israeli police in suppressing demonstrations in October 2000, which resulted in the death of thirteen unarmed protestors. The Or Commission, set up to investigate the incident, concluded that despite the fact that the legal prohibition of discrimination is in place, Israel's "Arab citizens live in a reality in which they are discriminated against as Arabs."[11] The incident suggests how a vicious cycle can be set in motion that perpetuates the legitimation problems associated with the ethnic citizenship model and disrupts the rule of law: when minority grievances are expressed they become interpreted as an attack on the state, and the unrestrained or discriminatory response of the agents of the state, in turn, further exacerbates such grievances.

In the case of Kuwait, the challenges that ethnic citizenship presents for the rule of law are dramatized by demographic factors. As in other states in the Gulf, most of the workforce there consists of migrants whose proportion of the population has been rising. In these societies the categories "minority" and "majority" have different connotations because the citizens are often outnumbered by foreign workers. The forms of exclusion and dominance engendered by ethnic citizenship in the Gulf are also differently expressed and codified, most notably in the system of *kafālah* or "sponsorship," which reflects its own peculiar logic. The role of the state in managing migrants is limited by the formalization of relationships that bind foreign workers directly to their local sponsors. As Paul Dresch (2005: 22) explains, "Instead of governments simply limiting the

---

[11] Or Commission, Report of the State Commission of Inquiry to Investigate the Clashes between the Security Forces and Israeli Citizens in October 2000, quoted in Peled (2005: 94).

overall number of foreign residents and assigning their distribution
to the market or to state control, foreign residents are placed directly
under the control of specific individuals and local companies who act
as the foreigner's *kafīl* or sponsor."

This system of migrant control renders foreign workers particularly
vulnerable given their precarious legal status and the degree to which
the *kafīl* can exercise discretion. In her analysis of "civic ethnocracy" in
Kuwait, Anh Nga Longva (2005) stresses the role of Kuwaiti citizenship as a foundation of the ethnocratic regime, as what serves as the key
marker of ethnicity in this context is not religion or language but citizenship on the basis of descent. The Nationality Law of 1959 distinguished
between "originally Kuwaiti" and "Kuwaiti by naturalization" and
established a system based exclusively on *jus sanguinis*; subsequent revisions have introduced further restrictions, for example an annual limit
of fifty naturalizations, thus lengthening the distance between Kuwaiti
citizens and foreign workers. A combination of restrictive nationality
laws and the *kafālah* system provides the basis of Kuwait's model of
ethnic citizenship. This particular combination perpetuates patterns of
highly uneven relations of power, manifested in forms of ethnic stratification and dominance but also expressed in class and gender terms and
affecting Kuwaiti society as a whole.[12] Nevertheless, this regime renders
migrants particularly vulnerable to arbitrary treatment and exploitation, given the prominent role of discretion and the limited or lacking
recourse to public authority. Fundamental tenets of the rule of law such
as access to justice, although they may be available to Kuwaiti citizens,
appear to be suspended for many non-Kuwaitis, especially for the most
vulnerable segments that are employed in the household:

[12] This is the main point of Longva's (2005: 118) analysis of the role of migrant workers
in Kuwaiti society:

More than oil prosperity per se, it is the presence of non-Kuwaiti workers and their
legal, social and political subjection to Kuwaiti citizens that allows for (1) the reproduction of a political structure with quasi-autocratic features, and (2) the continued
marginalisation of Kuwaiti women from productive work, their willing confinement
within the role of biological reproducers and their formal absence from political life.

Whereas my focus here is on forms of dominance and exclusion framed in cultural
terms, it is clear that ethnic citizenship also has important implications for women and
gender relations. See the examination of the intersections of gender, nation, and nationalism in Yuval-Davies (1997)

The power of the *kafīl* or sponsor over his employees is much more extensive than one might expect. Sponsorship is not a labour-contract through which an agreed amount of labour is performed and an agreed salary is paid. It is in essence a moral contract in which the written clauses are less important than the unwritten expectations. Because of the impending threat of sponsorship-withdrawal, expatriate employees will more often than not feel obliged to perform more than the tasks required by a formal job description. In the case of domestic workers, the power of the *kafīl* is practically limitless, the only real constraints being those that sponsors set upon themselves. Actual treatment of servants varies from case to case, and not all sponsors take advantage of the power over employees. But there is a disturbing pattern of exploitation and mistreatment.(Longva 2005: 126)

These two illustrations, although very different in many respects, make legible the distinctiveness of the model of ethnic citizenship and the ambivalent functions performed by the law in this context. The tendency to articulate ethnic citizenship in the idiom of law suggests an attempt by nation-states to express and integrate its operation, at least nominally, in a rule of law framework. Indeed, this tendency is evident in the amendments to Israel's Basic Law and the repeated revisions of the Nationality Law in Kuwait. The central place of law in the ethnic citizenship construct reflects efforts to stabilize it but also helps to explain the strategies adopted by many marginalized and excluded groups, which often focus their struggles on changing the law through constitutional and other nonviolent means, rather than seeking to challenge the political and legal order of the state in a more radical way. Such strategies have been pursued for the most part by the Ainu in Japan, Turkish migrants in Germany, and Russian minorities in the Baltic states. In each of these cases, the flexibility of citizenship as a legally expressed and formalized status has allowed for at least some measure of adaptation and renegotiation of the terms of membership, with varying implications for the affected groups and the relationship between ethnic citizenship and the rule of law.[13]

---

[13] This capacity of citizenship to adapt and accommodate change is implicit in much of the scholarly literature. See, for example, T.H. Marshall's (1992) classic work on social citizenship, and the idea of citizenship as an incompletely theorized contract in the work of Saskia Sassen (2006).

DYNAMICS OF RENATIONALIZATION: CONTESTED CITIZENSHIP IN A GLOBAL ERA

The model of ethnic citizenship sits uneasily in the scholarly debates over citizenship. The mushrooming literature that has turned citizenship studies into a separate, multidisciplinary field in the social sciences in recent decades tends to focus on trends and transformations of citizenship that emphasize globalizing, rather than nationalizing, logics. The commitment of Western liberal democracies to the project of multiculturalism is increasingly called into question; nevertheless, the overall direction of change in the institution of citizenship is often assessed to reflect broader processes of denationalization (Bosniak 2000; Sassen 2006) and liberalization (e.g., Joppke 2007a). Citizenship in a global era is seen as fragmenting into separate discourses of rights, responsibilities, participation, and identity, reflecting worldwide social transformations driven by forces such as capitalism and democracy (Delanty 2000). The unity of status, rights, and identity in the nation-state, which characterizes the twentieth-century model of citizenship, is currently destabilized by a realignment of its constituent elements with multiple scales and domains of governance. The increasing complexity and layering of citizenship can be observed in Europe, where civil rights often migrate to the supra-state level of international and European instruments, political rights are no longer exclusively bounded by the nation-state and take on a European dimension, and social rights become differentiated in devolved units at the substate level (Bauböck and Guiraudon 2009; Keating 2009).

Seen in this context, the model of ethnic citizenship may appear as exceptional if not obsolete, reflecting attempts to reconstruct a version of the unitary model of citizenship in moments of intense nation-building, such as those precipitated by the collapse of multinational states at the end of the Cold War, or to maintain such frameworks in the face of overwhelming forces that are pulling in the opposite direction. Moreover, the significance of ethnic citizenship as an encompassing status contrasts sharply with accounts that emphasize how citizenship is deflated and devalued at the current juncture. On the one hand, substantive citizenship rights are eroded by forces associated with neoliberal globalization; as one study put it, "Welfare entitlements are removed at the behest of international lenders, labour rights are curtailed, and trade agreements are concluded with little or no citizen participation" (Brysk and Shafir 2004: 6). On the other hand, states are enforcing universal human rights and not only national rights, diminishing the value of citizenship from another direction. This is the thrust of Yasemin Soysal's (1994) seminal work on the emergence of "postnational citizenship" in Europe. Migrants become incorporated by the host state via their universal personhood rather than nation-hood, as states are challenged to reconcile their sovereignty with the "transnational discourse and structures celebrating human rights as a world-level organizing principle" (Soysal 1994: 3).

However, in some sense, these developments are reinforcing the analytical value of ethnic citizenship as a lens into the relationship between nationalism and the rule of law in a global era. The more apparent becomes the decline of citizenship in a substantive sense, as signaled by the advent of corporate globalization or the develop-ment of denizenship arrangements premised on universal human rights, the greater are the incentives for revaluation of citizenship as a symbolic resource for the nation-state in managing questions of iden-tity. A symbolic revaluation of citizenship can be detected in salient processes of renationalization, which are unfolding alongside the vari-ous dynamics of denationalization that are often emphasized in the literature. Globalizing conditions such as migration and deterritorial-ization can provide a fertile ground for the reconstruction of national identities in new ways, as captured by Benedict Anderson (1992) in his account of "long-distance nationalism." Similarly, in the citizen-ship arena such conditions may become entangled with some contra-dictory developments. Christian Joppke (2003: 3) suggests that when it comes to immigration, cross-border migration "forces the state to de-ethnicize citizenship, in the sense of grounding citizenship more on residence and birth on territory than on filiation," whereas with respect to emigration, it "tips the balance in the opposite direction, toward re-ethnicization, in the sense of providing incentives for states to retain links with their members abroad, particularly across genera-tions." The growing acceptance of dual nationality by many states can be seen as one example of the symbolic import of citizenship, in this case highlighting the significance of maintaining symbolic links with co-ethnics abroad, in an era of intensified migration and long-distance nationalism.

A symbolic revaluation of citizenship can be discerned also in the ongoing debates over immigration and Islam in the West, which have been fueled by the perceived failures of multiculturalism, the terrorist attacks of 9/11 in the United States, and concerns about homegrown Islamic terrorism in Europe. These debates are associated with the rise of new sites of identity politics and mobilization of nationalist, xeno-phobic, and anti-Islam rhetoric by populist movements, but also by political parties that sometimes manage to shift the entire mainstream discourse to the right (see, e.g., Boomkens 2010; Brochmann and Seland 2010). In this environment, the "cultural" dimension of citizenship acquires new significance that is reflected, for instance, in the pervasive anxieties about "illiberal" practices of ethnic and religious minorities and growing concerns about "social cohesion." The integration of immigrants in the host society is reimagined as participation in a shared national culture and acceptance of a related set of values, and the immigrant's route to full citizenship is endowed with a new symbolism. These dynamics have become apparent, for instance, in the shift to "civic integration" policies across Europe, which often require immigrants to undertake language training or civic education courses; to demonstrate command of the national language and knowledge of polity and society; to pass citizenship tests and partake in various symbolic contracts, oaths, and ceremonies.[14]

Some observers have interpreted such developments as manifesting the illiberal tendencies inherent in liberalism itself, in particular the disciplining and repressive import of its neoliberal version associated with contemporary globalization, rather than as a resurgence of "anachronistic" nationalist and racist impulses (Joppke 2007b: 267–271).[15] Questions of national identity and "culture," however, cannot be

---

[14] See, for example, the series of essays in the special issue on cultural citizenship of *Citizenship Studies* 14.3 (2010) and Joppke (2007b).

[15] On this argument, what we are seeing after September 11, 2001, is a shift from the liberalism of toleration, which supported multiculturalism, to the liberalism of autonomy, which is "much less patient and compatible with any one creed" (Joppke 2007a: 46). But liberal states and societies have shown varying degrees of toleration for different creeds and have responded very differently to the range of illiberal practices that have come to the fore in this period. For instance, the decade of the War on Terror has also

easily extricated from the semantics of integration and cohesion that permeates the discourse of citizenship. Indeed, for students of nationalism, the turn to civic integration is reminiscent of some of the classic nationalization projects pursued by states in the nineteenth and twentieth century, which often involved large-scale educational enterprises and diffusion of a single language and societal culture, famously captured by Eugène Weber (1979) in the transformation of "peasants into Frenchmen."[16] Viewed in this light, the paradigms of civic integration and ethnic citizenship can be situated on a spectrum of contemporary state policies of renationalization, which reflect a revaluation of citizenship as a symbolic resource for the nation-state precisely at a time when other forces may be increasingly serving to decouple cultural and political units. These dynamics are deeply implicated in contemporary processes of identity construction and mobilization and may become even more important in the context of further erosion of the substantive content of citizenship by the forces of neoliberal globalization.

It is instructive that some of the rule of law challenges associated with policies signaling a renationalization of citizenship, whether such policies are pursued by liberal or ethnic states, often emerge from similar sources and become expressed and negotiated in similar ways. Joppke (2007a) argues that the symbolic reappropriation of citizenship by the liberal state as manifested, for instance, in recent campaigns for "unity" and "integration" and a turn to more restrictive naturalization

been a period of seemingly endless revelations about sexual abuse of children implicating the Catholic Church. Affected states have responded to these shocking allegations with careful investigation of specific incidents and abuses, precisely the sort of restraint that became suspended in the context of the War on Terror. Catholics have not been subjected to a process of "othering" similar to one that has affected many Muslims, nor has their religion become entangled in contentious debates over social cohesion and citizenship policy. See, for example, Ireland's Cloyne Report and the international reactions to its release: Report of Commission of Investigation into Catholic Diocese of Cloyne, December 2010, retrieved from http://www.justice.ie/en/JELR/Pages/Cloyne_Rpt (accessed 23 October 2011); Muted International Coverage of Cloyne, *IrishTimes.com*, 14 July 2011, retrieved from http://www.irishtimes.com/newspaper/breaking/2011/0714/breaking32.html (accessed 23 October 2010).

[16] From this perspective, the persistence of various forms of ethnic citizenship in parts of the postcolonial world could be understood in terms of incomplete and ongoing nation-building.

policies in Europe, is inherently limited by well-entrenched liberal democratic principles and human rights norms. Such principled commitments of European states, however, have not prevented attempts for renationalization of citizenship and immigration policy by more or less illiberal means, even if the overall objectives of such policies are often rhetorically justified on the terms of liberalism. The ensuing tensions and contradictions between nationalism and the rule of law can be observed in the field of antidiscrimination in the European Union (EU), playing out as contestations between member states and European law and institutions.

Consider, for example, the resistance of some member states and the controversies surrounding the implementation of the EU's Race Directive of June 2000, which extends the ambit of European antidiscrimination legislation to "all persons" – citizens and noncitizens of EU member states – and targets both direct and indirect forms of discrimination on the basis of racial and ethnic origin.[17] Another example is the backlash provoked by the *Metock*[18] decision of the European Court of Justice (ECJ), which was met with vigorous protests from several member states. The decision affirms the right of noncitizen spouses of EU citizens to move and reside with them in the Union without having previously been lawful residents of a member state, thus challenging the restrictive immigration rules of several countries in the EU.[19] *Metock* caused an outcry in Denmark, where many saw the ruling as an attack on the country's restrictive immigration legislation, and the prime minster, Anders Fogh Rasmussen, described it as "hijacking" national immigration policy.[20] The point of the controversy was that

[17] Council Directive 2000/43/EC of 29 June 2000, implementing the principle of equal treatment of persons irrespective of racial or ethnic origin (see Articles 3.1 and 2.2.a). For an illuminating discussion of the controversies that have accompanied the implementation of the EU's Race Directive, see Joppke (2007b: 256–267).

[18] *Metock and Others v. Minister for Justice, Equality and Law Reform*, C-127/08, European Union: European Court of Justice, 25 July 2008.

[19] The ruling was based on Directive 2004/38/EC of the European Parliament and of the Council of 29 April 2004, on the right of citizens of the Union and their family members to move and reside freely within the territory of the Member States.

[20] Quoted in Ana Lansbergen, "Testing the Limits of European Citizenship," European Policy Brief, The Federal Trust for Education and Research, May 2009, retrieved from http://www.fedtrust.co.uk/admin/uploads/Testing_Limits_of_Citz.pdf (accessed 11 October 2011). See also the discussion of the backlash triggered by the *Metock* ruling in

by upholding free movement and residence rights within the EU, the ECJ effectively allowed certain migrants to circumvent the carefully charted national "integration" paths and their symbolic milestones and requirements, such as immigration tests.

Similar contestations over state policies breaching the principles of equality and non-discrimination have also accompanied the articulation of ethnic citizenship in the past two decades, implicating a range of regional and international bodies. Diane Orentlicher (1998) has drawn attention to the responses of such bodies to the restrictive citizenship policies adopted by Estonia, Latvia, and the Czech Republic after the fall of communism, illuminating the role of ethnic citizenship as a catalyst for the development of international law in this domain. She suggests that the critical interventions of the Council of Europe, the Organization for Security and Cooperation in Europe, and the United Nations in these cases signal a normative shift, as international law constrains state discretion in respect of citizenship – seen to be limited by international human rights norms such as non-discrimination – and implicitly reinforces "a territorial/civic model of citizenship in preference to an ethnic model" (Orentlicher 1998: 299).

There is also a move toward growing judicialization of questions arising from ethnic citizenship by regional bodies such as the European Court of Human Rights (ECtHR). In *Sejdić and Finci*,[21] for example, the ECtHR challenged the peculiar form of ethnic citizenship engendered by the post-Dayton constitutional order of Bosnia and Herzegovina, which allows only members of the three so-called constituent peoples (Bosniaks, Croats, and Serbs) to stand for election to the Presidency and the House of Peoples, thus effectively excluding and discriminating against members of the country's Jewish, Roma, and other minorities. Another example is the involvement of the ECtHR in the case of the "erased" in Slovenia, which I examine later

Simon Taylor, "Protecting Citizens Does Not Mean Closing the Borders," *European Voice*, 2 October 2008, retrieved from http://www.europeanvoice.com/article/imported/protecting-citizens-does-not-mean-closing-the-borders/62519.aspx (accessed 10 October 2011).

[21] *Sejdić and Finci v. Bosnia and Herzegovina*, Application nos. 27996/06 and 34836/06, Council of Europe: European Court of Human Rights, 22 December 2009.

in the book.[22] The point here is that such parallels arising in diverse contexts highlight the analytical traction of the model of ethnic citizenship for broader explorations of the symbolic revaluation of citizenship that we are witnessing. Ethnic citizenship affords a lens that makes legible multiple dynamics of renationalization at the current juncture and draws attention to a range of ensuing conflicts and contestations that implicate the rule of law, both within and beyond the state.

In conclusion, I have argued that the concept of ethnic citizenship is useful in clarifying several important dimensions of the relationship between nationalism and the rule of law. The various strategies of incorporation and exclusion associated with the model of ethnic citizenship suggest how the pursuit of such state-driven nationalist projects may serve to undermine the rule of law and, at the same, highlight the ambivalent role of law. The legal articulation of ethnic citizenship can serve as a moderating factor and afford opportunities to renegotiate the terms of membership in line with alternative, more inclusive conceptions of nationhood. The role of legitimacy in mediating the relationship between nationalism and the rule of law becomes apparent in this context. Ethnic citizenship and the rule of law emerge as competing frameworks and principles of legitimation, which are increasingly not only domestic but also regional and international in character. Finally, the analytical traction of ethnic citizenship is underscored by the concurrent unfolding of dynamics of denationalization and renationalization at the current juncture, in particular the revaluation of citizenship as a symbolic resource for the nation-state at a time when global forces are challenging its ability to shape collective identities.

---

[22] See Chapter 4, § "Europeanization."

2   TRANSITIONAL JUSTICE

In a recent decision, the French Constitutional Council struck down a bill intended to criminalize the denial of genocides recognized by France, most notably the Armenian atrocities from the First World War, with the reasoning that the legislation caused "unconstitutional harm to the exercise of freedom of expression and communication."[1] The controversies sparked by the bill in Turkey, France, and elsewhere is the latest example of the use of law to address historical legacies of mass atrocities that implicate nations and nationalism, which increasingly take the form of judicial and quasi-judicial responses to past experiences of mass violence and abuse. These developments suggest yet another way of approaching the relationship between nationalism and the rule of law, raising a set of questions about the promise and limits of law as a form of reckoning with the "dark side" of nationalism. Should the law be used to promote one representation of the past over others? What is the role of law and legal institutions in validating collective memories and experiences of injustice and challenging the national projects and identities that may be entangled with such grievances? Can legal processes be harnessed to manage and transform nationalism?

In the following pages I examine some of these questions in the context of *transitional justice* – the multiplicity of responses and mechanisms that address legacies of large-scale human rights violations

[1] Scott Sayare, "French Council Strikes Down Bill on Armenian Genocide Denial," *New York Times*, 28 February 2012, retrieved from http://www.nytimes.com/2012/02/29/world/europe/french-bill-on-armenian-genocide-is-struck-down.html (accessed 28 February 2012).

associated with armed conflict and repressive rule. The origins of transitional justice are often traced to what Huntington (1991) calls the "third wave of democratization," which affected some thirty countries in Southern Europe, Latin America, Eastern Europe, and parts of Africa and Asia between the mid-1970s and the early 1990s, although some histories go back to the Nuremberg Trial and the post-war period. The field of transitional justice has expanded enormously over the past two decades and now provides a focal point for a broad range of responses, including criminal prosecutions and truth telling, constitutional and institutional reforms, and various forms of recognition, reparation, and redress for victims and survivors.[2] Moreover, we are witnessing a normalization and entrenchment of transitional justice across a range of contexts and situations (democratization scenarios but also conflict and post-conflict settings, exceptional periods of political change as well as late unfoldings after many years and decades), and a proliferation of actors, claims, and purposes that become enmeshed in the politics of transitional justice (Teitel 2003; Rangelov and Teitel 2011).

Among the various modalities of transitional justice, domestic criminal trials represent a form of reckoning that most directly implicates the rule of law. There is a substantial body of literature on trials but few scholars engage with the semantics of nations and nationalism.[3] Moreover, even when nationalism is discussed, it is usually to examine the narratives advanced by the prosecution, defense, and judges, rather than to illuminate the ways in which diverse actors and audiences outside the courtroom may be engaging with these narratives and the larger issues they raise. As Christiane Wilke points out, "Trials restage violence for distinct audiences. Yet in research on trials, the audience remains literally in the dark" (Wilke 2011: 147). In contrast, the "deliberative" interpretation of transitional justice developed in this chapter emphasizes the role of trials as a vehicle for public debate, which affords opportunities to manage and transform the discourse of nationalism. I examine France's trials for crimes against humanity from the Occupation and Vichy period as a paradigm of deliberative transitional justice, highlighting their role in opening up for public

---

[2] See the discussion of different modalities of transitional justice in Teitel (2000).
[3] For two notable exceptions, see Wilke (2011) and Aptel (2011).

discussion the "dark side" of nationalism and encouraging critical reassessment of accepted narratives of national unity and transformation. Finally, I briefly discuss Turkey's "Armenian problem" as an example of "transition without justice," and examine some of its implications. I draw attention to the nature of the ensuing public conversation about the past, which often involves incessant contestation of the "facts" of past atrocities, rather than engagement in productive debate over their significance and interpretation. If transitional justice processes may create opportunities to open up and renegotiate questions of national identity and state legitimacy in the aftermath of mass atrocity, I argue that transitions without justice risk entrenching the problems of legitimation and encouraging further nationalist mobilization.

TRANSITIONAL JUSTICE AND THE CHALLENGE OF NATIONALISM

Law is often seen as a blunt instrument for addressing traumatic experiences of large-scale violence and abuse, even in societies where justice may be in high demand. Can general rules of law be applied to exceptional massacres and atrocities without distorting or normalizing them? Are legal procedures too formalistic and rigid to comprehend multiple experiences of suffering and injustice? Katherine Franke (2006: 821) highlights the inherent limits of the law in this respect, noting that "the translation of human suffering into the language of law and rights will always satisfy the interests of legal authorities more than those who are called to narrate their pain." Such problems are compounded when the reopening of legacies of mass atrocity may involve raising unsettling questions that implicate national projects and collective identities. When nations and nationalisms reflect the fault lines of enmity and violence, how prudent is it to revive such polarizing grievances and relive them in the rituals of law? Criminal prosecutions after mass violence inevitably select some crimes and neglect others and are often used by the state to promote its preferred representations of the past. In such contexts, are trials likely to inhibit the emergence of shared narratives and to complicate reconciliation processes?

I propose a deliberative interpretation of transitional justice, emphasizing the potential of trials to engender productive forms of reckoning with legacies of mass violence and abuse, which becomes legible outside the courtroom and encourages more contestation than closure in the public domain. This is a distinctive conception of the process and purpose of transitional justice, which draws attention to the role of trials in affording opportunities for discursive engagements of diverse actors and publics with the subject matter at stake, and locates the significance of the proceedings in the ensuing public articulation of plural representations and interpretations of the past. There are three characteristics that distinguish a deliberative understanding of transitional justice.

First, trials are reinterpreted as vehicles for public debate. Beyond the impact of the proceedings on those directly involved, trials provide opportunities to open up a broader conversation about the past that engages diverse audiences and publics outside the courtroom. The judicial process becomes particularly important when it furnishes a set of reference points that shape the nature of the discussion, shifting the focus of public contestation from the "facts" at stake to their significance and interpretation. To be sure, the ways in which trials become appropriated in public discourse can never be predicted and controlled. The prosecution, defense, and judges may resort to various rhetorical strategies in order to shape public reactions, but equally important is the possibility that diverse actors and audiences outside the courtroom may use the trial as an opportunity to advance a range of other claims and purposes in the ensuing discussions. When the emphasis shifts from the courtroom to public discourse, there is an inherent uncertainty as to who may engage with the trial and in what ways, what interpretations and representations of the past might be articulated and debated in the public domain, but this is precisely the significance of the process: indeterminacy is seen here as pregnant with opportunity.

The second aspect of this conception of transitional justice concerns the focus of the public conversation sparked by the trials, particularly when questions about the role of nationalism and complicity of nations loom large. In such contexts, trials often tell a rather limited story, distancing the state and nation from the offenses listed in the indictment by framing them as exceptional in character. The political projects and ideologies implicated in the atrocities may be neglected by the court, or invoked only to draw a line between the past and the present and to reinforce appealing narratives of "transition" and "transformation." However, the significance of the public deliberation encouraged by the trial may be precisely in challenging such narratives of progressive change. When the court frames a particular period of violence and abuse as an exception or "rupture" in the history of the nation, the public conversation is useful precisely as a counterweight to such claims and representations, affording opportunities to illuminate the issue of continuity and the persistence of certain forms or strands of nationalism that may be implicated in the criminal legacies at stake. Just as the trial is most effective when it sparks a broader conversation that goes beyond the confines of the court, the ensuing public debate is most productive when it shifts back and forth between the past and present, drawing attention to salient but often neglected continuities in nationalism and submitting them to critical scrutiny and reassessment.

Finally, in this approach the significance of transitional justice stems from the process of deliberation and contestation itself and the ensuing opportunities for diverse actors with stakes in these issues to articulate multiple interpretations and representations of the past. It is far less ambitious than conceptions of justice that invest such processes with expectations for political reconciliation or the construction of shared narratives of the past. In fact, a deliberative interpretation of transitional justice calls into question the prudence of such aspirations. The assumption is that public discourse has to be fluid and contentious in order to enable public articulation of private memories, dissident accounts, and subversive interpretations, which are often suppressed when the focus is on finding a common ground or reaching a consensus. Whereas the courts may choose to tell a story of national unity and transformation, or to promote ideas of reconciliation and redemption, an emphasis on critical public deliberation pulls in the opposite direction by encouraging those who may be excluded or marginalized in such narratives to engage and contest them. Minority experiences of injustice become validated through the medium of public discourse itself, articulating memories and identities and challenging the accepted narratives of nationalism that may have little or no space for them. Ultimately, what is at stake in such debates is the legitimacy of the state and the national projects and identities that are opened up for public reassessment and renegotiation.

The idea of deliberative transitional justice is foreshadowed in some of the classic texts in the field, particularly in the work of Osiel (1997) and Teitel (2000). A perspective sensitive to the challenge of nationalism, however, goes further in several ways. Osiel (1997: 2) notes that in the aftermath of large-scale brutality, conducting criminal prosecutions is justified beyond the usual goals of deterrence and retribution: "At such times, the need for public reckoning with the question of how such horrific events could have happened is more important to democratization than the criminal law's more traditional objectives. This is because such trials, when effective as public spectacle, stimulate public discussion in ways that foster the liberal virtues of toleration, moderation, and civil respect." On this account, trials become public spectacles aimed at engaging and provoking their audiences. Such trials are liberal but not only in the sense that they tell a liberal story, one that rewards liberal virtues and renounces illiberal ones. When disagreement about the past is channeled into a single conceptual framework, it becomes "civil dissensus" and the logic of discursive engagements produces a form of solidarity that accords with liberalism: "[T]he kind of solidarity embodied in the increasingly respectful way that citizens come to acknowledge the differing views of their fellows" (ibid.: 22–23). The role of law after mass atrocity is not to encourage political reconciliation but to facilitate society's return to civility, by staging a pedagogic drama in the courtroom and fostering discursive solidarity in the audience. Crucially, these functions of criminal law are geared not to suppress but to uphold moral disagreement.

An approach that takes into account the challenge of nationalism articulates with Osiel's conception but also qualifies it, raising certain questions about the pedagogic and liberal goals of criminal law. Trials for mass atrocities may be conducted with a number of objectives in mind, but these rarely include a sustained interrogation of the role of nations and nationalism in past episodes of violence, or a probing of the limits of national transformation in their aftermath. The trial may tell a liberal story about the specific offenses in the indictment and at the same time neglect or distort the broader national story. The problem here is not only that "a few bad apples" may be convicted without scrutiny (or precisely to avoid scrutiny) of the regime and chain of command to which they belong – a possibility that Osiel anticipates and confronts.[4] There is also the risk that the court frames the story as an aberration or rupture in the history of the nation, even if an entire regime such as the Third Reich or Vichy France is condemned in the course of the trial. Such representations of the past may obscure important continuities in nationalism and provide easy answers to the difficult questions of national unity and transformation.

Teitel (2000: 9) notes that legal responses to repressive pasts are "both performative and symbolic of transition." Seen in this light, transitional justice is significant because it offers a narrative that enables transformation. Courts, however, are organs of the state with its preferred versions of national history and identity, and they are likely to favor such constructs for multiple reasons when addressing legacies of past abuse. Trials may provide the occasion and impetus for opening up these questions but it is the broader public conversation set in motion by the proceedings that is more likely to expose the "dark side" of nationalism and submit it to a critical reevaluation. In this sense, the significance of transitional justice as a narrative that enables transformation often hinges on its ability not to represent "transition" and "transformation," but instead to call them into question: to encourage reckoning with the nation's past as it persists in its present and expose salient continuities that may be veiled by the attractive rhetoric of change. On this account, then, deliberative transitional justice starts with the stories and interpretations offered by the participants in the courtroom drama; it is sparked by the trial, but takes on a life of its own.

PROBING THE NATION THROUGH THE LAW: LATE JUSTICE IN FRANCE

The idea of deliberative transitional justice can be explored further by examining France's protracted struggle to come to terms with the

[4] Osiel (1997: 163) describes the situation where the court tells a story of the few bad apples leading an innocent nation astray as a failure of criminal law.

legacy of the Vichy regime and the Occupation during the Second
World War. Public discourse was captured by the memory of Vichy
in the 1970s and remained in its grip for several decades. The endless
debates and controversies sparked by the trials of Klaus Barbie, Paul
Touvier, and Mourice Papon for crimes against humanity became a
mirror reflecting the struggle over French nationalism. The representations of the past promoted by the French judiciary in the course of
the trials often appeared inadequate and unsatisfactory; in fact, these
readings of French history seemed to reveal more about the state's
political objectives and ideological justifications than about the nature
of the Vichy regime and the Occupation. It was the broader public discussion sparked by the trials that afforded opportunities to interrogate
the "dark side" of French nationalism and contest accepted understandings of national identity and transformation.

French historian Henry Rousso (1991) argues that the Occupation
and Vichy period of 1940–1944 represents an archetype of the Guerre
franco-française, a political and ideological conflict going back to the
late nineteenth century and expressing the persistence of extreme
right-wing and antirepublican traditions in French political life. He
highlights three factors that help account for the contested memory
of Vichy in post-war France: the emergence of Pétanism and its view
of history as an ideal for those subscribing to a counterrevolutionary
Catholic tradition; Vichy's own origins in right-wing and extreme right-
wing political traditions, reflecting deeply rooted political divisions in
France; and, lastly, the persistence of anti-Semitism as "a constant in
French history since the Dreyfus affair: the existence of a political,
nonreligious, antisemitic tradition, which at intervals has surfaced to
create a division within French society" (Rousso 1991: 300).

These deep rifts in French politics and national identity came to
the fore in the public debates surrounding the trials for crimes against
humanity from the Vichy era, alongside the more apparent themes of
French collaboration and resistance in the period of the Occupation.
The trials marked the peak of what Rousso calls the "Vichy Syndrome"
in France, but its origins go back to the immediate post-war period:

> Between 1944 and 1954 France had to deal directly with the after-
> math of civil war, purge and amnesty. I call this the "mourning

phase," whose contradictions had a considerable impact on what came afterward. From 1954 to 1971 the subject of Vichy became less controversial, except for occasional eruptions in the period 1958–1962. The French apparently had repressed memories of the civil war with the aid of what came to be a dominant myth: "resistancialism." This term, first coined after the Liberation by adversaries of the purge, is used here in a rather different sense. By resistancialism I mean, first, a process that sought to minimize the importance of the Vichy regime and its impact on French society, *including its most negative aspects*; second, the construction of an object of memory, the "Resistance," whose significance transcended by far the sum of its active parts (the small groups of guerrilla partisans who did the actual fighting) and whose existence was embodied chiefly in certain sites and groups, such as the Gaullists and Communists, associated with fully elaborated ideologies; and, third, the identification of this "Resistance" with the nation as whole, a characteristic feature of the Gaullist version of the myth.

Between 1971 and 1974 this carefully constructed myth was shattered; the mirror was broken. This was the third phase of the process, which is analyzed here as a "return of the repressed." In turn this inaugurated a fourth phase, continuing to this day: a phase of obsession, characterized on the one hand by the reawakening of Jewish memory and, on the other, by the importance that reminiscences of the Occupation assumed in French political debate. (Rousso 1991: 10 (emphasis in the original))

The initial legal response in postwar France involved a series of prosecutions, purges, and amnesties, but left largely untouched the legacy of Vichy's repression of Jews and the disturbing question of French complicity in the Holocaust. With hindsight, these developments represented only the first phase of transitional justice in France, and later debates often recast them as a failure of justice that needed to be remedied in what became a period of "late justice" from the 1970s onward. The immediate post-war trials were conceived to punish treason and collaboration – "intelligence with the enemy" – rather than cases of torture, killings, and deportations of Jews (Fraser 2005: 181), but it was the latter crimes that came to preoccupy the judiciary and the public in the 1980s and 1990s. The High Court that tried René Bousquet in 1949, for example, was not interested in his role in crafting Vichy

policies toward the Jews while serving as a secretary-general of the
regime's police. When Bousquet was shot dead in his apartment in
Paris in the summer of 1993, however, a second trial was imminent –
this time for his role in the Final Solution.[5] In 1964 France suspended
the statute of limitations for crimes against humanity, shortly after it
had granted amnesties for offences committed in the Algerian War.
Rousso (1991: 93) notes the intention to forget the excesses of the latest Guerre franco-française but to remember the monumental crimes
of the Nazis, and to forge national unity on both counts. Ironically,
three decades later the 1964 crimes against humanity legislation provided the basis for the trial of Maurice Papon, which among other
things helped open up the taboo subject of French abuses in Algeria.

Subsequent reassessments of the initial reckoning with the legacy
of the war and Occupation in France raise important questions about
the role of amnesties in promoting national unity and reconciliation.
Scholars often highlight the utility of amnesties as an instrument that
enables divided societies to put the past behind them and move forward (Cobban 2007; Huntington 1991). In an attempt to unite and
reconcile the nation, France granted amnesties in 1951 and 1953,
released most prisoners, and marked the end of the post-war purges.
But twenty years later, a single pardon sparked a public controversy
that reopened old wounds and resurrected the spectre of the "Dark
Years" of the Occupation. The occasion was provided in November
1971, when President Pompidou quietly granted a pardon to Paul
Touvier, a former officer of Milice, Vichy's quasi-military arm that
brutalized the enemies of the regime.

When information about the pardon was revealed to the public
several months later, the reaction was astonishing: "The press was
unleashed in one of the most spectacular outbursts of journalistic
attention to the Occupation since the 1950s: 350 articles appeared in
the month of June alone, 2,000 in 1972, and some 5,000 through 1976.
With a series of 'exclusive reports,' 'revelations,' and 'new documents'
added to an already thick dossier, the media kept up constant pressure"
(Rousso 1991: 177). The reaction also appeared disproportionate to

---

[5] Many saw the Touvier case as an inadequate substitute for the trial of René Bousquet,
who had come to symbolize French complicity in the Holocaust. See Golsan (2000a:
24–42); Beigbeder (2006: 213–220).

the profile of the villain. After the Liberation, Touvier remained in France but went into hiding, engaged in petty crime, married, and had two children. He was tried in absentia for intelligence with the enemy and sentenced to death in 1946 and 1947, by courts in Chambéry and Lyon. When Pompidou's pardon became public knowledge, the scandal was fueled by the fact that Touvier had succeeded in evading French justice for so long with the help of powerful patrons in the Catholic Church. At the heart of the controversy was the role of the Church in Vichy France and its long-standing association with antire-publican and anti-Semitic currents in French nationalism:

> Throughout the Vichy and post-war periods, up to controversies surrounding Pope John Paul II's 1996 visit and connections with the debate around the conversion of Clovis to Christianity as the founding moment of *la vraie France* (true France), parts of French Catholicism have been associated with anti-Republican, antisemitic agitations and political movements. Here, Touvier's case raises profound questions which echo in the legal context with Richard Weisberg's troubling thesis about a latent and vital Catholic anti-semitism at the heart of French national identity and legal politics. (Fraser 2005: 193–194)[6]

The Touvier Affair was going to preoccupy France for the next two decades, ending with his conviction in 1994 and death in prison a couple of years later. But the public furore provoked by the presiden-tial pardon raises important questions about the use of amnesty as a form of legally sanctioned forgetting (*oubli juridique*) in the interest of national unity and reconciliation. What had changed between 1951 and 1971? In a speech justifying the pardon, Pompidou argued that it was time to draw a veil over the past and look to the future – completely out of line with the prevailing public sentiment, which pulled in the opposite direction. That disconnect meant that "the effects of the par-don were precisely the opposite of what was intended" (Rousso 1991: 126). In fact, the very act of official forgetting appeared to engender public demand to remember, as the presidential pardon marked the beginning of an era of public reckoning with France's national past. This is the other aspect of the incident that deserves attention: should

---

[6] See also Weisberg (1996).

law be used to encourage nations to "forget" their pasts in the first place? Amnesties may or may not be effective depending on the yardstick used to assess them, but are they desirable? The Touvier Affair encouraged public discussion of the role of Catholicism in shaping French national identity before and beyond the Dark Years, the myth of resistancialism, and the fiction of the seamless French nation of De Gaulle's era. The debates sparked by Touvier's pardon and subsequent arrest and trial helped interrogate both the official narratives of French nationalism and its more opaque underside.

The first man tried for crimes against humanity in France was not Touvier, however, but the German Lieutenant Klaus Barbie. At the end of the war Barbie had served as the head of the Gestapo in Lyon, where he built a reputation as the Butcher of Lyon for overseeing the killing and deportation to death camps of some 12,000 suspected Resistance members and Jews. His cardinal crime, which eventually ensured his arrest and prosecution, implicated him in the torture and death of the Resistance martyr Jean Moulin. Barbie had a colorful post-war career that included providing intelligence services to the Americans and eventually relocating to Bolivia, where he became involved in various business ventures and local politics. Sustained pressure from Nazi hunters and Resistance groups were starting to bear fruit, however, and with a favorable political dispensation emerging in Bolivia in the early 1980s, President Mitterrand eventually managed to secure Barbie's extradition to France. The trial started in May 1987 and was marked by unprecedented interest from the media and civil society: 800 journalists were following the proceedings and 40 representatives of the victims and their families were acting as civil prosecutors (Binder 1989: 1325–1328). The French state was ready to perform a pedagogic trial of Nazi atrocities, a lesson in history and ethics that was about to tell precisely the limited story discussed earlier in the chapter: "To that end [the government] presented Barbie as a symbol of Nazi barbarism: the man who tortured Jean Moulin would be judged in the name of the law and of the impossibility of forgetting the past" (Rousso 1991: 201).

The 1964 crimes against humanity legislation was invoked to tell the story of Nazi barbarity and French resistance. But the French judiciary had gone through a series of revisions of the charges against

Barbie before the road was cleared to use the law as intended. The problem was the amnesty legislation from 1964 and 1968 for offenses committed by French forces in suppressing the Algerian revolt: how to prosecute Barbie for crimes against members of the Resistance without undermining the validity of the amnesty laws, given the similarities between the two cases? The response of the Court of Appeals was to drop the charges against suspected members of the Resistance and focus on the deportation of Jews, defining crimes against humanity as "the persecution extending to the extermination, in peacetime as well as in wartime … of any noncombatants because of their race or their religious or political beliefs in application of a deliberate state controlled policy, useless to the operations of war."[7] Barbie's attorney, Jacques Vergès, found himself arguing on the same side as the Resistance groups: crimes against humanity must also cover the murder of Jean Moulin. Vergès was seeking to stir public controversy by raising questions about the complicity of Moulin's fellow *résistants* in his death; the Resistance associations were seeking a legal sanction of Moulin's martyrdom.

In the end, the Cour de Cassation found a way to reinstate the charges involving deportation of suspected members of the Resistance by redefining crimes against humanity: as long as the offenses were committed in the name of a state practicing "a policy of ideological supremacy" against opponents of that policy, the racial and religious identity of the victims did not matter.[8] Binder (1989: 1338) notes that as far as the French courts were concerned, crimes against humanity

> [C]ame to mean all and only crimes undertaken on behalf of a state committed to Nazi ideology. Hence, Barbie's prosecutors were required to identify the Nazi ideology his crime enforced, and the ideals for which the Resistance was martyred and France liberated. And every noble ideal attributed to France in such a trial served to distinguish France's repression of Algeria as a mere crime of war because, after all, the French were not Nazis.

Were the French "remembering in vein," as Alain Finkielkraut (1992) argued? In the course of the trial, Vergès kept raising the spectre of

---

[7] Judgement, 20 December 1985, quoted in Binder (1989: 1321).

[8] Ibid., 1337.

colonialism, suggesting that France had no right to judge Barbie without judging its own crimes in the colonies. Osiel (1997: 279) notes that one of the implications of the trial was that "the French were ultimately asked to accept responsibility for all of their twentieth-century massacres, as in resisting independence movements in Algeria and other former colonies."[9] But the trial was also used as an opportunity to focus public attention on more contemporary problems in French politics and society. Foreign Trade Minister Michel Noir, whose father had died in a Nazi concentration camp, created a political storm by calling on the governing conservative coalition to distance itself from the extremist National Front of Jean-Marie Le Pen and its anti-immigration rhetoric against North Africans. Noir warned that racism and anti-Semitism were on the rise in France once again, and argued that the lesson of the Barbie trial was that the government should choose electoral defeat over cooperation with the National Front: "Are we ready to sacrifice our soul so as not to lose the elections?"[10] It was these issues and the ensuing debate in the public domain that generated much of the press coverage of the trial (Binder 1989: 1343).

The more France became preoccupied with the legacy of Vichy, the more the judicial response appeared unsatisfactory. In April 1992, the Paris Court of Appeal dismissed the case charging Paul Touvier with a massacre of seven Jews at Rillieux. The definition of crimes against humanity inherited from the Barbie trial required that the acts were committed in the service of a regime practicing a policy of ideological supremacy. The court found that unlike the Nazis, Marshal Pétain's regime had not practiced such a policy; therefore, Touvier could only be charged with war crimes for which the statute of limitations had already expired.[11] The interpretation of Vichy's historical record advanced by the Court of Appeal was seen as "tendentious in the extreme" (Golsan 2000a: 22) and created a public uproar. The

---

[9] For a critical account underscoring the problems with the strategy pursued by Vergès, see Binder (1989).

[10] Paul Lewis, "Barbie Is a Specter in a Cabinet Rift in France," *New York Times*, 20 May 1987.

[11] See *Touvier*, France, Court of Appeal of Paris (First Chamber of Accusation), 13 April 1992, Court of Cassation (Criminal Chamber), 27 November 1992, *International Law Reports* 100: 337–364 (1994).

Court of Cassation quashed the controversial ruling, but it allowed the case to proceed on the grounds that the murders had been instigated by an officer of the Gestapo.[12] Touvier was finally convicted in 1994 as an accomplice to a state practicing a policy of ideological supremacy, but that state was the Third Reich rather than Vichy France. French law redefined crimes against humanity once again, suggesting that a Frenchman could perpetrate such atrocities only on German orders. The Court, in other words, told a liberal story about Touvier but refused to tell the larger national story.

The Touvier Affair was not the last episode of judicial reckoning with the legacy of the Dark Years. If anything, it kept public interest alive in the run-up to the spectacular finale: the trial of Maurice Papon in Bordeaux. In April 1998, at the end of the longest trial held in France, Papon was convicted of complicity in crimes against humanity for his role in the deportation of Jews from the Bordeaux region to Nazi death camps, and sentenced to ten years in prison. During the trial, Papon insisted that he had not been aware of the destination of the trains and the Final Solution. In the end, he was found guilty of complicity in the illegal arrest and detainment of the victims but not in their extermination (Curtis 2002: 288). The trial of Maurice Papon gripped French politics and society in a way that none of the previous trials for crimes against humanity could. Unlike the German fugitive Barbie and the underground thug Touvier, Papon had enjoyed a successful career as a high-ranking civil servant stretching from the Third to the Fifth Republic. For the media and the public, the trial of Papon became "the symbolic trial of Vichy itself" (Golsan 2000b: 3).

The many different questions and discussions opened up by the trial of Maurice Papon cannot be recounted here. Pierre Nora captured the spirit of the time in *Le Monde*: "Today, everything converges on the haunting memory of Vichy."[13] What was unprecedented was the activism and soul searching outside the courtroom. Jewish associations staged demonstrations and read the names of French victims of the Holocaust and the Catholic Church issued an apology for its role in the Dark Years and asked for forgiveness. Similar apologies followed

[12] Ibid.
[13] Nicolas Weill and Robert Solé, "Interview with Pierre Nora," *Le Monde*, 1 October 1997, reprinted in Golsan (2000b: 171–178).

from the national organizations of the doctors and police (Golsan 2000a: 160). The judgment of the court in Bordeaux was received with the same stormy debate that had accompanied the proceedings: was Papon really unaware of the destination of the trains? Was Vichy only an accomplice in the Holocaust? Again, the court's reading of national history appeared unsatisfactory. Even critics of the trial, however, acknowledged its value as an opportunity to engage in further debate, including debate over the problems with the story told by the court: "The confusion [the trial] arouses will at least have the virtue of making us think about it, ask ourselves questions, debate the past without hiding behind the legal decision and without assuming that this verdict closes the historical case just because it concludes the legal one."[14]

The Papon Affair had another intriguing dimension, which concerned the brutal suppression of the Algerian protest in Paris on 17 October 1961. Papon had overseen the violent crackdown as a prefect of the Paris police and helped to cover it up. Exploding shortly after the end of his trial for crimes against humanity in Bordeaux, the Algerian controversy appeared to confirm Papon's fears expressed in an interview for *Libération*: "I am a kind of expiatory victim for the evils of our age."[15] Papon's second legal battle involved a defamation suit against historian Jean-Luc Einaudi, who in May 1998 wrote in *Le Monde* that the suppression of the Algerian protest of 17 October constituted "a massacre," and was perpetrated by the police on Papon's orders. Papon lost the case against Einaudi as French law confronted the wounds of the Algerian War for the first time. The court rejected the officially accepted version of the events of 17 October 1961 as being "largely inspired by reasons of state," and ruled that "the extreme brutality of the crackdown at that time should today call for a different analysis that does not exclude the word 'massacre.'"[16]

---

[14] Laurent Greilsamer and Nicolas Weill, "An Interview with Henry Rousso," *Le Monde*, 7 April 1998, reprinted in (Golsan 2000b: 205).

[15] Anette Lévy-Willard, "An Interview with Maurice Papon," *Libération*, 6 March 1996, reprinted in (Golsan 2000b: 166).

[16] Philippe Bernard, "The Magistrate's Court of Paris Acknowledges the 'Extreme Violence' of the Police Crackdown on 17 October 1961," *Le Monde*, 28–29 March 1999, reprinted in Golsan (2000b: 240).

The analogy between the France of Pétain and the France of De Gaulle emerged as one of the axes of the ensuing public discussion, despite protests by historians that the analogy was untenable and stifled understanding of either period. De Gaulle's era disregarded the repression of Jews during the Dark Years and the role of the Vichy regime in the Final Solution, and was marked by its own atrocities in Algeria. It tried to forget both legacies of abuse by passing amnesties for the Second World War and Algerian War. There was enough to detect a pattern, and the media seized it. The figure of Maurice Papon embodied the idea of continuity and loyalty in service to the French state: police prefect in Bordeaux at the time of the deportations to Nazi death camps; inspector-general of administration in Constantine during the Algerian War; police prefect of Paris in October 1961; and, finally, minister in the government of Valéry Giscard d'Estaing.

The Papon "effect" involved public reckoning with some of the deep national traumas that these historical periods had inflicted. To the extent that it helped crack the taboo on discussing the troubling legacies of the Algerian War, it paved the way for subsequent discussions of French atrocities in Algeria (MacMaster 2002). But equally important was the role of Papon's legal battles in provoking a public conversation that interrogated the limits of national transformation after the Dark Years and focusing public attention on some of the troubling continuities in French nationalism and statism. The analogy between Vichy and Algeria was so controversial and subversive because it invited reflection on these continuities:

> What unites the two, in the person and personality of Maurice Papon, is the idea that the French state is the representative of the French nation and obedience to that state is required at all times. Whether the state defines its enemies as "Jews" or as "Arabs," French police and government officials have shown themselves ready, willing and able to commit torture and killing in the name of the nation. (Fraser 2005: 207)

The Barbie, Touvier, and Papon Affairs opened up for public reassessment accepted narratives and mythologies, such as resistancialism, but they also served as a catalyst to discuss and debate the "dark side" of French nationalism: the influence of Catholicism and antirepublicanism; the persistence of racism; and the idea of blind loyalty to the state. These themes were engaged and interrogated in the public domain alongside the civic and republican referents, which are usually invoked to represent French national identity. The interpretations of national history offered by the courts often appeared problematic and unsatisfactory, and themselves became a subject of much controversy and contestation. The judicial drama unfolded in conversation with contemporary politics and society, and was appropriated in a discursive framework connecting a series of disturbing events for the French nation and its evolving self-understanding: Dreyfus; Vichy; the purges; colonialism; and the Algerian protest of 17 October 1961. The significance of the trials for crimes against humanity in France was in this unintended spillover from the courts that served to expose, as it were, the skeletons in the closet.

TRANSITION WITHOUT JUSTICE?

Rousso (1991) argues that the French became obsessed with Vichy because they couldn't assimilate the "rupture" that the Dark Years constituted. My analysis points in the opposite direction: Vichy instigated so much controversy in France because it raised the question of continuity. Episodes of mass violence and atrocity can be easily forgotten, rationalized, or confined to a distant past. Nations and nationalism, however, transmit unsettling continuities that are much more difficult to exorcise and transcend. It is precisely these continuities that need to be opened up for public deliberation and submitted to critical reassessment in order to address the legitimacy dilemma inherent in the question of mass atrocity and create opportunities for renegotiating the terms of membership in the political community. A legitimacy dilemma is often unavoidable in the aftermath of large-scale violence and abuse, but it becomes particularly destabilizing when the legacy of atrocities lends itself to politicization along national and ethnic lines. The deliberative conception of transitional justice advanced here, which emphasizes the role of the judicial process as a vehicle for public debate, offers one answer to this dilemma.

An intriguing question for further research is to what extent the absence of sustained public reckoning with the legacy of colonialism can explain the persistence of other troubling continuities in French nationalism and racism, which today single out Islam and Muslims as the main targets. Todd Shepard argues that what prevented discussion of the Algerian War as an opportunity to interrogate French republicanism, racism, and imperialism, was the "invention of decolonization" at war's end: "[It] helped circumscribe what lessons could be drawn, in the West as in the former colonies, about the role of colonialism in state institutions and national pasts. This made it more difficult to address such tensions in the future" (Shepard 2006: 272). Many of these tensions come to the fore in contemporary debates over the perceived "danger" that Islam represents for the French nation and its commitments to republicanism and universalism. In her examination of the "politics of the veil" in France, Joan Wallach Scott (2007) contrasts the successful integration of Jews with the difficulties experienced by Muslims, for whom a similar integration path is seen as foreclosed. Her analysis highlights the importance of public reckoning with past wrongs in explaining the differences:

> The Jews from the Maghreb pose many of the same challenges to French universalism that Arab/Muslims do, and yet the animus of those who worry about the fracturing of the nation is directed at Muslims, not at Jews. I am not arguing that Jews should be targeted; not at all. I do want to point out that one positive legacy of France's history during the Second World War is a decline in anti-Semitism, an admission of the wrongs that were committed because of that racism, and the acknowledgement that the full integration of Jews is possible, even as some forms of their identification newly stress a collective identity. (Scott 2007: 78)

It is important, then, to consider not only the potential of deliberative justice processes but also the implications of their absence. The risk associated with situations of *transition without justice* is that important opportunities to interrogate issues of state legitimacy and national identity through the medium of critical public discourse may be foreclosed; instead, the question of mass atrocity can become a latent source of further nationalist mobilization and radicalization. It is hard to predict when demands for reckoning with legacies of past abuse may become politically significant and the need may arise to renegotiate the underlying questions of identity and legitimacy in light of such legacies.

In post-war France, the resurfacing of Jewish memories of the Second World War engendered a need to reconsider the dominant representations of that historical period. Rousso (1991: 303) notes that "deportees, especially Jewish deportees, had no place in the idyllic saga of the Resistance. It was the reawakening of their memories in the 1970s that made it necessary to revise the widely accepted picture of the wartime years." When such need arises, the virtue of a judicial process is that it provides a forum for establishing some reference points, thus helping to diminish the space for denial and shifting the focus of public deliberation from the question of whether or not atrocities were committed to questions about their significance and interpretation.

Transitions without such justice processes and the ensuing opportunities for public deliberation risk setting in motion a different dynamic, whereby public energies become channeled in incessant denial and contestation of the "facts" of mass atrocity, transforming the past into an object of policing for the state and nation. Particularly when the criminal legacies at stake are associated with periods of national and ethnic conflict, they easily become a cause célèbre for nationalists and other activists of identity politics. In such contexts, when certain memories and experiences of injustice that are suppressed in accepted narratives of nationalism come to the fore and seek validation, they often encourage a backlash and further attempts to suppress them. As a result, the legitimacy dilemma engendered by the question of mass atrocity becomes entrenched both by demands to remember and by efforts to deny or forget. On both sides of the divide, identities coalesce around conflicting claims and narratives of injustice, reifying the past and precluding the sort of discursive engagements that may bring it into a productive dialogue with the present.

There are few cases that illustrate these risks better than Turkey's "Armenian problem," the issue in which France sought to intervene with the genocide-denial legislation mentioned at the very beginning of the chapter. The involvement of the French state in the historical dispute between Turkey and the Armenians suggests that we need to think about these issues in a different way in the twenty-first century, when some of the key "activists of memory" can be third states or non-state actors and the legitimacy dilemma associated with the question of mass atrocity often plays out in transnational frameworks. In this environment, the ways in which identities coalesce around legacies of past abuse and become harnessed for nationalist mobilization increasingly reflect the rise of diaspora politics and "long-distance nationalism" (Anderson 1992). In the Turkish-Armenian dispute, for example, much of the action appears to be driven by diasporic communities and their organizations, such as those aligned with the Armenian Revolutionary Federation, Dashnaktsutyun, and the Assembly of Turkish American Associations.[17]

Turkey's continuing resistance to demands for recognition of the Armenian atrocities as constituting genocide has an intriguing history, which starts with the limited legal response of the Ottoman Empire shortly before it was superseded by the Turkish Republic. After the 1918 Mondros Armistice, both the Ottoman government in Istanbul and the nationalist movement led by Mustafa Kemal Atatürk initially acknowledged that massacres of Armenians and Greeks had been committed. In fact, at that stage both sides appeared to favor trials of members of the Committee of Union and Progress implicated in the atrocities. The position of the nationalist movement shifted in response to the policies adopted by the Entente Powers in the Treaty of Sèvres, which envisioned prosecuting those responsible for the massacres, but also raised the spectre of partitioning Anatolia:

> The main change in the attitude adopted by the nationalist movement toward trying those guilty of war crimes and massacres occurred after the contents of the Treaty of Sèvres became clear. In this agreement, the Entente powers essentially showed that they interpreted the punishment of the "the Turks" as the elimination of the Ottoman's state right to sovereignty. For that reason, the Entente powers included in their program the punishment of the leaders of the nationalist movement. As a result of their pressure, the court-martial in Istanbul started trying not only those who were accused of war crimes and massacres but also important members of the Turkish nationalist movement. In April 1920, the First Extraordinary Court Martial in Istanbul began to try the leaders of the Anatolian movement, and Mustafa Kemal foremost among them (in absentia). (Akçam 2004: 203)

---

[17] See Armine Ishkanian, "Civil Society Resistance to Normalizing Turkish-Armenian Relations," Box. 13.3, in Rangelov and Teitel (2011: 173–174).

The Istanbul trials were dealt a decisive blow by the proceedings against Atatürk, the future founder and secular deity of the Turkish Republic. More importantly, the significance of such prosecutions could no longer be separated from the other provisions of the Treaty of Sèvres. The Armenian massacres became intertwined with the issue of Turkish sovereignty, blurring the lines between the nation's responsibility and its survival. When the nationalist forces prevailed in the Turkish War of Independence and the Treaty of Lausanne restored Turkish sovereignty in Anatolia, Atatürk attempted to foster national unity by renouncing the divisive legacy of the Ottoman era. Class, ethnicity, and religion were effectively erased from Turkey's new republican citizenship, propagating these identities became criminalized, and the army was given special powers to counter the menace of leftist, Kurdish, and Islamist threats. Akçam (2004: 25) notes that the new Turkish state "was established on the foundation of a national psychosis forged in the struggle and preservation of its existence against internal and external enemies. This psychosis continues to the present."

Turkey's transition without justice meant that the Armenian atrocities were never confronted with a judicial process or another form of public reckoning. But that was only one of the challenges for the rule of law in the decades that followed. Turkish law became an instrument for forging national unity by policing the past and punishing those who dared to question its officially sanctioned representations, as in the prosecutions for "denigrating Turkishness" under Article 301 of the Turkish Penal Code.[18] The purpose of such judicial interventions

---

[18] The relevant part of Article 301 was amended to "denigrating the Turkish nation" in 2008. Charges have often been brought for statements about the Armenian atrocities, and attracted international attention in 2005–2006 when high-profile cases involved novelists Orhan Pamuk and Elif Shafak and Turkish-Armenian journalist Hrant Dink. After Dink's subsequent assassination by radicals, Pamuk stated:

In a sense, we are all responsible for his death. However, at the very forefront of this responsibility are those who still defend article 301 of the Turkish Penal Code. Those who campaigned against him, those who portrayed this sibling of ours as an enemy of Turkey, those who painted him as a target, they are the most responsible in this. And then, in the end, we are all responsible.

See Sebnem Arsu, "Turkish Court Drops Charges against Novelist," New York Times, 24 January 2006; "Orhan Pamuk: We Are all Responsible for Dink's Death," Hürriyet, 21 January 2007, retrieved from http://www.hurriyet.com.tr/english/5817673.asp (accessed 28 February 2012).

is clear – to silence dissident voices and preclude critical public discussion of the national past – but their effectiveness is questionable. The
"Armenian problem" persists and continues to raise troubling questions. Should the massacres be understood as a rupture or a bridge
between the empire and the Republic?[19] Are the "founding fathers" of
the Republic heroes or criminals?[20] Are the efforts to forget and deny
the Armenian atrocities symptomatic of deeper anxieties at the heart
of Turkish nationalism, which are also reflected in the suppression of
Kurdish demands and the militant secularist response to the rise of
Islam?[21]

In sum, this chapter draws attention to the productive potential of
the tensions between nationalism and the rule of law and underscores
the importance of the deliberative character of legal processes for
managing and transforming nationalism. A deliberative understanding of transitional justice suggests one way of recovering this potential,
reinterpreting the judicial process as a vehicle for public debate over
questions of national identity and state legitimacy. It highlights the role
of trials in encouraging critical reassessment of nationalist continuities that may be obscured by the appealing rhetoric of transition and
transformation or masked by accepted narratives of national unity and

---

[19] Taner Akçam (2004: 150) discusses the Armenian atrocities as the last stage in the
process of Turkification and homogenization of Anatolia, suggesting that "the precon-
ditions for the establishment of the Turkish Republic were in large measure created by
this massacre."

[20] Some of those who established the nationalist movement also participated and enriched
themselves in the Armenian atrocities. Serving in the forces of Atatürk apparently
offered refuge to Unionists wanted by Istanbul and the Occupation authorities for
their role in the atrocities. After the war, some of them assumed high positions in the
government. Indeed, Akçam (2004: 240–241) argues:

[T]he main reason that Turks avoid any discussion on history and make it a taboo lies
in the reality of this connection between the Armenian Genocide and the foundation of
the Turkish Republic. The devastation that would ensue if Turks had to now stigmatize
as "murderers and thieves" those whom they are used to regarding as "great saviours"
and "people who created a nation from nothing," is palpable.

[21] Again, the analysis of Akçam (2004: 150) is provocative and illuminating:

While during the first nation-building process the Muslim communities succeeded in
adopting a shared, religion-based attitude toward the non-Muslim communities, in a
similar fashion today the different ethnic groups within Turkish society have managed
to unite around a shared approach towards the Kurds. In a sense, the Kurds today
replaced the non-Muslim communities of the 19th and early 20th centuries as both a
source and a target of intergroup and intercommunal conflict.

reconciliation. The question of mass atrocity engenders a legitimacy dilemma that cannot be easily addressed without interrogating the "dark side" of nationalism and renegotiating the underlying issues of identity and legitimacy that it raises. In the absence of a judicial process that may encourage such public reckoning and provide key reference points for the discussion, transitions without justice face the risk of incessant contestation of the "facts" of mass atrocities, precluding debate over their significance and interpretation that may bring the past into a productive dialogue with the present.

3 INTERNATIONAL CRIMINAL JUSTICE

The historical origins and evolution of international criminal justice are inextricably linked with the spectre of extreme nationalism in the twentieth century. The birth of international justice at the Nuremberg and Tokyo Trials and its revival half a century later, during the war in Bosnia, unfolded in the shadow of nationalist projects that had inflicted intolerable levels of violence and destruction, propelling the question of individual criminal responsibility on the international agenda. Both periods were marked by the ascendance of internationalist and humanitarian sentiments and heightened expectations for redefining the relationship between law and violence in the international sphere. The ensuing articulation of an international rule of law premised on individual criminal responsibility reflects these wider aspirations of the post-war and post–Cold War moments. At the same time, however, the distinctive pursuits of justice at the International Military Tribunals and the International Criminal Tribunal for the Former Yugoslavia (ICTY) have been deeply embedded in the particular forms of nationalism and warfare that sparked the impulse for international prosecutions at these junctures.

This chapter treats the rise of international criminal justice as an opportunity to examine the evolving relationship between nationalism and the rule of law beyond the state. It starts with a discussion of nationalism as a catalyst for the development of international legal norms and structures and highlights its role in shaping the substantive crimes and underlying concepts of the regime of international criminal law. My analysis emphasizes in particular the movement from "crimes against peace" to "crimes against humanity" as a central dimension of the historical trajectory of international criminal justice, seeking to recover from this narrative the influence of nationalism on the changing character of this legal regime and, more broadly, its constitutive role in the development of the international rule of law in the second half of the twentieth century. At the center of the analysis is a shift in paradigms from "total war" at Nuremberg to "ethnic cleansing" at the Yugoslav Tribunal, which seeks to capture the dynamic relationship between nationalism, war, and international criminal justice at these junctures.

In the final section, I approach the relationship between nationalism and the rule of law from an alternative perspective. If the rise of international criminal justice could be seen as embodying a constitutive tension between nationalism and the rule of law, what are the implications of the actual exercise of international justice? Scholarly debates over the impact of international justice on affected societies are often framed as dichotomies: justice either promotes peace and reconciliation or serves to compromise them; the international "colonizes" the local or becomes subverted and manipulated by domestic actors, and so forth. I examine the role of the ICTY in the Balkans over the past decade and detect a less conclusive but still intriguing dynamic, suggesting that international justice has set in motion an ongoing process of *pluralization* of public discourse, politics, and law in the region. In my reading, the ICTY itself is important, but pluralization is engendered by the pervasive interactions of diverse political and social actors with the processes and structures of international criminal justice. I examine the role of international justice in the emergence of transnational discourse, regional politics, and hybrid legal orders, and interpret these pluralized spaces as sites where the tensions between nationalism and the rule of law are expressed and negotiated.

CRIMES AGAINST PEACE AND THE FOUNDATIONS OF INTERNATIONAL JUSTICE

Histories of international criminal justice often start with Versailles and Leipzig. The view that the Axis Powers were employing methods breaching the "laws of humanity" gained salience during the First

World War and put criminal trials on the agenda of the peace negotiations. The spectre of criminal prosecutions was already raised by
Britain, France, and Russia in May 1915 in the Declaration to the
Ottoman Empire, which characterized the ongoing Armenian atrocities as "crimes of Turkey against humanity and civilization."[1] Public
opinion was also agitated by the mounting reports of German war
crimes, and Britain and France, both heavily affected, kept up the pressure for punishment.[2] At the Preliminary Peace Conference convened
in early 1919, the Allies created a special commission to consider the
question of accountability for war crimes and the enforcement of penalties. The commission proposed the establishment of an international
"high court" comprising representatives of the Allied governments to
dispense justice for the use of "barbarous or illegitimate methods in
violation of the established laws and customs of war and the elemen-
tary laws of humanity."[3]

The United States and Japan did not endorse the recommendations
of the commission, their reluctance to invoke international jurisdiction
prefiguring the eventual failure of the endeavour. The U.S. delegation
was concerned about the uncertainty of the law to be administered,
especially the "laws of humanity," and argued instead for domestic
war crimes trials. The international option appeared to be set aside
by doubts about moral universalism: "There is no fixed and universal
standard of humanity."[4] The Treaty of Sèvres envisioned the establishment of a tribunal to punish those responsible for massacres of
Armenians and Greeks, thus entertaining the idea of holding a government accountable for abuses against its own citizens, but it was
abandoned and the subsequently agreed on Treaty of Lausanne was
accompanied by a declaration of amnesty (United Nations War Crimes
Commission [UNWCC] 1948: 45).

---

[1] "Declaration to the Ottoman Empire," 28 May 1915, cited in McCormack
1997: 45.
[2] In Britain, for example, Lloyd George successfully campaigned with "Hang the
Keiser" slogans in the 1918 elections. See Bass (2000: 73–75).
[3] Report on the Responsibility of the Authors of the War and on Enforcement of
Penalties to the Preliminary Peace Conference, 29 March 1919, reproduced in
American Journal of International Law 14: 95–154 (1919).
[4] Ibid., Annex II: Memorandum of Reservations Presented by the Representatives of
the United States to the Report of the Commission on Responsibilities, 144.

The Treaty of Versailles incorporated accountability provisions but they remained on paper. Wilhelm II was arraigned for offenses against international morality and the sanctity of treaties; moreover, the Treaty envisioned the establishment of both military tribunals and an international body to prosecute individuals charged with war crimes against nationals of more than one of the Allied Powers.[5] The kaiser, however, sought exile in the Netherlands, which was reluctant to extradite him to stand trial. In the end, instead of conducting the prosecutions themselves, the Allies accepted the proposal of the German government to try perpetrators domestically, at the Supreme Court of the Empire in Leipzig. The Leipzig trials turned into a fiasco:

> The net result of the trials was that out of a total of 901 cases of revolting crimes brought before the Leipzig Court, 888 accused were acquitted or summarily dismissed, and only 13 ended in a conviction; furthermore, although the sentences were so inadequate, those who had been convicted were not even made to serve their sentence. Several escaped, and the prison wardens who had engineered their escape were publicly congratulated.(UNWCC 1948: 48)

Unfortunate as it was, the outcome was hardly surprising. Historically, defeated enemy leaders were not seen as war criminals that should be put on trial. If punished, their fate was more likely to be execution or exile, such as Napoleon's detour to St. Helena (Bass 2000: 56–57). In this sense, the war crimes debacle after the First World War failed to break new ground. Nevertheless, its significance was in entertaining the possibility of pursuing individual criminal responsibility in the first place. Versailles set a precedent by conceiving of justice as a policy in international affairs, while also demonstrating its limitations.[6] The debate over punishing the kaiser and his proxies involved governments, lawyers, and the broader public. In the course of the discussions, some early arguments in favor of international justice were aired, suggesting that national courts might be too biased to prosecute war crimes properly, but also noting that breaches of international law should be

---

[5] Treaty of Peace with Germany, signed at Versailles, 28 March 1919, T.S. No. 4 (1919) (Cmd. 153), Articles 227–230.

[6] On the "policy of justice" in this context, see Shklar 1986: 143.

adjudicated by international courts so that the rule of law of the "family of nations" could be restored (McCormack 1997: 52–53). The Armenian atrocities raised questions about state sovereignty and treatment of its own citizens. The existence of certain "laws of humanity" was also given some consideration, foreshadowing the idea of crimes against humanity.

In the end, the lasting legacy of Versailles might have been Leipzig: "When planning [the trials at] Nuremberg, Allied leaders sometimes remembered with chagrin this earlier catastrophic effort" (Bass 2000: 58). The turn to "legalism"[7] gained momentum toward the end of the Second World War, and these considerations certainly played a role, but the establishment of the International Military Tribunals in Nuremberg and Tokyo was anything but predetermined. In his gripping account of the run-up to Nuremberg, Bass (2000) conveys the competing positions in the Allied camp on the question of punishment. Stalin entertained the idea of executing large numbers of Germans and later argued for show trials, rehearsed in his own purges in the Soviet Union; Churchill called for the execution of major war criminals, after a brief procedure to confirm their identity; the American administration was divided between Henry Morgenthau Jr., in charge of the Treasury, who advocated mass executions, and the Secretary of War Henry Stimson, who pushed for trials. Roosevelt endorsed trials, but only after Morgenthau's plans to "pastoralize" Germany had become public and embarrassed the administration, and that option eventually prevailed.

Despite growing awareness of the scale of Nazi atrocities, decisions about the forum and crimes to be prosecuted were not made until late in the day. The Moscow Declaration, issued by Churchill, Roosevelt, and Stalin in November 1943, stated that German war criminals would be sent to the country where they had committed the offenses and stand trial there; major war criminals would be "punished by a joint decision of the Governments of the Allies."[8] The declaration came shortly after the UNWCC had been set up to investigate war crimes and identify

---

[7] Shklar (1986: 1) defines legalism as "the ethical attitude that holds moral conduct to be a manner of rule following, and moral relationships to consist of duties and rights determined by rules."

[8] Moscow Declaration, 1 November 1943, reproduced in UNWCC (1948: 107–108).

suspects. One of the questions on the agenda was what crimes should be punished. At the first meeting of the Commission's legal committee in March 1944, the Czechoslovak delegate presented a report making a case for what later became "crimes against peace":

> His thesis was that the paramount crime was the launching and waging of the Second World War, and that individuals responsible for it should be held penally liable and tried accordingly. The criminal nature of the last war was found to derive from its aims and methods. The aims were to enslave foreign nations, to destroy their civilisation and physically annihilate a considerable section of their population on racial, political or religious grounds. The methods arose from the fact that it was a "total" war, which disregarded all humanitarian considerations lying at the root of the laws and customs of war, and introduced indiscriminate means of warfare and barbaric methods of occupation.(UNWCC 1948: 180)

This argument was prefiguring the principles that eventually underpinned and justified the exercise of international criminal justice at Nuremberg and Tokyo. The central offense was the violation of state sovereignty, pursued through military conquest and occupation; all other crimes – from conventional war crimes to the destruction of civilian populations – emanated from this paramount crime. The policy of waging "total war" was at the root of all other offenses and atrocities, and it was first and foremost the architects of the Second World War who should be held accountable. In the ensuing discussions at the Commission, supporters of the Czechoslovak position invoked the Kellogg-Briand Pact of 1928 in asserting that aggressive war was illegal, but others argued that the treaty was binding only on ratifying parties. Moreover, even if aggressive war was illegal under the terms of the treaty, some delegates expressed doubts whether it entailed individual criminal responsibility. The Commission concluded that the issue of prosecuting individuals for launching and waging a war of aggression could not be resolved on the basis of the existing international law and required a political decision, referring the matter to the Allied governments without clear recommendations (UNWCC 1948: 180–185). The political leaders had to determine the law after their lawyers had failed. The Allies finally resolved the issue in favor of prosecution at the London Conference in August 1945. Robert Jackson, the chief prosecutor for the United States at Nuremberg, had already made up his mind that the time was ripe to criminalize aggressive war in international law. Judith Shklar (1986: 176) notes that Jackson "did not believe that, by outlawing aggressive war in the course of trying the Nazi leaders, future war could be prevented, but he thought that aggressive war might becomes less likely, or at least controlled."[9]

The Charter of the International Military Tribunal at Nuremberg established the court's jurisdiction over crimes against peace, war crimes, and crimes against humanity, committed in the interest of the European Axis. The list of crimes starts with crimes against peace, defined as "planning, preparation, initiation or waging of war of aggression, or a war in violation of international treaties, agreements or assurances, or participation in a common plan or conspiracy for the accomplishment of any of the foregoing."[10] Eschewing legal niceties such as the issue of retroactivity (*nullum crimen sine lege*), the Allies codified crimes against peace and placed them at the top of Article 6, confirming their status as the paramount crime of the Second World War. The Charter of the International Military Tribunal for the Far East made the hierarchy of crimes even more explicit, providing that "the Tribunal shall have the power to try and punish Far Eastern war criminals who as individuals or members of organizations are charged with offenses which include Crimes against Peace."[11] Without the link to aggression, war crimes and crimes against humanity were not sufficient for assuming jurisdiction at Tokyo.

Jackson's passion and eloquence in arguing the charges of crimes against peace were rewarded in the Nuremberg Judgment, which included a strong statement of the "supreme" status of these offenses in the international legal order:

> The charges in the Indictment that the defendants planned and waged aggressive wars are charges of utmost gravity. War is essentially an

[9] See also Jackson's domestic considerations in pressing the criminal nature of the Second World War, aimed at vindicating U.S. involvement in the war and fighting America's isolationist impulses, in Shklar (1986: 170–179).

[10] Charter of the International Military Tribunal, annexed to the Agreement for the Prosecution and Punishment of the Major War Criminal of the European Axis, 8 August 1945, 59 Stat. 1544, 82 UNTS 279 (hereinafter Nuremberg Charter), Article 6.

[11] Charter of the International Military Tribunal for the Far East, reproduced in *International Military Tribunal for the Far East, Established at Tokyo, Jan. 19, 1946*, U.S. Department of State Pub. No. 2675 (1946), Article 5.

evil thing. Its consequences are not confined to the belligerent States alone but affect the whole world.

To initiate a war of aggression, therefore, is not only an international crime; it is the supreme international crime differing only from other war crimes in that it contains within itself the accumulated evil of the whole.[12]

The Nuremberg Trials were marked by the invention and triumph of crimes against peace at the founding moment of international criminal justice. Their significance was dramatized by the horrors of the war and the aspirations for "peace through law," which came to the fore in the post-war moment. The taboo on waging aggressive war continued to evolve through other means, from the Charter of the United Nations to global condemnation of Iraq's invasion of Kuwait and more recent interventions. But the prosecution of individuals for crimes against peace remained confined to the Nuremberg and Tokyo Trials. Aggression virtually disappeared from the "courtrooms of humanity."

A glimpse of the problems with the offense was already offered at the Tokyo Trial. In his dissenting opinion, Justice Pal from India challenged the hegemonic politics implicit in the American-led prosecutions in the Far East:

No term is more elastic or susceptible to interested interpretations, whether by individuals, or by groups, than aggression.... The question involves further difficulty in view of the fact that the fundamental basis of these trials has been declared to be the organization of international life on the footing of humanity, but as a matter of fact, there are still nations under the domination of another nation. The question would naturally arise whether the term aggressive would have reference to the interests of the dominated nation as distinct from that of the dominating power, or whether it would have reference to the *status quo*.[13]

As Shklar has pointed out, "With or without a natural law justification, aggressive war, defined as any resort to violence aimed at altering the international *status quo*, could and did appear as nothing but

---

[12] International Military Tribunal (Nuremberg), Judgment and Sentences, 1 October 1946, reproduced in *American Journal of International Law* 41(1): 172–333 (1947), 186.

[13] Judgment of the Honourable Mr. Justice Pal, Member for India, Tokyo Trial, quoted in Boister and Cryer (2008: lxxx).

an ideological defence of colonialism" (Shklar 1986: 180). Seen in this light, the retreat of crimes against peace in the post-war decades goes hand in hand with the rise of decolonization. But other developments have also been important, from the interventionist projects of the Superpowers in Vietnam and Afghanistan during the Cold War to the advent of humanitarian intervention in the 1990s and later the War on Terror. Aggression was included in the Rome Statute of the International Criminal Court, adopted in 1998, but the provisions remained inoperative until an agreement was reached for "defining the crime and setting out the conditions under which the Court shall exercise jurisdiction with respect to this crime."[14] A definition of aggression was finally agreed on in 2010, at the Review Conference of the Rome Statute in Kampala; however, the Court's exercise of jurisdiction over the crime of aggression has been deferred until at least January 1, 2017, subject to a further decision of the state parties after that date.[15] In the meantime, other offenses have come forward to claim the status of supreme international crime.

CRIMES AGAINST HUMANITY AND THE REINVENTION OF INTERNATIONAL JUSTICE

The other major innovation at Nuremberg was crimes against humanity, often seen as its lasting legacy: "Today almost nobody remembers the quixotic American crusade to outlaw war itself, but the category of crimes against humanity is well-established" (Bass 2000: 283). By the end of the war, the scale of Nazi atrocities against Jews and occupied populations had dispelled any doubts of the Allies about the existence of a universal standard of humanity. The Nuremberg Trials revealed shocking facts about the Holocaust and other atrocities, eliciting universal condemnation. Even critics of the Tribunal suggested that in

---

[14] Rome Statute of the International Criminal Court, UN Doc. A/CONF.183/9, 17 July 1998, 2187 UNTS 90, Article 5(2).

[15] Resolution RC/Res.6 of the Review Conference of the Rome Statute, adopted at the 13th plenary meeting, on 11 June 2010, by consensus. See the discussion of crimes against peace after Nuremberg in Antonopoulos (2001). See also Trahan (2011), for an account of the Kampala negotiations.

this particular case, the novelty and iniquity of the offenses justified international prosecution and punishment, despite the issue of retro-activity and the problematic wartime record of the prosecuting pow-ers. Shklar, for example, notes that these crimes were unprecedented, and after Dresden and Hiroshima, they represented the only offense in which the Allies themselves could not be implicated: "The argument suggested here is that as far as the Trial concerned itself with crimes against humanity it was both necessary and wise" (1986: 155).

In the hierarchy of crimes of the Nuremberg Charter, however, crimes against humanity were listed last, after crimes against peace and war crimes, and defined as "murder, extermination, enslavement, deportation, and other inhumane acts committed against any civilian population, before or during the war; or persecution on political, racial or religious grounds in execution of or in connection with any crime within the jurisdiction of the Tribunal, whether or not in violation of the domestic law of the country where perpetrated."[16] Moreover, the Charter established a nexus to international armed conflict that appeared more symbolic than real. Hannah Arendt and others have criticized the connection between crimes against humanity and aggressive war:

> And what had prevented the Nuremberg Tribunal from doing full justice to this crime was not that its victims were Jews but that the Charter demanded that this crime, which had so little to do with war that its commission actually conflicted with and hindered the war's conduct, was to be tied up with the other crimes. How deeply the Nuremberg judges were aware of the outrage perpe-trated against the Jews may perhaps best be gauged by the fact that the only defendant to be condemned to death on a crimes-against-humanity charge alone was Julius Streicher, whose specialty had been anti-Semitic obscenities. In this instance, the judges disre-garded all other considerations.(Arendt 1994: 258)

The evidence of Jewish suffering under the Nazis was overwhelm-ing, and the sentencing practices of the judges at Nuremberg appeared to subvert the presumed hierarchy of crimes. As one study put it, "Each of those executed was convicted of war crimes, crimes against humanity, or both. The death sentences reflected much

---

[16] Nuremberg Charter, Article 6(c).

more the Tribunal's attitude to these offences than to the aggressive war charge" (Clark 1997: 175). Nevertheless, crimes against peace dominated the policy of justice at the Nuremberg Trials. Crimes against humanity were not seen as a priority because they were not central to the launching and waging of aggressive war. The emphasis on the logic of the total-war paradigm ensured, for example, that deportation to slave labor was included in the Nuremberg Charter as a war crime; clearly, the setting up and running of labour camps had facilitated the war effort. But the persecution, concentration, and extermination of Jews were puzzling and shocking, because if anything, they had encumbered the war effort. As a result, crimes against humanity were seen as a horrible aberration at Nuremberg, offenses that were not dictated by military strategy and necessity and even contradicted their logic. The same understanding applied when the victims were enemy civilians. As one observer put it at the time, "It should be remembered that these crimes are committed chiefly against enemy innocent civilians, non-combatants; that these violations have no relationship with military and strategic considerations" (Myerson 1944: 230–231).

Cold War politics was inimical to the project of international justice, but unlike crimes against peace, crimes against humanity did not disappear; instead, they were taken up by domestic courts in trials of Nazi war criminals. The best-known case is the trial of Adolf Eichmann, kidnapped in Argentina and brought to Jerusalem to answer for his role in the Holocaust. Arendt criticized the ideological goals of the trial, conducted by the Israeli State to prosecute not just Eichmann but "anti-Semitism throughout history." She also emphasized the failure of the proceedings to advance an adequate definition of crimes against humanity (the most serious charge was "crimes against Jews," which couldn't capture the humanity aspect), and to comprehend the type of criminal at stake – the "banality" of Eichmann, an ordinary bureaucrat unable to grasp the evil of his deeds and insisting on lack of intent (Arendt 1994: 4–5). Elsewhere in the book, I discuss the crimes against humanity trials in France, which also proved to be highly controversial.[17]

---

[17] See Chapter 2, § "Probing the Nation through the Law."

Beyond domestic trials, in the Cold War years the law of crimes against humanity continued to evolve through international treaties. International human rights law was seen as "soft law," and generally safe for states to sign up to.[18] Indeed, critical legal scholars have noted the irony of the burgeoning human rights regime, originally conceived as a defence against state power: "The government-operated international human rights law is the best illustration of the poacher turned gamekeeper" (Douzinas 2000: 119). But certain types of human rights violations were attracting wide condemnation, even by states. Raphael Lemkin successfully lobbied at the United Nations for a convention criminalizing the novel crime of the Holocaust. He first attempted to establish genocide in international law while serving as a legal adviser to Robert Jackson at Nuremberg (Segesser and Gessler 2005: 463). Lemkin's efforts were finally rewarded when the UN General Assembly adopted the Genocide Convention in December 1948, defining certain acts as constituting genocide when "committed with intent to destroy, in whole or in part, a national, ethnical, racial or religious group, as such."[19] Other international treaties dealing with crimes against humanity were adopted in subsequent decades, including the Convention on Non-Applicability of Statutory Limitations to War Crimes and Crimes Against Humanity (1968) and the Torture Convention (1984).[20]

The end of the Cold War gave a new lease of life to international criminal justice, and this time crimes against humanity were front and center. The opening up of authoritarian states under pressures from globalization heralded a new era of instability, including an upsurge in nationalist mobilization and ethnic violence. The Yugoslav wars of disintegration from 1991 to 1995 started with brief hostilities in Slovenia, followed by vicious wars in Croatia and Bosnia and Herzegovina.

---

[18] Some observers go further: "Convention-based approaches to human rights reflect the interests of state power, but they may do so at the expense of law's normativity." See Koller (2005: 239).

[19] Convention on the Prevention and Punishment of the Crime of Genocide, 9 December 1948, 78 UNTS 171, Article 2.

[20] See Convention on the Non-Applicability of Statutory Limitations to War Crimes and Crimes Against Humanity, 26 November 1968, 754 UNTS; International Convention against Torture and Other Cruel, Inhuman or Degrading Treatment or Punishment, 10 December 1984, 1565 UNTS 85.

The media reports from the region employed the novel term "ethnic cleansing," the English translation of *etničko čišćenje*, allegedly chosen by the Yugoslav People's Army (JNA) for the military strategy of securing territory by forcibly removing non-Serb populations from ethnically mixed areas (Petrovic 1994: 343).

Alarmed by the mounting reports of atrocities in the Balkans, in October 1992 the UN Security Council requested from the Secretary General to appoint a Commission of Experts to investigate violations of international humanitarian law.[21] The report of the Commission described the ongoing ethnic cleansing, involving mass killings, rape, torture, and destruction of civilian, cultural, and religious property, and proposed the establishment of an international criminal tribunal.[22] The record of the deliberations at the Security Council reveal the awareness of its members that ethnic cleansing was not a by-product of the war in the former Yugoslavia, but rather a policy pursued in a systematic fashion, at that time particularly by Bosnian Serb forces. The discussions included statements that the deliberate targeting of civilian populations through ethnic cleansing was an instrument of war (Venezuela), which outraged the conscience of humanity (Brazil), and constituted a threat to international peace and security (France). The creation of an international tribunal to prosecute and punish the perpetrators was seen as reaffirming the Nuremberg Principles at a time when international humanitarian law was clearer, agreed on, and enforceable (United States), and a step toward the establishment of a permanent international criminal court (United Kingdom) with universal jurisdiction (Spain).[23]

In February 1993, the Security Council unanimously decided to establish the ICTY in The Hague, endowing it with jurisdiction to prosecute violations of international humanitarian law committed in the territory of the former Yugoslavia since 1991, and within three

---

[21] S.C. Res. 870, UN Doc. S/RES/870 (1992).

[22] Interim Report of the Commission of Experts, reproduced in Annex I of Letter dated 9 February 1993 from the Secretary General addressed to the President of the Security Council, UN Doc. S/25274 (1994).

[23] Record of the 3175th meeting of the Security Council, 22 February 1993, UN Doc. S/PV.3175 (1993).

months approved its statute.[24] The unfolding genocide in Rwanda soon propelled international justice back on the agenda of the Security Council, and in November 1994 the International Criminal Tribunal for Rwanda (ICTR) was established as a twin court based in Arusha.[25] The creation of the two ad hoc tribunals was celebrated by many as a revival of the Nuremberg legacy and a stepping stone to a permanent international criminal court; that was the spirit of the deliberations at the Security Council. Others, however, argued that the international community was setting up courts to prosecute atrocities it could have prevented, conducting trials instead of putting its soldiers on the line: "Law became a euphemism for inaction" (Bass 2000: 215).

The reluctance of major powers to risk their soldiers' lives in places such as Bosnia and Rwanda was palpable but hardly new. There seemed to be more to the sudden turn to international criminal justice. It has been noted that the development and enforcement of international humanitarian law since the nineteenth century has generally followed a different logic, driven by the interests of states "to legitimate ever more destructive methods of combat" (af Jochnick and Normand 1994: 51). And yet, the Security Council established the twin courts before the international community intervened in the Yugoslav conflict and after the violence in Rwanda had subsided without its involvement, a far cry from the exercise of "victors' justice" at the end of the Second World War. What appeared to favor a revival of international criminal justice at that particular juncture was the global visibility and humanitarian framing of ethnic conflict, in particular the growing awareness and condemnation of the systematic policy of targeting civilians with persecution, expulsions, and killings (Chinkin and Rangelov 2011: 118).[26]

There were important similarities with the Nuremberg Trials, but they concerned crimes against humanity. The atrocities in the Western

---

[24] S.C. Res. 808, UN Doc. S/RES/808 (1993); S.C. Res. 827, UN Doc. S/RES/827 (1993) adopted the Statute of the International Tribunal as annexed to Report of the Secretary General pursuant to paragraph 2 of Security Council Resolution 808 (1993), UN Doc. S/25704 (1993) (hereinafter ICTY Statute).

[25] S.C. Res. 955, UN Doc. S/RES/955 (1994) and Annex: Statute of the International Criminal Tribunal for Rwanda (hereinafter ICTR Statute).

[26] Bass (2000: 282) argues that this moral strength of the ad hoc tribunals was also their practical weakness, evident in the reluctance of the international forces in Bosnia to put soldiers at risk in order to apprehend war criminals.

Balkans revived haunting memories of the Holocaust and the Second World War, which may help to explain why so many states supported the idea of international justice for the first time in fifty years. The significance of this particular framing of the crisis in the former Yugoslavia has been noted by Madeleine Albright, herself a refugee from the Second World War, who represented the United States at the Security Council and spearheaded the effort for the establishment of the Tribunal:

> We were besieged in many ways by endless photographs and news stories about the horrors that were taking place through-out the region ... it became very evident, to anyone really watch-ing, what was going on were reminisces of pictures that reminded one of World War II. I am a child of Europe, having been born in Czechoslovakia, and spent the war in England. I am very familiar with the horrendous pictures that came out during that time, and it seemed to me a repeat of seeing people herded into buses and trains, being taken away, families separated, and horrendous stories coming out in terms of the crimes that were taking place. So when I arrived at the United Nations, I was fully familiar with the brutality that had been taking place in the region.[27]

With hindsight, the concerns at the Security Council were clearly jus-tified, but the response didn't go far enough. The final report of the Commission of Experts concluded that in the course of the conflict, ethnic cleansing and rape were "carried out by some of the parties so systematically that they appear to be the product of a policy."[28] In 1995 this policy reached genocidal dimensions at the UN "safe haven" of Srebrenica: Bosnian Serb forces killed more than 7,000 Muslim men and boys, handed over by the Dutch peacekeepers entrusted with their protection, in what became Europe's worst massacre since the Second World War. In the same year, Croatian forces launched Operation Storm, a military offensive that many saw as aimed at "the permanent removal of the Serb civilian population from the Krajina [region of Croatia] by force or threat of force, which amounted to and

[27] Madeleine Albright, Statement at the ICTY, 17 December 2002.

[28] Final Report of the Commission of Experts, annexed to Letter dated 24 May 1994 from the Secretary-General addressed to the President of the Security Council, UN Doc. S/1994/674 (1994).

involved persecution (deportation, forcible transfer, unlawful attacks against civilians and civilian objects, and discriminatory and restrictive measures)."[29] The Dayton Peace Accords helped end the violence in Bosnia and Croatia but ignored the critical situation in Kosovo, which toward the end of the decade was engulfed by another wave of ethnic cleansing, driving from their homes the majority of the population of the province. In the wake of the NATO air campaign in the spring of 1999, the expelled Albanians started to return, but a process of reverse ethnic cleansing targeted the remaining Serbs.[30]

The ad hoc tribunals for Yugoslavia and Rwanda were conceived as a revival of the Nuremberg legacy, but they also marked a break with the earlier paradigm of international justice. Crimes against peace are not included in the jurisdiction of the ICTY and ICTR. The place of aggression is taken by genocide as the new supreme international crime, and it is the genocide charge that has dominated the prosecution of the highest-ranking Serb defendants and the bulk of the jurisprudence on Rwanda.[31] The definition of crimes against humanity is expanded to incorporate imprisonment, torture, and rape, and the nexus to international armed conflict is broken.[32] These crimes have dominated the exercise of international justice at The Hague and Arusha because they are better suited to comprehend the nature of the conflicts and atrocities that engulfed the two regions. Whereas at Nuremberg crimes against humanity were construed as aberrations that contradicted the war effort, the ad hoc tribunals were confronted with situations where these offenses were at the very heart of military strategy and seemed to capture both the goals and methods of warfare.[33]

---

[29] *Prosecutor v. Ante Gotovina, Mladen Čermak, Mladen Markač*, Case No. IT-06–90-T, Judgement, 15 April 2011, para. 2314.

[30] For a detailed analysis of the Kosovo crisis, see Independent International Commission on Kosovo 2000.

[31] See *Prosecutor v. Slobodan Milošević*, Case No. IT-01–51-I, Indictment, 22 November 2001; *Prosecutor v. Ratko Mladić*, IT-09–92-PT, Third Amended Indictment, 20 October 2011; *Prosecutor v. Radovan Karadžić*, IT-95–5/18-PT, Third Amended Indictment, 27 February 2009. For a high-profile genocide case from Rwanda, see *Prosecutor v. Jean Kambanda*, Case. No. ICTR-97–23-S, Judgment and Sentence, 4 September 1998.

[32] ICTY Statute, Article 5; ICTR Statute, Article 3.

[33] Arendt (1994: 291) criticizes the treatment of crimes against humanity as aberrations at Nuremberg, suggesting that in the Nazi order they had in fact been normalized as the rule.

International criminal justice had to be reinvented to take into account the new forms of conflict and violence it was confronting. As Teitel (2011: 30) notes, "While humanitarian norms originated in settings of interstate conflict, contemporary developments challenge accepted understandings as to how to draw the line between war and peace, international and internal conflict, state actors and private actors, and combatants and civilians." One of the questions that focused attention concerned the character of the conflicts in Bosnia and Rwanda: Were these conflicts international or internal? A lot was at stake given the discrepancy in the laws of war applicable to interstate and internal armed conflict, which Steven Ratner (1998) calls one of the "schizophrenias" of international criminal law.

The limitations of the Nuremberg paradigm became particularly apparent in the former Yugoslavia, where borders were shifting and contested, and the conflict didn't fit easily either the interstate or civil war model. The distinction between internal and international armed conflict was becoming increasingly untenable; if anything, the conflict appeared to be regional and transnational in character. The Security Council abstained from determining the character of the conflicts when it established the ICTY and the ICTR. Given the nature of the atrocities that came before the ad hoc tribunals, the distinction also seemed unjustifiable. As the ICTY argued in its first case, "What is inhumane, and consequently proscribed in international wars, cannot but be inhumane and inadmissible in civil strife…. In the area of armed conflict the distinction between interstate wars and civil wars is losing its value as far as human beings are concerned."[34]

The Nuremberg law was also based on clear distinctions between combatants and civilians, and military and civilian targets, which became increasingly muddled in the context of conflicts where ethnic cleansing and genocide were the central goals. Other aspects of the law appeared inadequate because they relied on an obsolete state-centric view of war. The Bosnian War was fought by networks of state and non-state actors, including military and police forces, paramilitary formations, irregular police units, militias, and criminal groups. A new

[34] *Prosecutor v. Duško Tadić*, Case No. IT-94–1, Decision of the Defence Motion for Interlocutory Appeal on Jurisdiction, 2 October 1995, paras. 119 and 97.

type of war criminal came to the fore in the first case before the ICTY: Duško Tadić, a Serb from a small town in Northwestern Bosnia, was running a café and karate courses, not armies and ministries. The Tribunal had to acknowledge the growing role of such actors, noting that "the law in relation to crimes against humanity has developed to take into account forces which, although not those of the legitimate government, have de facto control."[35] A more substantive notion of the international rule of law was starting to take shape in the workings of international criminal justice, but it required developing and adapting the law to the changing character of war.

FROM CRIMES AGAINST PEACE TO CRIMES AGAINST HUMANITY: NATIONALISM, WAR, AND THE PURSUIT OF INTERNATIONAL JUSTICE

The trajectory of international justice from crimes against peace to crimes against humanity underscores the constitutive role of nationalism in the articulation of the international rule of law in the twentieth century. The origins of international justice in the 1940s and its revival half a century later emerged from efforts to suppress two specific forms of extreme nationalism and criminalize their preeminent expressions: external expansion and ethnic cleansing. Fascism has been defined as "a genus of political ideology whose mythic core in its various permutations is a palingenetic form of populist ultra-nationalism" (Griffin 1991: 44); especially in its Nazi version, it involved the pursuit of both expansion and cleansing.[36] Nevertheless, for the Allies the paramount offense at stake, which justified prosecution and punishment at the international level, was the offense against other states and the international system – the "goal of empire, expansion, or a radical change

---

[35] *Prosecutor v. Duško Tadić*, Case No. IT-94–1, Trial Judgment, 7 May 1997, para. 654.
[36] Paxton (2004: 235), for example, defines fascism as:

[A] form of political behaviour marked by obsessive preoccupation with community decline, humiliation, or victimhood and by compensatory cults of unity, energy, and purity, in which a mass-based party of committed nationalist militants, working in uneasy but effective collaboration with traditional elites, abandons democratic liberties and pursue with redemptive violence and without ethical or legal restraints goals of internal cleansing and external expansion. See also, Midlarsky (2011: 85–86).

in the nation's relationship with other powers" (Payne 1995: 7). In the midst of the Bosnian War five decades later, the emphasis shifted, and this time international justice was invoked in response to ethnic cleansing, pursued in a systematic manner, and framed as a threat to international peace and security. Extreme nationalism was once again at the heart of the turn to criminalization in the international legal order; in establishing the ICTY, however, the Security Council was concerned with mass atrocities and expulsions rather than violations of sovereignty.

The evolution of international criminal justice from the Nuremberg Trials to the Yugoslav Tribunal is deeply embedded in the particular historical forms of nationalism to which it responds. The ensuing changes pertaining to the central offense, jurisdiction, definition of crimes, and other aspects of the law reflect the changing nature and manifestations of extreme nationalism from the 1940s to the post–Cold War era. One way of grasping these developments in international criminal law is to consider the relationship between the dominant conceptions of war and nationalism in the twentieth century. Approached in this way, the decisive shift is from the total-war paradigm of the Second World War, premised on conquest and expansion, to the ethnic-cleansing paradigm that emerged from the Yugoslav wars of disintegration, where control over territory was established through displacement and persecution of civilians.

In a sense, this is a shift in emphasis and framing to the extent that both wars had elements of cleansing and expansion, from the Holocaust to the Greater Serbia project in the 1990s. But precisely because they signal a shift in emphasis and framing, these developments illuminate the ways in which particular forms of warfare and nationalism have shaped the evolution of international criminal justice. Kaldor's (1999) discussion of "new" and "old" wars is useful here in illuminating the issue at stake. The Second World War is a paradigm for what Kaldor calls "old war," fought by states in pursuit of ideological and geopolitical goals with conventional military forces and battles, financed through taxation, and often associated with intensified state-building. The war in Bosnia and Herzegovina, on the other hand, is a typical "new war," characterized by claims to power on the basis of identity and blurring boundaries between political and criminal violence, internal and external, and public and private. In such wars battles are rare and most of the violence is directed against civilians. The conflict is sustained by polarizing identity politics and a globalized war economy, and often involves state un-building. But what the distinction between new and old wars ultimately gets at is a shift in how we think about and imagine war; it seeks to interrogate the underlying conception of war that informs international policies and responses, as well as to illuminate the changing character of organized violence itself.[37] Seen in this light, the shift from crimes against peace to crimes against humanity reflects the changing relationship between war and nationalism – from total war to ethnic cleansing – but it also reveals how international criminal justice emerges from historically situated understandings of the specific forms of war and nationalism that are selected for criminalization and suppression.

My interpretation of the trajectory of international justice from Nuremberg to The Hague seeks to illuminate the role of nationalism as a catalyst for the development of the international rule of law and show how the latter has been shaped by particular forms of war and nationalism in the second half of the twentieth century. The movement from crimes against peace to crimes against humanity, however, may also be interpreted in more expansive ways and related to broader normative changes. Teitel (2011), for example, draws on developments in the law of war, human rights law, and international criminal law to illuminate the rise of "humanity law," signaling a growing recognition of persons and peoples as subjects of international law and a reframing of the rule of law in terms of their preservation and protection. In this context:

> The increasing recognition of crimes against humanity goes to the heart of the emerging global rule of law. It expresses the change in the rule of law by sending a message that "humanity rights" are inviolable, and by expressing the value of protection – that is, of freedom from persecution by the state and other state-like entities – on a global basis. (Teitel 2011: 58)

---

[37] This point is often missed by critics of the "new-wars" thesis, who point out various similarities between contemporary conflicts and premodern wars or classic civil wars. See Kalyvas (2001); Mello (2010).

A parallel dynamic can be detected in the discourse of *human security*, defined as freedom from fear and freedom from want. Moving away from traditional conceptions of national and international security, or borders and sovereignty, human security shifts the focus to individuals and communities; at the sharp end, it also serves to propel the issue of protection from genocide and large-scale human rights violations on the global agenda.[38]

AFTER THE WAR: THE ROLE OF INTERNATIONAL JUSTICE IN THE BALKANS

The Allies conducted the Nuremberg and Tokyo Trials as occupying powers of countries they had defeated in war. Whatever goals they sought to achieve with these prosecutions, they were addressed to the post-war order. The revival of international criminal justice in the 1990s occurred in a very different setting. The Security Council established the ICTY in the midst of ongoing hostilities in the former Yugoslavia, recasting international justice as an instrument for containing and managing an active conflict. The purposes of the legal intervention were inextricably linked to this changing context, calling for international action to stem the tide of extreme nationalism and ethnic cleansing in the region. Indeed, the creation of the ICTY appeared to raise expectations that international justice could help contain the violence and prevent atrocities on the ground even before the court had any suspects in the dock.

The architects of the ad hoc tribunals for Yugoslavia and Rwanda had an ambitious catalogue of objectives in mind, reflecting a vision of international justice as an instrument of peace building. The immediate goal was to facilitate the emergence of peace and deter further

---

[38] See, e.g., United Nations Development Programme, *Human Development Report 1994: New Dimensions of Human Security* (1994); International Commission on Intervention and State Sovereignty, *The Responsibility to Protect: Report of the International Commission on Intervention and State Sovereignty* (2001); United Nations General Assembly, Outcome Document of the 2005 World Summit, A/60/L.1, 15 September 2005; Human Security Centre, *Human Security Report 2005: War and Peace in the 21st Century* (2005). See also MacLean, Black, and Shaw (2006).

atrocities; over the longer-term, the courts were intended to counter collective guilt and facilitate post-war reconciliation. The ICTY was established on the understanding that it "would contribute to the restoration and maintenance of peace,"[39] and with respect to ongoing atrocities, "to contribute to ensuring that such violations are halted and effectively redressed."[40] It was these policy objectives that justified the creation of the ICTY and ICTR in the first place, aligning the decisions of the Security Council with its mandate to maintain international peace and security. Skeptics, however, argued that the threat of prosecution may end up radicalizing the leaders of the warring factions, exacerbating atrocities, and ultimately obstructing the emergence of peace. These arguments hark back to earlier concerns about Nuremberg, put starkly by Raymond Aron: "Would statesmen yield before having exhausted every means of resistance, if they knew that in the enemy's eyes they are criminals and will be treated as such in case of defeat?"[41]

The issue was dramatized by the indictment of the key leaders of the Bosnian Serbs, Radovan Karadžić and Ratko Mladić, in the run-up to the Dayton peace talks. The ensuing disagreement over the indictments set the terms of the so-called Justice-versus-Peace debate, which has dominated subsequent discussions of the role of international justice in ongoing conflicts.[42] Although early assessments of the (potential) role and implications of the ICTY pulled in opposite directions, most observers seemed to agree that the Tribunal was going to be judged on "its contribution to deterrence, reconciliation, peace" (Alvarez 1996: 264). In a sense, the role of international justice in the Balkan conflicts has been disappointing for both sides in the debate. On the one hand, the establishment of the ICTY did not prevent major atrocities, such as Srebrenica, and large-scale ethnic cleansing in Krajina and Kosovo. On the other hand, the threat of prosecution did not obstruct the emergence of peace in Bosnia and Kosovo either, despite

---

[39] S.C. Res. 808.
[40] S.C. Res. 827.
[41] Quoted in Bass 2000: 285.
[42] For a taste of the different positions in the debate, see Akhavan 1998; Allen 2006; Snyder and Vinjamuri 2003/2004. See also the essays in Ambos, Large, and Wierda (2009).

the highly controversial timing of the indictments of Karadžic, Mladić, and Milošević. As for reconciliation, the evidence so far is inconclusive at best, and in any case it may be too early to judge, given the pace of political change in the region and the long-term horizon of reconciliation processes.[43]

With hindsight, these early debates appear somewhat misguided in emphasizing the potential influence of the ICTY on the dynamics and termination of the conflict. The role of international justice in the Balkans has been much more significant in the post-war period of transition. The 1995 Dayton Peace Accords did not mark a decisive transitional moment for the region: they ended the hostilities in Bosnia and Herzegovina but ignored the festering problem in Kosovo, and if anything served to strengthen the regimes of Slobodan Milošević and Franjo Tuđman. The ICTY was seen as a weak and irrelevant institution in the second half of the 1990s, a "paper tiger" that was largely ignored by post–Yugoslav elites and an international community reluctant to risk the lives of peacekeepers to apprehend suspects. The situation started to change only at the turn of the new century, when the Kosovo crisis and the rule of Tuđman and Milošević had come to an end, and accession to the European Union (EU) had emerged as a consensus project for all countries in the region. The exercise of international criminal justice was becoming relevant in the Balkans, but its significance was bound up with the politics and problems of transition, addressing the post-war states and societies that inherited legacies of mass atrocity. In this sense, at least, the Yugoslav Tribunal is reminiscent of earlier war crimes trials. Shklar notes about Nuremberg:

> It was to the political classes of Germany, a great part of which are trained in law, that this Trial was addressed. If one judges it in terms of its foreseeable effects upon those Germans who inevitably would and did write West Germany's constitution and dominate its political life, the Trial was not only justified, but it was the only justifiable way of dealing with the Nazi leadership. (1986: 168)

[43] With respect to such ambitious goals, some of the direct participants and observers of the exercise of international justice in the Balkans urge caution and suggest that we might have to look elsewhere for a more adequate assessment of the legacy of the ICTY. See Mégret (2011).

And for Arendt, "There is no doubt that the Eichmann trial had its most far-reaching consequences in Germany" (1994: 16).

Scholarly debates over the impact of the ICTY in the countries of the former Yugoslavia are often framed in terms of dichotomies. Assessments tend to start with a set of normative goals such as peace, reconciliation, and democracy, and then proceed to analyze the evidence in order to show how the exercise of international criminal justice has served to advance or undermine such goals (e.g., Akhavan 1998; Snyder and Vinjamuri 2003/2004). Moreover, the "domestic" and the "international" are usually conceived as two separate realms, which are animated by different logics and reflect the pursuit of competing interests and objectives. In such accounts, international justice is either harnessed by powerful international actors seeking to manage Balkan politics (McMahon and Forsythe 2008), or "hijacked" by domestic elites and used for their own political purposes (Subotić 2009). The impact of the ICTY in the region depends on what forces and dynamics are emphasized (local or international) and what goals of international criminal justice are selected to guide the inquiry.

In the remaining part of this chapter, I develop an alternative understanding of the role of international criminal justice in the post–Yugoslav space. My approach starts not with the normative goals of the ICTY, but with analysis of the multiplicity of actors and processes that international justice has implicated and stimulated in the course of the past decade. I shift the focus away from the grand narratives of international justice, such as peace, reconciliation, and democratization, and recover a core dynamic of pluralization that may be more inconclusive and normatively ambiguous, but is nevertheless intriguing and illuminating for the inquiry of this book. I argue that international criminal justice encourages an ongoing process of pluralization of public discourse, politics, and law in the Balkans, which is set in motion by the existence and workings of the ICTY, but becomes fully legible in the pervasive interactions of a range of other actors with the norms and structures of international justice. I also suggest that pluralization involves a growing interpenetration of the international and the domestic, evident in the emergence of new spaces and forms of hybridity that blur the boundaries between the inside and outside. I examine the emergence of transnational discourse, regional politics, and hybrid legal orders, and interpret them as sites where the tension between nationalism and the rule of law becomes expressed and negotiated.

Given the political context of the revival of international criminal justice in the early 1990s, the establishment of the Yugoslav Tribunal was bound to engender a struggle for discursive hegemony. Two dominant arguments framed the debate from the start, reflecting competing ideological positions and interpretations of the purpose of international justice in the Balkans. One is the "liberal" argument, formulated early on by Madeleine Albright in the following way:

> [T]he tribunal will make it easier for the Bosnian people to reach a genuine peace. The scars left on the bodies and in the minds of the survivors of this war will take time to heal. In too many places, neighbors were betrayed by neighbors and friend divided from friend by fierce and hostile passion. Too many families have assembled at too many cemeteries for us to say that ethnic differences in Bosnia do not matter. But responsibility for these crimes does not rest with the Serbs or Croats or Muslims as peoples; it rests with the people who ordered and committed the crimes. The wounds opened by this war will heal much faster if collective guilt for atrocities is expunged and individual responsibility is assigned.[44]

At heart, the liberal argument is an attack on extreme nationalism in the Balkans and an appeal for the construction of a liberal order. If the advent of identity politics and ethnic cleansing serves to polarize and break up communities in the region, the international judicial intervention is intended to restore the bonds severed by war and mass atrocity. The central contribution of international criminal justice is its ability to focus on the individual in establishing responsibility (as a perpetrator) and extending rights (as a defendant). As Alan Norrie (1993: 10) has noted, "Criminal law is, at heart, a practical application of liberal political philosophy." On this argument, the purpose of the ICTY is first and foremost to counter the narrative of collective guilt, promoted by nationalists and reinforced by the experience of ethnic cleansing across the region. As the former chief prosecutor of

[44] Madeleine K. Albright, Address at the U.S. Holocaust Memorial Museum, Washington, DC, 12 April 1994, retrieved from http://www.silent-edge.org/mt/rwanda/albright.html (accessed 12 January 2012).

the ICTY, Carla Del Ponte, put it in her opening statement at the trial of Slobodan Milošević, "The accused in this case, as in all cases before the Tribunal, is charged as an individual.... No state or organization is on trial here today. The indictments do not accuse an entire people of being collectively guilty of the crimes, even the crimes of genocide."[45]

Del Ponte's statement was addressed to the audience in Serbia – which was following the trial on national television – but also to the proponents of the "nationalist" argument. This argument comes in a variety of forms, but at its core it depicts the Yugoslav Tribunal as a political institution meting out collective guilt and punishment. On trial is not just the individual defendant but the people, the nation, the state that the defendant represents. In Serbia, for example, one popular version of the nationalist argument portrays the ICTY as an instrument of the West to put the blame for the disintegration of Yugoslavia on the Serbian nation.[46] Another version, prevalent in Croatia, suggests that the prosecution of Croatian generals at the ICTY amounts to an attack on the legitimacy of the "Homeland War" and Croatia's independence (Peskin and Boduszynski 2003: 1117–1118). Vojislav Šešelj spoke for an entire field of argument when he declared from the dock at The Hague: "My political conviction is that the [indicted] Radovan Karadžić and Ratko Mladić must never face this tribunal alive. This is their historical responsibility to the Serbian people because through them, the entire Serbian nation, the entire Serbian people, would be tried."[47]

Finally, the "pragmatist" argument has come to the fore in the past decade as all post-conflict states in the Balkans have pursued membership in the EU and confronted its accession conditionality, which includes a requirement for full cooperation with the ICTY. The pragmatist argument negotiates between the liberal and nationalist positions, treating international criminal justice and its requirements as a fact of life. If, say, Croatia or Serbia wants to join the EU and avoid a return to the international isolation of the 1990s, it has no other choice but to cooperate with the ICTY and transfer suspects and evidence to

[45] *Prosecutor v. Slobodan Milošević*, Case No. IT-01–51-I, Transcripts, 12 February 2002, 4.
[46] See Chapter 6, § "Nationalism Reframed."
[47] *Prosecutor v. Vojislav Šešelj*, Case No. IT-03–67-PT, Transcripts, 5 June 2007, 1214.

The Hague. Proponents of the pragmatist argument sometimes imply that state interests are better served by compliance with the demands for cooperation, given the possibility that the accused might be exonerated, than by resisting and agitating the international community. This appears to be the position adopted by Croatia's former Prime Minister, Ivo Sanader, when the news that a high-ranking Croatian general had been arrested in the Canary Islands sparked protests across the country. "It is in Croatia's interests," Sanader argued in parliament, "to establish the full truth in the case of General Gotovona."[48]

My purpose here is not to relate all nuances that can be detected in debates over the ICTY.[49] What I want to convey is the pluralization of public discourse and the nature of the discursive spaces constituted by these arguments and their proponents. The liberal argument of Albright and Del Ponte is also advanced by sections of civil society in the region, from human rights organizations to prominent public intellectuals, and by reformists in the political classes of post–Yugoslav states. Indeed, the idea to create an international criminal tribunal emerged from civil society in the region itself and was promoted with liberal justifications from the start (Rangelov and Teitel 2011: 167–168). The nationalist argument is popular in the region but not limited to it. It is prevalent among many diaspora groups and underpins the emergence of an "anti-globalist" discourse connecting diverse actors – from the Serbian Radical Party to the International Committee for the Defence of Slobodan Milošević, which had enlisted figures such as Harold Pinter (Rangelov 2013a). The pragmatist argument is continuously adapted by governments to address multiple audiences, "nationalized" for domestic consumption and "liberalized" in conversations with Brussels. The ensuing pluralization of discourse reflects the emergence of transnational discursive spaces, where these arguments are continuously articulated, contested, and negotiated.

In some sense, the pluralization of politics has mirrored the discourse, unfolding along the dominant nationalist, liberal, and pragmatist lines. If The Hague appeared to be far away and largely irrelevant in the 1990s, since then it has become the stuff of politics: galvanizing

---

[48] Quoted in OSCE, Mission to Croatia, Spot Report: Reaction in Croatia to the Arrest of Ante Gotovina, Zagreb, 13 December 2005.

[49] I discuss these in more detail in Chapters 5 and 6.

media controversies and street protests, dominating cabinet meet-
ings and election campaigns, and mobilizing political parties and civil
society in shifting alliances and coalitions. Serbian playwright Borka
Pavičević told me once that Yugoslavs were still connected because of
the court in The Hague.[50] I remembered her words when the ICTY
delivered its judgment in the Vukovar Three case, acquitting one of
the former officers of the Yugoslav People's Army tried for a massacre at the Vukovar hospital in 1991, and sentencing another to five
years in prison.[51] I was in Belgrade when the news was reported by
the local media and hailed as a triumph for Serbia; at the same time,
the Croatian parliament was busy adopting a declaration denouncing
the verdict as "morally and legally unjustifiable."[52] Two years later, the
arrest of Radovan Karadžić unleashed protests and disturbances in
Belgrade and celebrations on the streets of Sarajevo.

Perhaps the most significant aspect of the pluralization of politics
encouraged by international justice in the Balkans is its growing regionalization. The EU adopted a regional approach to the post-conflict
countries of the former Yugoslavia by establishing the Stabilization and
Association Process (SAP) for Southeast Europe. The SAP provides
a common framework and set of conditions for applicant countries,
one of which requires them to demonstrate full cooperation with the
ICTY. Arresting and transferring suspects to The Hague has been the
most contentious issue in the negotiations, and has often dominated
the politics of "Europeanization" in the Balkans, most notably when
the EU suspended accession talks with Croatia and Serbia over their
failures to cooperate.[53] In an interesting turn of events, the EU itself
has become increasingly involved in enabling state cooperation with
the ICTY by working alongside a range of domestic and international
actors in the region. Miroslav Lajcak, former High Representative and
EU Special Representative in Bosnia and Herzegovina, notes that his

---

[50] Borka Pavičević, interviewed by the author in Belgrade, 31 October 2006.

[51] *Prosecutor v. Mile Mrkšić, Mirolsav Radić and Veselin Šljivančanin,* Case No. IT-95–
13/1-T, Trial Judgment, 27 September 2007.

[52] Declaration on the Judgement of the International Criminal Tribunal for the Crimes at
Ovcara and the Cooperation of the Republic of Croatia with the International Criminal
Tribunal for the Former Yugoslavia, *Official Gazette* 108/2007, 12 October 2007.

[53] For a detailed discussion of the EU's war crimes conditionality in the context of the
SAP, see Batt and Obradovic-Wochnik (2009).

office in Sarajevo "cooperates with and supports the activities conducted by the ICTY, NATO, EUFOR, the Republika Srpska police, the BiH Intelligence and Security Agency (OSA), and others involved in efforts to bring the four remaining [Bosnian] fugitives to justice."[54] The dynamics of regionalization are also evident in the efforts of other regional organizations to promote the agenda of international justice and dealing with the past in their interactions with post–Yugoslav countries, in particular the Organisation for Security and Cooperation in Europe (OSCE) and the Council of Europe.[55]

Another dimension of the regionalization of politics, which is often overlooked in discussions of the role of the ICTY in the Balkans, reflects the emergence of bottom-up processes and coalitions that in various ways engage with and make use of international criminal justice in regional frameworks. The politics of the EU's war crimes conditionality has enabled civil society groups to address their concerns directly to Brussels, putting pressure on national governments to strengthen cooperation with the ICTY, but also seeking to encourage domestic debate about dealing with the past.[56] The most important regional development from below, however, is the emergence of the Coalition for RECOM – a regional civil society initiative, which advocates the creation of a regional commission to establish the facts of war crimes and address the issue of the remaining 15,000 missing persons.

The Coalition has enlisted more than 1,000 members from all post–Yugoslav countries, including associations of victims and war veterans, human rights NGOs, women's and youth groups, religious communities, and media and public intellectuals. Over the past 5 years, the initiative has conducted 150 consultations with survivors, civil society groups, and affected communities at the local, national, and regional

---

[54] Office of the High Representative and EU Special Representative, *33rd Report of the High Representative for Implementation of the Dayton Agreement on Bosnia and Herzegovina to the Secretary-General of the United Nations (1 October 2007 – 31 March 2008)*, New York, 13 May 2008.

[55] See, e.g., the thematic Web page of the Council of Europe's Commissioner for Human Rights on post-war justice and reconciliation in the former Yugoslavia, which details his continuous dialogue on these issues with national authorities and civil society in the region, retrieved from http://www.coe.int/t/commissioner/activities/themes/Post-war/Default_en.asp (accessed 17 February 2012).

[56] See Chapter 6, § "Pluralization and the Role of Europe."

level. In the course of this consultative process, the Coalition has managed to develop a draft statute of RECOM and collect 600,000 signatures from citizens in support of the establishment of a regional commission.[57] Although the RECOM initiative emerges from the discursive and political space opened up by the advent of international justice in the region, it is also conceived as a response to its increasingly apparent limitations:

> The initiative for RECOM is not an alternative to war crimes trials conducted before the ICTY and national war crimes chambers in the region, but it represents a response to the limitations of the approach to the truth about the past conflict, which is directed at the perpetrator. War crimes trials [have] failed to inspire a significant public debate on war crimes within or among the countries in the region, nor were they accepted as a mechanism for transitional justice that can give a comprehensive explanation of what happened and why the war crimes happened.
>
> The RECOM initiative is a local response "from the bottom up" to a growing societal need to deal with the past. Its legitimacy originates from a very strong feeling of ownership within various organizations of civil society in all of the former Yugoslav states which have found a common interest in establishing the facts about war crimes, victims, and other serious human rights violations. Victims and their families are entitled to that kind of truth.[58]

Finally, international justice has encouraged pluralization in the legal domain, evident in the growing interpenetration of international and domestic law and governance and the emergence of hybrid legal orders.[59] For most of the 1990s, international law and jurisdiction were separated from their domestic counterparts in the region by a high fence, and debates over the Yugoslav Tribunal often emphasized the problems of compliance and enforcement in a highly unfavorable political environment. Already at that time, however, Anne-Marie

---

[57] See the Web site of the Coalition for RECOM at http://www.zarekom.org/The-Coalition-for-RECOM.en.html (accessed 17 January 2012).

[58] Coalition for RECOM, *Report for May-December 2009: Review of Opinions, Suggestions, and Recommendations* (on file with the author), 2.

[59] This dimension of hybrid governance in conflict-affected states is often overlooked by scholars who emphasize the coexistence and interaction of modern/state and traditional/non-state actors and institutions. See, e.g., Boege, Brown, and Clements (2009).

Slaughter (1998: 136–140) anticipates the potential of the ICTY to foster a dialogue and establish a set of links with domestic courts, foreshadowing a scenario where "domestic courts function not as domestic actors invisible and unaccountable behind the opaque shield of the state, but rather as agents of a higher corporate body," and where "courts play a dual role as servants of both the domestic and the international legal system."

International justice stimulates pluralization in the post–Yugoslav space by partially removing domestic courts from their national encasement and subjecting them to international monitoring and supervision, but also by contributing to the emergence of new legal processes and structures that are hybrid by design. These developments reflect the intensifying interactions of the ICTY with domestic legal spheres, especially in the context of the Tribunal's transfer of cases to domestic jurisdictions, and the involvement of various other international actors in promoting and monitoring war crimes trials in the region. In Serbia, a special War Crimes Chamber has been established at Belgrade District Court with much international involvement and resources, whereas in Croatia four courts (Osijek, Rijeka, Split, and Zagreb) have been designated to try war crimes cases and endowed with extraterritorial jurisdiction. Although formally situated in the domestic legal system of each state, these institutions operate in the shadow of constant international scrutiny and oversight; the OSCE, for example, has been monitoring domestic war crimes trials and judicial standards and reporting regularly to the ICTY, as well as supporting the trials with training and outreach activities.

As a result, these structures tend to oscillate between the international and domestic – they have two masters, and their allegiance is always precarious, reflecting uneasy compromises and competing pressures. The War Crimes Chamber in Belgrade is regularly attacked in the press by nationalists, who see it as an extension of the "anti-Serb" ICTY, but it is also criticized for shielding the Serbian state from confronting its responsibility for atrocities.[60] War crimes trials are effectively serving to disaggregate the Croatian judiciary, as the top echelons increasingly align their practices with international

---

[60] See Chapter 6, § "Pluralization and the Role of Europe."

requirements and standards, whereas local courts continue to prosecute Serbs for war crimes in absentia and exhibit various other forms of ethnic bias in the administration of justice.[61] The logic of the hybrid legal order is most apparent in Kosovo and Bosnia, where the heavy involvement of the international community has engendered complex systems of hybrid governance. Kosovo's mixed panels for war crimes and ethnically motivated crimes are staffed by EU and local judges and prosecutors. The War Crimes Chamber of the State Court of Bosnia and Herzegovina is part of the domestic legal system, but has a mixed staff and applies both domestic and international law. The Chamber has been praised by the OSCE and ICTY for trying the bulk of the cases transferred back to the region and doing so according to international standards, but it has also become a favorite target of the political leadership of Republika Srpska, which seeks to curtail its operations and even calls for its dissolution.[62]

These dynamics of pluralization may be manifesting the inherent nature of international justice; as Gerry Simpson (2007: 30) notes, "One of the constituting relationships of the field of war crimes trials and international criminal law is that between two spaces: domestic and international, and between two modes of prosecution and defence: sovereigntist (or metropolitan) and cosmopolitan." Their significance stems from the fact that they contradict and partially reverse the homogenizing logic of the conflicts and transitions in the region. The pursuit of homogeneity is the animating logic of ethnic cleansing, but it is also a foundation of the post-war settlement in the former Yugoslavia, reconfiguring its political map by turning it into a patchwork of ethnic states, entities, and enclaves. The role of international justice in the region should be assessed by taking into account the political dispensations and relations of power produced by the conflicts and further entrenched by the post-conflict order, rather than

---

[61] See Chapter 5, § "Transitional Justice after Tuđman."

[62] See Human Rights Watch, *Narrowing the Impunity Gap: Trials before Bosnia's War Crimes Chamber*, February 2007, retrieved from http://www.hrw.org/reports/2007/02/11/narrowing-impunity-gap-0 (accessed 15 February 2012); David Tolbert, "EU Must Protect Bosnia's War Crimes Court," *Balkan Insight*, 8 February 2012, retrieved from http://www.balkaninsight.com/en/article/eu-must-protect-bosnia-s-war-crimes-court (accessed 15 February 2012).

by starting with normative goals and aspirations for ideal polities and politics. Seen in this light, pluralization is important because it emerges despite all odds, contradicting and challenging the powerful forces of homogenization that have dominated the region's wars and transitions since the early 1990s.

The ensuing pluralization of public discourse, politics, and law suggests one way of grasping the evolving relationship between nationalism and the rule of law in the post–Yugoslav space. If the rise of international justice embodies a constitutive tension between nationalism and the rule of law, as I have argued, the actual pursuit of international war crimes trials over the past decade has not been able to transcend or resolve that tension. Instead, the emergence of transnational discourse, regional politics, and hybrid legal orders has provided new sites where the tension between nationalism and the rule of law becomes expressed and negotiated by a multiplicity of actors, who in various ways connect to and make use of the ICTY in order to advance diverse political projects and purposes. The tension persists in the form of pervasive contestation but also limited accommodation; indeed, the pragmatist argument, the politics of Europe's ICTY conditionality, and the War Crimes Chamber, can be understood as ongoing attempts to manage the relationship between nationalism and the rule of law and negotiate the underlying tensions.

PART II   THREE CASES FROM THE FORMER YUGOSLAVIA

4   THE MAKING OF A LIBERAL DEMOCRACY

Ethnic Citizenship in Slovenia

The premises of the Association of the Erased – a dilapidated ware-house from the socialist era – contrast sharply with the affluence of central Ljubljana just minutes away. The founder of the Association, Aleksandar Todorović, is articulate and bitter when he tells the story of his "erasure." Todorović is an ethnic Serb who first came to Slovenia in 1977 to work on an archaeological project, and met his future Slovene wife. He left Serbia permanently in 1986 and settled in Slovenia, both republics of the Socialist Federal Republic of Yugoslavia (SFRY) at that time. Slovenia declared independence in June 1991. Todorović did not apply for citizenship in the new state, assuming that he would pre-serve his residence status and rights automatically. When he attempted to register the birth of his daughter with the local authorities two years later, however, he realized that he had been "erased" from the Registry of Permanent Residents without any notification, and was now an illegal alien in Slovenia. The officer destroyed his identification card and driving licence and informed him that as an illegal foreigner he could not be registered as the father. The covert act of the erasure was implemented in February 1992, and according to the latest official estimates, it affected at least 25,671 permanent residents of Slovenia. Reflecting on the plight of the "erased" over the years, Todorović speaks of "cleansing" and "fascism."[1]

I examine the case of Slovenia's "erased" as an opportunity to interrogate in greater depth the model of ethnic citizenship and rule

[1] Aleksandar Todorović, interviewed by the author at the Association of the Erased in Ljubljana, 18 June 2007.

of law issues that it raises. In the first part of the book, I theorize ethnic citizenship as a form of differentiated membership defined in ethnic terms and enshrined in law, and distinguish between strategies of incorporation and strategies of exclusion employed by the nation-state in its institutionalization.[2] Citizenship in post-independence Slovenia could be productively analyzed through the lens of incorporation, and indeed scholars have examined issues such as constitutional nationalism and the constitutionally established hierarchy of autochthonous and non-autochthonous minorities in Slovenia along those lines (Hayden 1992; Deželan 2011: 23–27). These issues are important because they go to the heart of the question of who "owns" the state, and bring into light diffuse forms of discrimination that shape the operation of Slovenia's model of ethnic citizenship. Nevertheless, I focus most of my discussion on the dynamics of exclusion as manifested in the case of the "erased," partly because of the severity of the measure and its consequences for those directly affected, and partly because it captures in a microcosm the wider implications of ethnic citizenship for the rule of law.

The erasure signaled a suspension of the legal status and rights of thousands of lawful residents, de facto excluding from the protection of the rule of law more than 1 percent of Slovenia's population. Moreover, the fact that the measure was implemented by executive decision and shrouded in secrecy for more than a decade further exacerbated the vulnerability of the "erased," exposing them to arbitrariness and abuse of power by agents of the state. But the Slovenian case is also useful because it illuminates broader themes concerning the relationship between contemporary forms of ethnic citizenship and the rule of law. The discussion of ethnic citizenship in Chapter 1 already prefigures a set of tensions between domestic and international arenas, highlighting the role of international monitoring and adjudication of human rights violations engendered by various regimes of ethnic citizenship. The legal and political contestations over the "erased" in Slovenia afford an opportunity to complicate the analysis, suggesting a growing embeddedness of human rights norms in domestic legal processes and structures and pointing

---

[2] See Chapter 1, § "Ethnic Citizenship."

to a multiplicity of actors – international and local, legal and political, state and non-state – who become implicated on different sides of the controversy. A detailed examination of ethnic citizenship in Slovenia also helps understand how liberal democracies, notionally committed to norms such as non-discrimination, may end up pursuing a renationalization agenda by illiberal means, illuminating the broader phenomenon of "symbolic revaluation" of citizenship at a time when its substantive content is becoming increasingly deflated and the power of the state to shape collective identities is called into question.[3]

Underlying my analysis is a conception of citizenship that emphasizes its flexible character: the ambivalent role of law in formalizing the citizenship construct on the one hand, and in keeping it open to the possibility of change and transformation on the other. This flexibility and reliance on legal articulation enables the state to revise the terms of membership and realign citizenship with shifting national projects and identities. Igor Štiks's (2010) analysis of the evolution of citizenship in the former Yugoslavia is particularly illuminating in this respect, suggesting how historical and contemporary polities have harnessed citizenship as an instrument of state- and nation-building in the pursuit of diverse and sometimes opposing goals. Citizenship, he argues, has been used:

> as a tool of national integration in the first Yugoslavia (1918–1941), as a tool of socialist re-unification after the failure of the previous national integration and the ensuing inter-ethnic conflicts (1945 to the mid-1960s), as a tool of cooperation among nations and their republics in a socialist multinational (con)federation (beginning in the late 1960s and continuing until 1990), as a tool of fragmentation and dissolution (1990–1991) and, finally, of ethnic engineering in Yugoslavia's successor states.(Štiks 2010: 3)

After discussing the erasure itself, I examine a set of broader dynamics of democratization, economic liberalization, and Europeanization in Slovenia since the 1980s, seeking to recover from these uneven transformations the pressures that have shaped the regime of ethnic citizenship and draw out its implications for the rule of law.

---

[3] See Chapter 1, "Dynamics of Renationalization."

THE ERASED

Slovenia is often viewed as the only "success story" that emerged from the dissolution of Yugoslavia in the early 1990s. Fostering this image internationally was one of the priorities for the transitional elites around the time of independence. Indeed, the need to build international legitimacy was particularly acute given widespread concerns in the West about the implications of Slovenia's secession from the federal state. In this environment, the political class ensured that the process of gaining independent statehood was legitimized by demonstrating respect for democratic principles and international human rights norms. The basis for declaring independence was the referendum of December 1990, in which an overwhelming majority expressed support for seceding from the SFRY. In preparation for the vote, a Statement of Good Intentions was adopted by parliament, seeking to reassure international publics and internal minorities that Slovenia was committed to protecting the rights of all residents without any discrimination. The Statement guaranteed the constitutional rights of the Hungarian and Italian minorities (Slovenia's so-called autochthonous minorities), but also "to all members of other nations and nationalities the right to an all-embracing development of their culture and language and to all those who have their permanent residence in Slovenia the right to obtain Slovenian citizenship if they so wish."[4] The latter reassurances were directed at migrants from other Yugoslav republics, and in the spirit of the Statement they were encouraged to participate in the referendum alongside ethnic Slovenes. The constitution of the Republic of Slovenia enshrined the principle of equality before the law and guaranteed human rights and fundamental freedoms to everyone, building a rule of law paradigm in the foundations of the state.[5]

As part of the corpus of law that was adopted for Slovenia's transition to independent statehood, the legislator provided a broad basis for acquisition of Slovenian citizenship by combining jus sanguinis and jus domicili principles. The citizenship framework of the SFRY included

---

[4] Statement of Good Intent, *Official Gazette*, no. 44/90-I (1990).
[5] Constitution of the Republic of Slovenia, *Official Gazette*, no. 33/91-I (1991), Article 14.

both federal citizenship, which all citizens of SFRY possessed, and republican citizenship in one of the constituent republics. This regime of "bifurcated citizenship" (Štiks 2010: 7) was largely inconsequential during the Yugoslav era, as federal citizenship established the equal rights and status of all Yugoslav citizens. When the federal state collapsed, however, republican citizenship acquired new significance, and unlike other republics of the SFRY, Slovenia had maintained detailed citizenship records at the republican level. The Citizenship of the Republic of Slovenian Act, adopted in June 1991, provided that all persons who possessed citizenship in the former Socialist Republic of Slovenia acquired Slovenian citizenship automatically. Article 40 of the Act enabled acquisition of Slovenian citizenship jure domicili for the 200,000 permanent residents from other Yugoslav republics, who comprised around 10 percent of the population:

> Citizens of another republic [of the SFRY] who on 23 December 1990, the day when the plebiscite on the independence of the Republic of Slovenia was held, were registered as permanent residents in the Republic of Slovenia and in fact live here shall acquire citizenship of the Republic of Slovenia if they lodge, within six months after the present Act enters into force, an application with the internal affairs authority of the municipality where they live.[6]

The vast majority of eligible residents from other republics of the SFRY applied within the six-month deadline, and 170,000 of them acquired Slovenian citizenship through the process. At least 30,000 permanent residents, however, did not obtain citizenship. Years of systematic research conducted at the Peace Institute in Ljubljana have clarified the range of individual circumstances that led to this outcome and paved the way for the erasure. There were a number of reasons why these residents did not obtain Slovenian citizenship:

• they did not apply for citizenship for various reasons (e.g., they missed the deadline, they chose not to apply and expected that they would keep their permanent residence in Slovenia, or they did not know they had to apply to prevent the loss of their permanent residence, etc.); or

---

[6] Citizenship of the Republic of Slovenia Act, Official Gazette, no. 1/91-I (1991), Article 40.

- they applied for citizenship, but their claim was rejected by the authorities (approximately 2,400 applications); or
- they wanted to apply but the authorities refused to accept their application under the pretext that it was not complete; or
- they applied for Slovenian citizenship, were issued a positive decision, but their citizenship was later withdrawn; or
- they applied for citizenship and they never received an answer from the Ministry of the Interior.[7]

These individuals were caught in a legal limbo because the Citizenship Act did not provide for any procedure that would allow them to regulate their status, either by retaining their permanent residence or by acquiring citizenship after the six-month deadline. The only legal provision in place was Article 81 of the Aliens Act, which stipulated that the Act was to apply to all citizens of other republics of the SFRY who had not applied for Slovenian citizenship within the period of six months or whose applications had been rejected.[8] Notably, the creation of a legal gap was anticipated in parliamentary discussions. In order to prevent this gap in the law, members of parliament from the Liberal Democracy of Slovenia Party had proposed an amendment to Article 81 of the Aliens Act, which would provide that residents from other former Yugoslav republics who did not apply for Slovenian citizenship would be issued permanent residence permits. The right-wing majority of the Democratic Opposition of Slovenia (DEMOS) voted down the proposal for the amendment, leading some observers to conclude that the subsequent enactment of the erasure was not some sort of mistake or omission but constituted a "purposeful *political act* of a discriminatory nature" (Dedić 2003: 47).

The provisions of the Aliens Act came into force on 26 February 1992, and on that day the erasure was implemented by the Ministry of the Interior ex officio. At least 25,671 former SFRY citizens lost their status as permanent residents and their names were erased from the register of permanent residents and entered into the register of aliens

---

[7] Neža Kogovšek and Roberto Pignioni, *The Erased People of Slovenia: Peace Institute Report on Discriminatory Practices in Slovenia Concerning Legal Statuses of Citizens of Other Republics of Yugoslavia*, Submitted to the Committee on Civil Liberties, Justice and Home Affairs at the European Parliament, Brussels, 26 June 2007.

[8] Aliens Act, *Official Gazette*, no. 1/91-I (1991), Article 81.

without a residence permit.[9] In effect, overnight, the "erased" became aliens or stateless persons who were residing in Slovenia illegally. The ECtHR was seized with the issue in the *Kurić* case, and described the predicament of the erased in the following way:

> In general, they [the "erased"] had difficulties in keeping their jobs, driving licences and obtaining retirement pensions. Nor were they able to leave the country, because they could not re-enter without valid documents. Many families became divided, with some of their members in Slovenia and others in one of the other successor States of the former SFRY. Among "the erased" were a certain number of minors. In most cases their identity papers were taken away. Some of "the erased" voluntarily left Slovenia. Finally, some were served removal orders and deported from Slovenia.[10]

The profile of those erased by the Slovenian authorities reflects the legal fiction of republican citizenship under the system of the former SFRY and a quasi-legal definition of who may be considered an "enemy" of the newly established Slovenian state. For example, children born to parents from two different republics who were not registered as Slovenian citizens should automatically have become citizens of another republic, but in practice republican-level citizenship records

[9] In 2002, when the erasure became publicly known, the Slovenian authorities estimated that 18,305 persons had been erased, but the arrival of new information technologies led to a recount in 2009, and the official figure was changed to 25,671. See *Kurić and Others v. Slovenia*, Application no. 26828/06, Council of Europe: ECtHR, 13 July 2010, paras. 42 and 65.

[10] *Kurić and Others v. Slovenia*, para. 43. Deportations in 1992–1995 had particularly severe consequences as both Croatia and Bosnia and Herzegovina were war zones at the time. The most detailed account of the erasure and its implications for those affected is available in Dedić, Jalušič, and Zorn (2003). A number of intergovernmental organizations and international NGOs issued reports on the erasure once it was exposed in the media. See, for example, Council of Europe: Office of the Commissioner for Human Rights, *Report by Mr Alvaro Gil-Robles, Commissioner for Human Rights, on His Visit to Slovenia, 11–14 May 2003*, CommDH(2003)11, 15 October 2003; United Nations Human Rights Committee, *Consideration of Reports Submitted by State Parties under Article 40 of the Covenant: Concluding Observations of the Human Rights Committee: Slovenia*, CCPR/CO/84/SVN, 25 July 2005; Amnesty International, *Slovenia: Amnesty International's Briefing to the UN Committee on Economic, Social and Cultural Rights, 35th Session*, AI Index: EUR 68/002/2005, November 2005; Council of Europe: European Commission Against Racism and Intolerance (ECRI), *Third Report on Slovenia, Adopted on 30 June 2006*, CRI(2007)5, 13 February 2007.

outside of Slovenia were often poorly maintained, and omissions became even more frequent once the region was engulfed by war. The war affected the "erased" in other ways, as well. In theory, citizens of former Yugoslav republics such as Serbia or Bosnia should have been able to acquire passports from the respective succession state; in practice, however, these states were cut off by ongoing hostilities and did not have any diplomatic representation in Ljubljana at that time (Dedić 2003: 60–61). After the military intervention of the JNA and the ensuing Ten Day War on the territory of Slovenia in the summer of 1991, a group of JNA officers found themselves on a list known as the "800 dangerous persons," and the Citizenship Act was amended later that year to preclude such elements from acquiring Slovenian citizenship. As one observer put it, "Another group seriously affected were officers of the Yugoslav People's Army who were designated as 'enemies' of, or 'aggressors' against, the newly formed state" (ibid. 62). The majority of the "erased," however, were internal migrants within the former Yugoslavia, such as Serbs and Bosniaks, and a number of Roma.

The contradictory character of Slovenia's citizenship policy in the wake of independence is as apparent as it is puzzling. On the one hand, the vast majority of permanent residents who were ethnic non-Slovenes were able to acquire Slovenian citizenship on the basis of the publicly adopted legislation and the procedures put in place for its implementation. On the other hand, the same body of law opened up the possibility for serious abuses and discriminatory policies adopted by executive decision and pursued covertly by the agents of the state. These contradictions can be comprehended as expressing a foundational tension between the rule of law and ethnic citizenship, each associated with powerful pressures that were set in motion at the time of gaining independence, and continued to pull in opposite directions throughout the period of transition. The issue of the "erased," more than any other transitional challenge, makes legible the competing logics of liberal constitutionalism and nationalist mobilization that have contested the meaning of citizenship in the Slovenian state in public confrontations implicating the political class, legal institutions, and civil society. More importantly, the story of the "erased" calls into question complacent assumptions about the rule of law in the liberal state, suggesting how formal commitments to non-discrimination and state policies producing the opposite effect may coexist and even reinforce each other.

The "erased" remained invisible and did not attract public attention for more than a decade, each of them pursuing their own individual struggle for status and survival. But the debate over citizenship became a permanent fixture of Slovenian politics during that period. One of the issues was a legislative proposal to withdraw the citizenship of ethnic non-Slovenes, envisioning a referendum to reverse the process that had granted citizenship to residents from other republics of the former SFRY under Article 40 of the Citizenship Act. The debate was fueled by claims that these persons possessed dual citizenship, which put ethnic Slovenes in a disadvantaged position. The discussions in Parliament invoked a range of arguments against the "immigrants" and called for setting up specific procedures to determine "the veracity of [their] Slovenization" and to prevent "the emergence of any national minorities."[11] In the end, the Constitutional Court intervened and put an end to the initiative, ruling that the request for a referendum on withdrawing citizenship was unconstitutional and contravened the principle of rule of law.[12] As it turned out, the decision was only the first in a series of interventions by the Constitutional Court on questions of citizenship; in particular, over the next decade and a half the Court was going to develop a large body of jurisprudence dealing with the "erased."

Concerns about the issue started to appear in the annual reports of Slovenia's Human Rights Ombudsman in the mid-1990s, noting that many individuals had difficulties regulating their status after being erased from the registry of permanent residents, and appealing for state action to resolve the problem (Jalušič and Dedić 2007: 107). The first decision of the Constitutional Court on the matter came in February 1999 in a case lodged by two individuals affected by the erasure that challenged the constitutionality of the relevant sections of the Aliens Act. The Court ruled that Article 81 of the Aliens Act was indeed unconstitutional because it created a legal void for citizens of the former SFRY (those with permanent residence at the time of

[11] Jelka Zorn, "The Ethno-Nationalism of Slovenia's Secession and Initial Citizenship Rules," unpublished manuscript on file with the author.

[12] Constitutional Court decision U-I-266/95, 20 November 1995.

independence who had not obtained Slovenian citizenship or whose applications had been dismissed), breaching the principles of rule of law, legal certainty, and equality, and gave the legislator six months to amend the law and regulate the special status of the affected persons.[13] The decision led to the adoption of the Act Regulating the Legal Status of Citizens of Other Successor States of the Former SFRY in the Republic of Slovenia (Legal Status Act) later that year. The legislation provided a three-month period in which the "erased" could file an application for a permanent residence permit; however, the status was granted only for the period after an application had been approved and only those individuals who had resided in Slovenia without interruption since 25 June 1991 were eligible to apply.[14] Simply put, this meant that those who had remained in Slovenia could not claim retroactive status from the time the erasure was implemented, whereas those who had left or had been expelled from the country could not claim any status at all.

The public silence about the "erased" was finally broken in 2002. The writings of Igor Mekina in the daily *Večer* and a press conference of the Association of the Erased on the tenth anniversary of the erasure propelled the issue into the public domain. At least some of the "erased" were mobilizing and pressing their demands collectively, and the media jumped on the story. A former constitutional judge, Matevž Krivic, assumed an active role in the legal representation and public advocacy on behalf of the "erased." In the ensuing public discussions, journalists and lawyers became involved alongside civil society actors and the political classes on different sides of the controversy. In particular, a series of public contestations over the issue of the "erased" ended up implicating the major legal and political institutions of the Slovenian state, including the Human Rights Ombudsman, Constitutional Court, parliament, and government.

The main positions and actors in these contestations crystallized in the period following another decision of the Constitutional Court, issued in April 2003. The Court found that the Legal Status Act was unconstitutional, firstly, because it did not extend permanent residence

---

[13] Constitutional Court decision U-I-284/94, 4 February 1999.

[14] Act Regulating the Legal Status of Citizens of Other Successor States of the Former SFRY in the Republic of Slovenia, *Official Gazette*, no. 61/99 (1999).

retroactively from the date of the erasure and, secondly, because it did not regulate the acquisition of permanent residence for those who had been forcibly removed from Slovenia. The judges also struck down the three-month deadline for lodging applications for permanent residence, and ordered Parliament to amend the respective provisions of the Legal Status Act within six months and the Ministry of the Interior to issue supplementary orders to those who had already obtained permanent residence effective from 26 February 1992.[15] The right-wing opposition, led by Janez Janša, accused the judges of taking over legislative powers and launched an attack on the center-left government, which had started to issue supplementary orders in line with the decision of the Constitutional Court. The effort of the government to resolve the issue was soon overwhelmed by the unleashed backlash from the right.[16] Janša launched a campaign to put the issue on a referendum, and the ensuing discussions in the parliament and media became infused with nationalist and xenophobic rhetoric, prompting the Council of Europe to express concerns that "intolerance, and even xenophobia, are sometimes found among politicians and representatives of public authorities, and that some media contribute to the development of such attitudes."[17] The heated debate over the "erased" helped to galvanize nationalist sentiment and support for Janša, who became the next prime minister and promptly suspended the process of issuing supplementary orders (Deželan 2011: 17, 19).

The Human Rights Ombudsman, Matjaž Hanžek, found himself in the middle of the controversy. The ombudsman had requested the constitutional judges to speed up the case of the "erased," and later publicly expressed his support for their decision. Speaking on national television,

[15] Constitutional Court decision U-I-246/02, 3 April 2003.

[16] On 25 November 2003, new legislation was adopted to regulate the procedure for implementing the decision of the Constitutional Court of April 2003, the Act on the Application of Point No. 8 of the Constitutional Court's Decision no. U-I-246/02–28, which has become known as the Technical Act. The right-wing parliamentarians managed to secure a referendum on whether or not the Technical Act should be implemented. The turnout was only 32.45 percent, with 94.59 percent opposed to implementing the legislation, and the Technical Act never entered into force. See *Kurić and Others v. Slovenia*, paras. 59–61.

[17] Council of Europe: Advisory Committee on the Framework Convention for the Protection of National Minorities, *Second Opinion on Slovenia adopted on 26 May 2005*, ACFC/INF/OP/II(2005)005, Strasbourg, 1 December 2005.

Hanžek denounced the proposal for a referendum on minority rights and argued that a Nazi referendum on the Final Solution in the 1930s, even if backed by the public, would not have changed the nature of Nazism. The statement unleashed a political storm and prompted right-wing politicians and media to launch an attack against him that lasted until the very end of his term in office. Hanžek's public statements over the years on various controversial issues such as the "erased," the rise of xenophobia, and the discriminatory treatment of members of the Roma minority provoked some parliamentarians to call for his impeachment and even for dismantling the institution of the Human Rights Ombudsman. When I met him in Ljubljana in the summer of 2007, Hanžek was still recovering from the relentless public campaign against him: "The Prime Minister [Janša] and the government attacked me repeatedly, saying that I was a traitor of the nation for publicizing information abroad, and asked me to apologize to the Slovenian nation."[18]

It is ironic that three years later an official apology was issued to the "erased" in Parliament by the speaker, Pavel Gantar. The apology followed the arrival of a new center-left government in 2008, which resumed the process of issuing supplementary orders, and the adoption of amendments and supplements to the Legal Status Act in 2010, which finally sought to implement the decision of the Constitutional Court from April 2003. Once again, a familiar scenario played out in Slovenian politics: the right-wing opposition requested a referendum on the changes and the Constitutional Court ruled that a referendum would be unconstitutional. Looking back at the years since the issue of the "erased" first attracted public attention, the level of contestation and controversy that it has elicited – parliamentary debates, legislative initiatives, calls for a referendum, decisions of the Constitutional Court, and so forth – appears truly astonishing. Gantar's apology to the "erased" recognized the human rights abuses they had endured over the years and validated their experiences of discrimination and injustice, but it raised as many questions as it answered. Why did the Slovenian state enact the measure in the first place? Why did it take so long to resolve the problem? And why did the issue become so contentious for Slovenia's political classes, institutions, and public?

---

[18] Matjaž Hanžek, interviewed by the author in Ljubljana, 21 June 2007.

RECOVERING THE MEANING OF THE ERASURE

Hanžek believes that the erasure was ultimately an act of "revenge after victory," pursued by nationalist dissidents-turned-politicians once Slovenia's independence had been secured.[19] A growing number of scholars have written about these issues in recent years, advancing a range of intriguing explanations and interpretations of the erasure. Tomaž Deželan makes an argument similar to Hanžek's:

> The main rationale of the erasure seems to have been in retaliation against members of the Yugoslav People's Army for their participation in the "Ten Day War" for Slovenian independence since the erasure affected individuals failing to or deciding not to acquire citizenship on the basis of art. 40 of the Citizenship Act. This is in line with the revision of the same act in December 1991, which introduced provisions about activities against the state. (Deželan 2011: 19)

Vlasta Jalušič examines the circumstances of the "erased" in the context of a larger transition, one that is signaled by the collapse of multinational states and the construction of nation-states in Eastern Europe. In the course of the transition, she argues, the totalitarianism of the all-controlling state is replaced by a normalization of practices of discrimination and exclusion associated with "a different, much more dispersed totalitarianism of mass society and enforced homogenization" (Jalušič 2003: 13). On this argument, the events in Slovenia should be located within much broader political and social transformations and geographies.

In Jasminka Dedić's (2003) more legalistic analysis, the spotlight is on the procedure for granting Slovenian citizenship and the systematic human rights violations that accompanied that process. The ensuing abuses, she argues, reflected both institutionalized forms of discrimination and a wider political consensus in the post-independence period, evident from the repeated appeals of mainstream political parties to disregard the decisions of the Constitutional Court. Brad Blitz is interested in the case of the "erased" because it reveals how the social construction of citizenship in periods of intense national homogenization may produce de facto statelessness. His study highlights the role

---

[19] Hanžek interview.

of political activists and state-owned media in devising elite-driven cultural policies and their subsequent institutionalization in discriminatory citizenship law: "These actions sought to reposition Slovenia in opposition to the former Yugoslavia and reinforce the specificity of the Slovenian nation, at the expense of non-Slovenes living within its borders" (Blitz 2006: 454).

Jelka Zorn analyzes the issue of the "erased" within the process of consolidation of Slovenian ethno-nationalism since the late 1980s. In particular, she emphasizes the role of dissident intellectuals gathered around the journal *Nova Revija* in constructing a narrative of suppression of Slovenian language and culture within the SFRY, providing the basis for a critique of the federal framework and subsequent demands for self-determination. Crucial in this respect was the formation of new political elites around the time of independence, which drew heavily on that dissident base. Zorn directs attention to other key issues such as the advent of neoliberal policies, unemployment, and social insecurity, which in her view served both to mask practices of ethnic exclusion and provide a justification for them. The erasure is grasped at the intersection of two dynamics that are simultaneously at play, one associated with an ethno-nationally framed state-building project from "above" and the other with popular anti-immigrant sentiments from "below." She notes that the issue of ethnic exclusion may be particularly stark in the case of the "erased," but its effects extend well beyond that group: "In Slovenia, immigrants from other republics of the former Yugoslavia and their descendents were depicted as a threat to Slovenian culture and language. Although the majority of them managed to become Slovenian citizens, ethnic oppression towards them continued."[20]

Finally, the erasure has been examined as one element of a larger transformation of citizenship in post-independence Slovenia. Interpretations of the broader terrain of Slovenian citizenship have often converged on employing the analytical framework of the "nationalizing state" advanced in the work of Rogers Brubaker (1996), which highlights the centrality of the "core nation" concept and the range of practices of political elites and bureaucracies in asserting its "ownership" of the state. Its logic allows for the countervailing force of international legal

[20] Zorn, "The Ethno-nationalism of Slovenia's Secession," 18.

norms and standards, but only to the extent that their incorporation represents a deliberate attempt on the part of national elites to foster the international legitimacy of the state, construed as a set of external constraints rather than an outcome of productive internal pressures and struggles. This is how Zorn (2009), for example, reinterprets the erasure in her more recent work. In his detailed analysis of the trajectory of Slovenia's citizenship regime over the past two decades, Deželan (2011) arrives at similar conclusions. He discerns the logic of nationalization operating across the various dimensions of citizenship policy and politics in Slovenia, from the regulation of dual citizenship and statelessness to the treatment of minorities and refugees. The erasure is only one manifestation of the logic that pervades this broader citizenship domain, where citizenship is understood as "membership in a 'nationalising state,' which is dominated by the principles of an ethno-cultural conception of nationhood primarily promoted by a right-wing political elite and constrained by its integration into the European Union and the wider international community" (Deželan 2011: 36).

In the remaining part of this chapter, I seek to recover the meaning of the erasure and the events that preceded, accompanied, and followed its implementation by drawing on three narratives of transition. These narratives capture three fundamental shifts that have unfolded concurrently and converged to reshape Slovenian politics, society, and identity in the course of a triple transition from authoritarian to democratic rule, socialist to capitalist economic order, and Yugoslavia to Europe. My analysis seeks to highlight the uneven and conflictual nature of democratization, economic liberalization, and Europeanization in the Slovenian context in order to map the contradictory pressures that have been engendered by each of these processes and understand how these pressures, in turn, have shaped the paradigms of ethnic citizenship and the rule of law and the emergence of the "erased" as an issue that manifests their incompatibility and tension.

DEMOCRATIZATION

Slovenia's secession is often seen as a catalyst for the disintegration of the former Yugoslavia, paving the way for a series of separatist claims and bloody wars that ended up engulfing most of the region. It is ironic that perhaps more than any other republic of the SFRY, Slovenia's road to secession during the 1980s was marked not by the resurgence of nationalism, which came late in the day, but rather by the emergence of a vibrant civil society that took the form of alternative ideas, autonomous spaces, and demands for human rights and democratic politics. The rise of social movements around issues such as peace, punk, feminism, sexual minorities, conscientious objection to military service, and the environment reflected an aspiration to redefine the relationship between state and society – not the relationship between Ljubljana and Belgrade. These new spaces of debate and dissent developed independently from the state and party apparatus, but also, for most of the decade, remained resistant to nationalist framing and appropriation. Indeed, many of the key actors in the awakening of civil society recall with chagrin the "nationalizing" of the spaces they had carved out and ultimately of Slovenian politics itself. In their accounts, the resurgence of nationalism emerges more as an outcome than a cause of Slovenia's push for independence.

Tomaž Mastnak (1994), a youth activist at the time, relates how the "alternative scene" and media that appeared in the early 1980s constructed a civil society discourse centered on the idea of plurality, which underscored the significance not of party politics but of social movements and civic initiatives and demanded respect for the rights of women and sexual, ethnic, and religious minorities. As the authorities in Slovenia became increasingly willing to accept and adapt to this process of internal pluralization, the tension with the centralizing forces operating at the federal level became more apparent. The pressures from Belgrade encouraged the convergence of civil society and reformers in positions of power at the republican level, and democracy became a national project: "Because sovereignty is, strictly speaking, indivisible, its politics are bound to be exclusionary; the fact that democratic society as it was formed in Slovenia needed national sovereignty in order to be able to survive was detrimental to its communications across internal Yugoslav borders. To a degree, Slovene politics became the mirror image of Serbian exclusivism" (Mastnak 1994: 107).

Vlasta Jalušič (1994), a prominent feminist activist and public intellectual, tells a similar story. She recalls how women's groups and concerns became increasingly marginalized in the so-called Slovenian Spring in the late 1980s. The mass movement that came to the fore at that time had its origins in the rich tapestry of earlier civil-society movements and struggles, when only one intellectual circle had championed the national issue and sought to put it on the agenda. Jalušič suggests that the turning point for pluralist civil society was the Trial of the Four in June–July 1988. Janez Janša and two other journalists from the dissident weekly magazine *Mladina* were preparing a story based on a leaked document of the Ljubljana Military District, which outlined a plan for introducing martial law in the republic. Together with the JNA officer who had leaked the document, the three journalists were tried by a military court in Ljubljana, and the proceedings were conducted in Serbo-Croatian. The trial provoked a storm of public protest and mobilization throughout the republic, spearheaded by a broad civil society coalition that called itself Committee for the Defence of Human Rights.

> The trial of the Four allowed all questions on the public agenda before 1988 to be subsumed under the national question. All questions that did not fit well enough into this shape became unimportant. If in the mid-1980s issues such as conscientious objection, obligatory military training for women, and the rights of homosexuals had equal or greater importance than other issues, after the military trial everything changed. Everything and everybody was mobilized for "our boys" and against the Yugoslav military. (Jalušič 1994: 148)

In some sense, the figure of Janez Janša could be seen as emblematic of the wider transformation that took place in Slovenian politics and civil society around the time of secession from the SFRY. Janša's career in the 1980s started as an activist in the communist youth organization and later a defense correspondent for the dissident magazine *Mladina*. In the course of the events that culminated with the Trial of the Four, Janša became well known for his radical anti-JNA and antimilitaristic views. Subsequently, however, he was appointed as the first post-independence minister of defense in the DEMOS government, and observers have noted that his approach during the Ten Day War of 1991 became so belligerent that the president, Milan Kučan, had to intervene and tame him.[21] This is how James Gow and Cathy Carmichael (2000: 162) describe the nature of Janša's remarkable transformation:

> Apart from going through a radical shift in his personal views in the space of four years – from favouring pacifist demilitarisation, through armed neutrality and territorial defence, to the creation of a Slovenian army and the standard Central and East European aspiration to join NATO, all this being reflected in policy positions – Janša was also prominent because of his alleged role in transferring arms to Bosnia and Herzegovina.

The logic of the struggle for national independence and spectre of violence raised by the Ten Day War – both of which played out in the context of an increasingly repressive and hostile federal state – helped eclipse the richness and pluralism of Slovenia's democratization movement and channel it in the imperative pursuit of national sovereignty. Opposing a Milošević-dominated Yugoslav state meant many different things in Slovenia at that time; democratic politics was associated with multiple civil society struggles, spaces, and agendas, which over time became increasingly tolerated by the communist elite in Ljubljana. As the question of national sovereignty gained momentum and the need for nation- and state-building came to the fore, however, powerful statist and nationalist forces were set in motion and pluralist civil society began to retreat. Some of the civil society actors from the earlier period adapted to the new environment by joining political parties and assuming positions of power; many others created NGOs, sought refuge in academia, or retreated from the public sphere.

In this changing context, one intellectual current from the civil-society scene became particularly important. By the mid-1980s a number of dissident intellectuals with nationalist leanings had gathered around the journal *Nova Revija*. In February 1987, the fifty-seventh issue of the journal published their "Contributions to a Slovene National Programme," which notably included a call for gaining independence from the SFRY. In his contribution to the volume, Dimitrij Rupel,

---

[21] Hanžek interview.

who later became minister of foreign affairs in the government that implemented Slovenia's secession, argued that Slovenian had become a second-class language in Yugoslavia, and articulated an ethnocultural understanding of a revived Slovenian nationhood (Rupel 1987). Some scholars have emphasized the importance of these ideas for under-standing subsequent developments in Slovenia, including questions about citizenship and the "erased," noting that "certain ideas of the intellectual circle of Nova Revija are firmly embedded in the Slovene political system and political culture."[22] Mastnak, however, insists that when the National Programme first appeared, its impact was much greater in the rest of Yugoslavia than in the democratic move-ment in Slovenia itself: "Only later, when, with Demos, people from the journal's circle came to power, did the 'Contributions' become an historic event" (Mastnak 1994: 106). In the intellectual milieu of dis-sent and alternatives that emerged in Slovenia in the 1980s, the ideas and figures associated with *Nova Revija* represented only one posi-tion among many. Some have even questioned the authenticity of the National Programme, suggesting that it was simply a response to the Memorandum of the Serbian Academy of Sciences and Arts issued in 1986, which provided a platform for the resurgence of Serbian nationalism.[23] Whether the articulation of Slovenian nationalism in the "Contributions" represented a mere reaction to events in Belgrade or not, its significance was initially limited by the fact that it represented the views of one of the many currents in Slovenia's democratic move-ment; it gained momentum only with the Trial of the Four, Ten Day War, and emergence of some of its protagonists as key political actors in the post-independence dispensation.

The peculiar articulation of ethnic citizenship in Slovenia is illumi-nated by this uneven and unpredictable trajectory of democratization. The ethos of the civil society movements, which associated democracy with pluralism and respect for minorities, coexisted with a conception

---

[22] Zorn, "The Ethno-nationalism of Slovenia's Secession," 5.

[23] When I interviewed Matjaž Hanžek about these events (himself an active participant in the democratization movement), he emphasized the importance of a meeting that took place in Ljubljana between the future authors of the "Contributions" and the Serbian intellectuals responsible for the Memorandum of the Serbian Academy of Arts and Sciences. See also Ramet (1999: 18–19).

of democracy that conflated "ethnos" and "demos." The fact that the new Slovenian state allowed the vast majority of non-Slovene residents to acquire citizenship, whereas the erasure targeted a smaller group and was implemented covertly, is perhaps indicative of the relative strength of the two positions and traction of these alternative understandings of the meaning of democracy prior to gaining independence. The question of membership in the political community was more closely intertwined with ethno-national belonging once the multiplicity and autonomy of the cultural sphere became eclipsed by concerns for sovereignty and statehood. Slovenian nationalism itself could be seen as oscillating between pluralist and exclusivist conceptions, the former dominating public discourse in the 1980s and the latter becoming more salient from the early 1990s. Its transformation and radicalization in the period of transition can be detected in debates over the proposed denaturalization of ethnic Slovenes in the mid-1990s and more recently over the "erased," which have often been accompanied by the unleashing of populist and xenophobic rhetoric in the parliament and media.[24] But the intensive public contestations and controversies elicited by the issue of the "erased" over the years could also be grasped in relation to the genealogy of the democratization process in Slovenia. On this reading, the earlier tension between the pluralism of the civil society movement and the monism of the national question, which goes back to the 1980s, becomes recast as a tension between pluralist and ethnic understandings of democracy in the new dispensation of independent Slovenia.

ECONOMIC LIBERALIZATION

The convergence of processes of democratization and nationalization, and in particular the harnessing of the former for the purposes of the

---

[24] Observers have noted, for instance, a tendency to conduct the public conversation over the future of the Slovenian nation in a discourse of fertility, which emphasizes perceived threats to the nation from rapidly procreating minorities, and even disappearing as a nation. Duška Knežević-Hočevar, interviewed by the author at the Socio-Medical Institute of the Slovenian Academy of Sciences and Arts in Ljubljana, 19 June 2007. See also Knežević-Hočevar (2004).

latter, could be seen as a somewhat unexpected and far from predetermined outcome of Slovenia's transition to independent statehood. Another set of forces that shaped Slovenia's transition, however, had a much more decisive direction and reflected far-reaching processes of economic liberalization and integration of postcommunist states in the global economy. These forces have operated in more diffuse ways at the level of economy and society, below the surface of Slovenia's citizenship policy as such; nevertheless, their impact on the regime of ethnic citizenship is recovered in scholarly accounts of prevalent attitudes and discourses, both before and after the erasure became publicly known and acknowledged. In particular, they have tended to reinforce negative attitudes toward migrants and refugees from the other republics of the former SFRY and strengthen the appeal of the populist rhetoric of the right, which in recent years has reframed for public consumption the intentions of the "erased" by suggesting that their struggle for recognition is driven by an exploitative economic agenda.

By the summer of 2007, when I arrived in Slovenia to start my field research, the vast majority of the "erased" that had remained in the country following the implementation of the measure had managed to regulate their status, either by obtaining Slovenian citizenship or securing permanent residence. At that stage, the thrust of their claims and legal struggle centered on the question of retroactivity. Restoring the status of all those affected by the erasure retroactively from February 1992, as required by the decisions of the Constitutional Court, was seen by some of the "erased" as amounting to an official recognition of the injustices perpetrated by the Slovenian state. In this sense, addressing the issue of retroactivity was interpreted as an official validation of their suffering and became invested with symbolic significance. The flip side of the question of retroactivity, however, involved the possibility for compensation claims for harms incurred as a result of the erasure, in particular for the infringement of social and economic rights related to loss of employment, housing, social security, pensions, children's allowances, and health care. The potential basis for such compensation claims by the "erased" can be glimpsed from the story of Irfan Biširević, a Bosniak who moved to Slovenia with his family when he was one year old. As a result of the erasure, he lost both his job and his health insurance, and over the years was unable to have vital surgeries on his legs and eyes. By the time I met him at the premises of the Association of the Erased, Biširević was permanently disabled as a result of complications that were preventable if he had been able to access health care: "On 13 October 2003," he told me, "I was finally granted Slovenian citizenship, but my health was already destroyed."[25]

Much of the continuing hostility against the "erased" among the Slovenian public may well be motivated by inflated fears that the state is asked to make enormous compensation payments to "Southerners" with the tax money of "hard-working Slovenes."[26] In such popular narratives, often encouraged by right-wing politicians, the workings of nationalist sentiment and economic grievance coalesce in ways that are impossible to disentangle in any meaningful way. The Third Report on Slovenia of the European Commission against Racism and Intolerance (ECRI), published in 2007, relates these developments:

> ECRI is deeply concerned at the tone prevailing in Slovenian pub-
> lic and political debate concerning the "erased" since its last report.
> It regrets that this part of the Slovenian population has in many
> occasions fallen hostage to merely political considerations, includ-
> ing the exploitation of their situation as vote gainer, and that the
> debate around the position of these persons has steadily moved
> away from human rights considerations. It is particularly regret-
> table that racism and xenophobia have been encouraged and fos-
> tered as part of this process, including through generalisations and
> misrepresentations concerning the loyalty of these persons to the
> Slovenian State or the economic burden that restoration of their
> rights would entail.[27]

For students of the SFRY, narratives invoking the spectre of economic predation by Southerners may be reminiscent of debates going back to the 1980s. Slovenia was the most economically developed repub-lic in the former Yugoslavia at the time and as such it made signifi-cant contributions to the federal fund established to provide economic assistance to the less-developed republics and regions of the SFRY.

---

[25] Irfan Biširević, interviewed by the author at the Association of the Erased in Ljubljana, 18 June 2007.

[26] Jasminka Dedić, interviewed by the author at the Peace Institute in Ljubljana, 20 June 2007.

[27] Council of Europe, ECRI, *Third Report on Slovenia adopted on 30 June 2006*, CRI(2007)5, 13 February 2007

Ljubljana repeatedly contested such payments to Southern regions such as Kosovo and Bosnia. As observers have noted, "Before 1989, the only aspect of Slovenia's economic problems that explicitly called its relationship with the rest of Yugoslavia into question was the much complained about aid to less developed regions" (Kraft et al. 1994: 201). Although the circumstances that may be engendering a sense of economic exploitation among the Slovenian population are very different in the case of the "erased," there are significant similarities in the framing and traction of these narratives expressing economic grievances against Southerners.[28]

But there are also important structural factors associated with Slovenia's economic transition after 1991, which favored popular acceptance of the model of ethnic citizenship and its normalization in Slovenian society. The process of economic liberalization and restructuring – from the self-management model of the former Yugoslavia to a full-blown market economy – was accompanied by a deflation of the welfare system and steep increase in unemployment, precipitated by privatization of some enterprises and closing down of others.[29] Zorn discusses the resulting "unemployment crisis" as one of the reasons why the plight of the "erased" remained invisible in the 1990s, becoming "somehow lost in the sea of other changes, which were also neither transparent nor foreseeable" (Zorn 2009: 293). Other scholars have underscored developments such as the mobilization of exclusionary identity politics as a response to the rise of economic inequalities and social cleavages in the transitional period. Peter Klinar (1994), for instance, notes that as the share of the poor was increasing, class conflict started to take the form of strikes and mass protest. He emphasizes the strategies deployed by Slovenia's political classes in seeking to deflect such grievances and conveys a trend toward a growing overlap of ethnicity and social class, rooted in the broader economic transformation:

> In the postsocialist period in Slovenia the old and the new political elite need unrealistic conflicts due to the critical conditions and

---

[28] It would be interesting to see whether similar complaints emerge once other post–Yugoslav states enter the EU, and whether Slovenia's contributions to the EU budget are viewed as part of the economic assistance for these states.

[29] Unemployment, for instance, increased from 1.6 percent in 1987 to 15.4 percent in 1993. See Kraft et al. (1994: 214).

because they want to take the pressure off themselves. The most
appropriate seem to be ethnic since they mitigate the concentration
of socio-economic conflicts.... Occurrences of ethnic stratification
which are accompanied by ethnic conflicts, distance, discrimination, ethnocentric nationalism and xenophobia are evident during
the transition period. Polarization of social stratification which has
been attained by parvenu rises and falls up to the poverty level is
reflected in the occurrences of ethnic stratification, in the harmony
of lower social statuses and statuses of underprivileged ethnic
immigrant minorities. (Klinar 1994: 102–103)

The Yugoslav wars of disintegration further contributed to these con-
vergent dynamics of social and ethnic stratification in post-independence Slovenia by stimulating the emergence of xenophobic public
discourse targeting refugees from the war-affected areas of the former
Yugoslavia, which has intensified and subsided at various junctures
since the early 1990s. Economic concerns emphasizing the strains
on the Slovenian state in dealing with the "refugee crisis" have provided one source of tension, but the public conversation has also been
shaped by allegations of prostitution and other criminal activities.[30]
Observers have noted the persistence of negative attitudes toward refugees in Slovenia and the tendency over the years to portray them "as
a threat to society, law and order, and later the nation-state" (Deželan
2011: 22).

The far-reaching consequences of economic transition and liberalization cannot explain the emergence of a regime of ethnic citizenship in Slovenia, but they help to illuminate a set of broader pressures
that have shaped its operation and traction in Slovenian society. These
pressures have contributed to the lengthening social distance between
ethnic Slovenes and non-Slovenes in ways that both encouraged and
justified various practices of discrimination and exclusion with respect
to ethnic minorities, refugees, and migrants. By the early 1990s, the
implications were already visible in public attitudes regarding employment opportunities, which in some sense mirrored the nationalizing
logics operating in the domain of citizenship: "There is a widespread

---

[30] Such allegations have been used to justify imposing severe restrictions on the freedom of movement of the first waves of refugees from Bosnia, including detainment in
former military barracks. See Gow and Carmichael (2000: 163).

opinion that immigrant workers should be dismissed from employment before ethnic Slovenes" (Klinar 1994: 108). The articulation of
ethnic citizenship serves to formalize certain exclusionary and discriminatory practices but such practices may be overlooked, normalized, or indeed openly defended much more easily in an environment
where larger socioeconomic forces are encouraging similar dynamics
from another direction.

EUROPEANIZATION

Europe has played an ambivalent role in the articulation of Slovenian
nationhood and the regime of ethnic citizenship during the period
of transition. This ambivalence stems in part from the emergence of
Europe as a compass for the reorientation of Slovenian national identity, first with respect to the former Yugoslavia and later in relation
to the EU. But it also reflects the tangible impact of European scrutiny, monitoring, and pressure in the initial determination of citizenship rules and the role of subsequent interventions of the European
Commission, Council of Europe, and ECtHR in resolving the issue of
the "erased." The uneven trajectory of the process of Europeanization,
by which I mean Slovenia's transition from the "Balkans" to "Europe"
and from Yugoslavia to the EU, captures yet another set of pressures
that have affected the implementation of the erasure and shaped its
handling by the state as an issue of domestic and international concern. This final narrative of transition is invoked here to illuminate the
complex interplay of nationalizing and Europeanizing dynamics in the
Slovenian context, seeking to understand how such interactions have
impacted the tension between ethnic citizenship and the rule of law.

In the drive to independence and the ensuing transformations of
Slovenian statehood and nationhood, Europe quickly emerged as a key
marker of differentiation from the rest of the former Yugoslavia and a
symbol of Slovenia's cultural and political revival. Enacting the symbolic shift from the Balkans to Europe became a central priority for
the transitional elites, as underscored in the recollections of Dmitrij
Rupel, Slovenia's minister of foreign affairs 1991–1993: "After persistent and tiresome lobbying with the European and other governments,

Slovenia managed to project the image of a peaceful and cooperative country, distinct from the rest of the former Yugoslav republics" (Rupel 1994: 193–194). One of the implications of such efforts to Europeanize Slovenia's international image and self-understanding involved the articulation of particular narratives of identity and difference, premised on a sharp contrast between a peaceful and progressive Slovenia and the backward, warring states and peoples of the Balkans. Indeed, the reimagining of national identity that accompanied Slovenia's symbolic "return to Europe" appeared to entrench a set of cultural stereotypes, which have remained salient in public discourse throughout the period of transition:

> Slovenia as well as its politicians envisioned Europe as a core political project, which was evident from their discourse since the adjective "European" always denoted something good, democratic, and worth aspiring to. The adjective "Balkan" (as Balkan-like) meanwhile had a diametrically opposite meaning and was usually employed to portray something rotten, undemocratic, and uncivilised. In that respect joining the EU meant a cultural leap from something supposedly "rotten" to something supposedly "heavenly" to which the nation belonged. (Deželan 2011: 32–33)

Ironically, the desired cultural leap ended up triggering its own set of anxieties about Slovenian culture and identity. Membership in the EU quickly emerged as a consensus project for the transitional state and Slovenia's political classes channeled their energies toward that objective, which was finally accomplished with the country's accession to the EU in 2004. As the prospect of accession became increasingly tangible and within reach, however, the significance of European integration started to shift and public discourse focused on the dangers of EU membership for Slovenian culture and identity. As one observer put it, "The debates on EU membership rarely if ever address the benefits and costs; the all-pervasive topic about the EU in political speeches, presidential addresses, and TV round tables is invariably the hypothetical danger of imminent 'loss of Slovenian identity' in the EU" (Šumi 2004: 78). These developments draw attention to the complex implications of Europeanization for Slovenian national identity, highlighting its capacity to engender and support divergent dynamics of nationalization in the cultural field.

The role of Europe is also crucial for understanding the specific circumstances of the implementation of the erasure and the more general tension between ethnic citizenship and the rule of law. European pressures around the time of declaring independence ensured Slovenia's formal compliance with international law in handling transitional citizenship arrangements. In the summer of 1991, Western governments supported a solution to the Yugoslav crisis within the framework of the federal state and discouraged calls for independence. The European position effectively meant that if Slovenia's bid for international recognition was to succeed, the state had to demonstrate respect for human rights norms and democratic principles. In these circumstances, even nationalist political groupings acknowledged the need to extend Slovenian citizenship to residents from other republics of the SFRY. Lev Kreft, an active participant in the parliamentary and public discussions at the time, recalls the understanding of the political classes: "We knew, and it was written in all documents and declarations, that if we wanted to get international recognition, we had to do everything concerning the independent state according to international law."[31] The combination of international scrutiny and domestic awareness of its implications suggests one way of grasping the contradictory features of the citizenship regime that emerged in Slovenia. The European pressures were reflected in the adopted citizenship legislation, premised on respect for human rights and the principle of non-discrimination, but also in the fact that the erasure was implemented by executive decree and shrouded in secrecy.

Since then, a range of European actors have become involved in the issue of the "erased" and in various ways have shaped the evolving legal articulation and politics of citizenship. As in the other successor states of the former Yugoslavia, the evolution of Slovenia's citizenship regime has been embedded in what Jo Shaw describes as "a 'constitutional mosaic' of overlapping and sometimes competing legal norms," derived from a range of national, European, and international sources (Shaw 2010: 1). The ambivalent role of Europe is underscored once again by considering the mechanisms through which Slovenia's compliance

---

[31] Lev Kreft, interviewed by the author at the Peace Institute in Ljubljana, 18 June 2007.

with international human rights norms has been encouraged by various institutions of the EU and Council of Europe. In theory, such compliance should have been ensured through the accession conditionality of the EU, which involved extensive monitoring and reporting on Slovenia's progress by the European Commission. In practice, although the pre-accession process opened up space for raising the issue of the erased and exerting some pressure, Slovenia was able to join the EU without changing its citizenship policy regarding the "erased" in a way that demonstrated respect for international norms and the decisions of the Constitutional Court (Shaw 2010: 22; Deželan 2011: 33).[32] In this sense, at least, the process of Europeanization appeared to expose the tension between ethnic citizenship and the rule of law in Slovenia, but failed to resolve it.

Once the erasure had attracted public attention, the Council of Europe also became involved in the issue and helped keep it on the agenda by drawing on the human rights instruments at its disposal.[33] Most significantly, in May 2007 the ECtHR admitted the *Kurić* case brought by eleven "erased" persons against Slovenia – three Serbian nationals, two Croatian nationals, two nationals of Bosnia and Herzegovina, and four stateless persons.[34] The act of the erasure itself was considered inadmissible because it was implemented before 1994, when Slovenia had acceded to the European Convention on Human Rights; however, the Court decided to consider the issues of retroactivity of permanent residence status and denial of effective remedy.

---

[32] When Slovenia became a member of the EU this window of opportunity was largely closed, although the European Parliament has become more involved, for example by referring the case of the "erased" to the Committee on Civil Liberties, Justice and Home Affairs in 2007.

[33] See, e.g., Council of Europe, Office of the Commissioner for Human Rights, *Report by Mr Alvaro Gil-Robles, Commissioner for Human Rights, on His Visit to Slovenia, 11– 14 May 2003*, CommDH(2003)11, 15 October 2003; Council of Europe, Advisory Committee on the Framework Convention for the Protection of National Minorities, *Second Opinion on Slovenia adopted on 26 May 2005*, ACFC/INF/OP/II(2005)005, Strasbourg, 1 December 2005; Council of Europe, Office of the Commissioner for Human Rights, *Follow-up Report on Slovenia (2003–2005): Assessment of the Progress Made in Implementing the Recommendations of the Council of Europe Commissioner for Human Rights*, CommDH(2006)8, Strasbourg, 29 March 2007.

[34] The application was lodged as *Makuc and Others v. Slovenia*, but the applicant Milan Makuc died in June 2008 and the case was renamed *Kurić and Others v. Slovenia*.

Seeking to preempt an unfavorable decision of the Court and deflect international attention at a time when Slovenia was preparing to take over the presidency of the EU, the Janša government drafted a constitutional bill that foreclosed the possibility of granting retroactive status and tried to overrule the relevant decisions of the Constitutional Court. The proposed legislation wasn't adopted but it managed to trigger a political storm, eliciting criticism from the parliamentary opposition and a coalition of human rights organizations, which included the Peace Institute, Legal Information Centre for Non-Governmental Organisations, Equal Rights Trust, and Open Society Justice Initiative.[35] These organizations became involved in advocacy on behalf of the "erased" and intervened as third parties in the proceedings before the ECtHR.

The judgement in *Kurić and Others v. Slovenia* was issued on 13 July 2010. The Court found a violation of Article 8, guaranteeing a right to respect for private and family life, and a violation of Article 13, a right to effective remedy. The Court ordered the Republic of Slovenia to "secure to the applicants the right to a private and/or family life and effective remedies in this respect." Significantly, the judges ruled that the question of compensation for damages resulting from the violations "is not ready for decision," and reserved that question for future consideration.[36] It remains to be seen what exactly will be the implications of the Court's decision to leave open the question of compensation. The involvement of the Court certainly reinforced the ongoing process of issuing supplementary orders granting retroactive status to the "erased," in line with the legislative changes and official apology adopted in 2010. This process may be closing one chapter in the decade-long controversy surrounding the "erased" but it may be opening another one, propelling the contentious issue of compensation claims on the agenda.

---

[35] See Public Statement concerning the confirmation by the Government of the Republic of Slovenia of the text of the Draft Constitutional Law amending the Constitutional Law for the Implementation of the Fundamental Constitutional Charter on the independence of the Republic of Slovenia, 30 October 2007, retrieved from http://www.mirovni-institut.si/Izjava/All/en/ (accessed 17 September 2011).

[36] *Kurić and Others v. Slovenia*, Application no. 26828/06, Council of Europe: European Court of Human Rights, 13 July 2010.

CONCLUSION

Slovenia offers a cautionary tale about the relationship between nationalism and the rule of law at the current juncture. At a time when struggles for democracy are back on the agenda and we may be witnessing the rise of another wave of political transformation and integration of states in the global economic order, both the temptations and dangers of the model of ethnic citizenship need to be fully appreciated as we think about the implications of democratization and economic liberalization. In many states with established liberal democratic institutions, harnessing citizenship as a symbolic resource in shaping collective identities may be equally tempting and dangerous: once the retreat of the rule of law is set in motion by succumbing to such temptations, reversing and redressing its consequences is a daunting task. In the context of global processes that encourage contradictory trends of denationalization and renationalization of citizenship, and continue to deflate the substantive aspects of citizenship while reinforcing its symbolic value for the nation-state, the story of the "erased" in Slovenia retains its relevance as a reminder of the lasting appeal of ethnic citizenship and the challenges it presents for the rule of law.

5 CONTESTING ATROCITY AND IDENTITY

The War Crimes Debate and Transitional Justice in Croatia

When I arrived in Zagreb on a sunny afternoon in the spring of 2008, there were two different conversations about *Oluja*[1] going on in the city. The cultural scene was preoccupied with the staging of Shakespeare's play *The Tempest*, one of the highlights of the season at the Croatian National Theatre. For those interested in contemporary politics and history, however, much more consuming were the ongoing trials of several high-ranking Croatian generals charged with war crimes and crimes against humanity. Three generals were prosecuted at the ICTY in The Hague, accused of expulsions and other abuses of Serb civilians during Operation Storm, the final chapter of the so-called Homeland War fought in Croatia between 1991 and 1995. At the same time, two generals were on trial in Zagreb for war crimes committed during Operation Medak Pocket in 1993, in the first case that was transferred from the ICTY to the Croatian judiciary.

The question of mass atrocity has been a recurrent subject of public controversy and contestation in Croatia since the 1980s. Over the past three decades, what is meant by "war crimes" in the public domain has changed several times, as both the underlying historical legacies of abuse and variety of projects and purposes pursued through their politicization have been shifting and evolving. In the late 1980s and early 1990s, public discussions of war crimes referred to the legacy of atrocities inherited from the Second World War. At that time, the public was preoccupied with the record of the wartime Independent State of Croatia (NDH) and the regime of the fascist Ustaša movement, as

---

[1] "Storm" or "tempest" in Croatian.

well as the issue of reprisals by the victorious Partisans and abuses perpetrated by the communist regime in the post-war period. During the
1990s, the focus of the public conversation shifted to the Homeland
War, and "war crimes" increasingly referred to atrocities committed by the JNA and local Serb forces in the course of the conflict.
Finally, in the new century the meaning of "war crimes" has shifted
once again, this time in response to allegations of ethnic cleansing and
abuse of Serb civilians by Croatia's armed and police forces during the
Homeland War.

I examine these three phases of the war crimes debate in Croatia as
an opportunity to illuminate the shifting relationship between law and
nationalism that each of them entails. My starting point is the framework developed in Chapter 2: contrasting the idea of deliberative transitional justice – which conceives of the judicial process as a vehicle for
public debate over questions of national identity and state legitimacy –
with the notion of transition without justice – which often involves
contestation over the "facts" of mass atrocities and encourages further
nationalist mobilization and radicalization. The Croatian case is useful as an illustration of these two concepts but it also suggests how
the law could be harnessed in yet another way: as an instrument for
pursuing wartime policies and agendas by judicial means, when the
courts themselves create a legacy of abuse that becomes a focal point
for subsequent claims for justice and redress. My discussion seeks to
recover the significance of the evolving war crimes debate since the
1980s as an arena of struggle over Croatian nationalism, highlighting
in particular how law has interacted with politics and public discourse
and raised important questions about identity and legitimacy in the
public domain.

ATROCITY AND IDENTITY: THE SPECTRE OF THE SECOND WORLD WAR

The founding of the Socialist Federal Republic of Yugoslavia (SFRY)
is a classic example of a transition without justice.[2] The legacy of

---

[2] See Chapter 2, § "Transition without Justice?"

egregious human rights violations inflicted during the Second World War was never addressed with a credible judicial process or fact-finding inquiry by the Yugoslav state; for several decades, the public discussion around these issues tended to reproduce the officially sanctioned historical account of the war. Tito's rule added further layers of abuse after the end of the war, in a period of reprisals and purges. When the taboo on discussing these issues more freely in the public domain started to crumble, the debate over mass atrocity quickly spiraled out of control. Suppressed histories of injustice and private memories of abuse were taken up in public discourse, fueling bitter contestation over facts and figures. The ensuing "calculus of death" involved recounting the victims on different sides of the war; in the public conversation, genuine grievances and concerns became intertwined with exaggeration and denial, blurring the distinction between facts and fabrications. In this environment, the question of mass atrocity emerged as a cause célèbre for nationalists in the republics, and the legitimacy of the Yugoslav state was increasingly attacked from ethnic and national positions.

In the official history of the SFRY, the complex fault lines and conflicts during the Second World War became simplified and recast in class terms. The emphasis on antifascist resistance and victory in such historical narratives allowed the communist regime to erase the legacy of Partisan abuses and dismiss the nationalists on all sides as class enemies. Tito's position highlighted their affinities and implicitly balanced their guilt: "If Croats had Ustashas, Serbs had Chetniks. What's the difference between them?"[3] The experience of wartime suffering in Yugoslavia had been so traumatic that it appeared to provide legitimacy to the officially promoted narrative of Yugoslav "brotherhood and unity." When the elements of this construct started to unravel in the early 1980s, the first target of public scrutiny was the communist regime itself.

The politicization of mass atrocity in the SFRY initially appeared as a critique of state repression, challenging the legitimacy of the totalitarian system, rather than the federal framework of the state. After Tito's death in 1980, various journalistic and artistic accounts started to uncover some of the large-scale abuses implicating his regime. Although these

[3] Quoted in Djokić (2002: 132).

accounts were subversive, they were mostly addressed to the Yugoslav public as a whole, rather than national audiences at the level of the republics. The fratricidal massacre at Goli Otok became one of the first taboo subjects taken up in the public domain. The camp at Goli Otok was set up by Tito after his split with Stalin in 1948, in an attempt to deal with those within the communist ranks who had sided with Moscow. In the early 1980s, a series of articles were published by a popular weekly magazine, the Belgrade *NIN*, revealing the scale of abuses perpetrated at the camp: "While the existence of this camp had never been denied, the nature of the cruelties practiced there, and the sheer numbers of people sent there on the basis of little or no evidence, came as a shock to the Yugoslav public" (Hayden 1994: 169). The theme of state repression after the breakup with Stalin was also taken up in artistic narratives, most notably in Emir Kusturica's acclaimed film *When Father Was Away on Business*, which won the Palm d'Or at Cannes in 1985.

The evolution of the legitimacy dilemma in the late 1980s and early 1990s, however, reflected a growing nationalization of the question of mass atrocity in the former Yugoslavia. The nationalist turn in the public discussion was partly precipitated by resurgent interest in war crimes committed during the Second World War, especially massacres attributed to the Croatian Ustaša and Serbian Četnik forces and Tito's Partisans.[4] The war crimes debate was increasingly retreating from the federal level to the individual republics and their bounded audiences, where the theme of state repression became supplanted by distinctly national accounts of past abuse and injustice. These dynamics of nationalization were particularly important in Croatia and Serbia. In both republics, that period was marked by the rise of discourses of national reconciliation – aimed at reconciling Partisans with Ustašas in Croatia and Partisans with Četniks in Serbia – and the growing traction of historical narratives that were reinterpreting legacies of past abuse in polarizing ethno-national terms. By the late 1980s and early 1990s, the war crimes debate had become so explosive that observers described the situation in Yugoslavia as a "verbal civil war" and a "Second World War II" (Hayden 1994: 181; Djokić 2002: 131).

---

[4] For an intriguing account of the complicated fault lines of the Second World War in Yugoslavia, see Djilas (1991).

In Croatia, the war crimes debate was increasingly dominated by the figure of Franjo Tuđman. A former Partisan and general of the JNA, Tuđman had left the military in the 1960s and worked as a full-time historian in Zagreb. His writings on military strategy in the Second World War became influential and accepted by the communist regime. But his openly nationalistic views and growing preoccupation with the victims of the Jasenovac camp, run by the wartime Ustaša regime, provoked the authorities and led to his expulsion from the Communist Party and a couple of detours to prison. In the official history of the SFRY, Jasenovac served as a symbol of antifascist struggle and martyrdom, commemorating the suffering of 700,000 victims, most of them Serbs. Tuđman's accounting, however, rejected the official estimate as a gross exaggeration. His position entailed a substantial revision of the history of Jasenovac, reducing the overall number of victims to just tens of thousands, and even suggesting that similar numbers of Serbs and Croats had found their death in the camp. Robin Okey (1999: 272–273) attributes Tuđman's motivations to long-standing suspicions, early signs of an imminent nationalist turn in Yugoslavia's historiography and politics:

> Why did Tudjman become so concerned about the exaggeration of what he dubbed the "Jasenovac myth"? It exemplified what he took from Belgrade historiography to be the subtext of the Serbs' view of the Croats, namely that they were a fascistoid and genocidal people who had brought Yugoslavia down in April 1941, and even whose Communists could not be trusted. He believed it to be a convenient device in the Communist authorities' strategy for keeping Croats on the leash and a main plank of Serb nationalism's bid for power after Tito's death. There was some truth in both surmises.

Any attempt to challenge the "Jasenovac myth" along those lines in Croatia was bound to stir anti-Serb sentiments in the public domain and water down the criminal record of the NDH. Shortly after Tuđman led the Croatian Democratic Union (HDZ) to victory in the first multiparty elections in Croatia and became president, the war crimes debate was fueled once again. The new government in Zagreb initiated a number of exhumations and church ceremonies aimed at exposing massacres committed by Partisan forces. In particular, public attention was focused on the reprisals against Ustašas and other noncommunists that had been handed over by the British forces at Bleiburg. Hayden (1994: 8) notes that the "recounting" of the Jasenovac victims and commemoration of Croatia's victims of communism were geared to relativize the criminal legacy of the Ustaša regime and weaken the largest opposition party, the League of Communists of Croatia. But the ensuing public discussion of Jasenovac and Bleiburg also activated two central themes in Croatian nationalism in the late 1980s and early 1990s: mobilization along ethno-national lines and demands for democratic politics. The question of mass atrocity blurred the lines between the two issues and offered a platform for pursuing independent statehood.

A main source of concern for Tuđman was the issue of Croatia's deeply rooted national divisions. He envisioned a consolidation of the Croatian nation by way of reconciling the victors and losers from the Second World War. Dejan Djokić (2002: 136) provides an intriguing account of the reconciliation debate in Croatia after HDZ's electoral success, emphasizing how the legitimation of Tuđman's power increasingly relied on a nationalist discourse that sought to downplay and collapse long-standing ideological differences in the name of national unity:

> Tudjman's argument was that a vast majority of Croats, regardless of whether they fought for the Partisans or for NDH, were neither indoctrinated Communists nor Fascist, but that they really fought for Croatia and Croatdom. Therefore, the continued division of "Partisan" and "Ustaša" Croats was meaningless, because they were, above all, members of one, Croatian, nation, and subjects of one, Croatian, leader. As the war was finished a long time ago, there was no longer any reason why the two sides should not reconcile."

The reconciliation initiative underscores the significance of Tuđman's efforts to minimize the atrocities of the NDH and "balance" them with Partisan crimes. The idea of reconciliation was unlikely to take root in Croatian society as long as the nation's internal fractures and divisions rested on polarizing histories of wartime massacres. Seen in this light, the attempt to revise the official history of the Second World War in Yugoslavia reflected a struggle to reframe and redefine Croatian nationalism.

The pursuit of national unity by bridging the long-standing divide between Partisans and Fascists, however, created an obvious problem for Croatia's minorities. In particular, the reconciliation rhetoric was bound to undermine the position of the large Serb minority, which accounted for 14 percent of the population of the republic. Despite regional differences, the loyalties of most Croatian Serbs were overwhelmingly Partisan and Yugoslav at a time when both of these identities and the political projects associated with them were coming under attack. The success of Tuđman's reconciliation initiative as an instrument of nation-building appeared to depend on alienating and excluding the Serbs. As Djokić (2002: 137) put it, "The minimization of the number of non-Croats (mainly Serbs) who perished in Jasenovac, by Tudjman and his authorities, paved the way for the Croat leader becoming a symbol of reconciliation between Ustašas and Croat Partisans." Here the question of mass atrocity illuminates an emerging tension at the heart of Croatian nationalism and the precarious position of the Serb minority in the new dispensation.

In sum, for several decades the legacy of brutality from the Second World War and its aftermath could be either neglected or submerged in the official historical narratives of the SFRY, but after Tito's death they came back with a vengeance. Whereas in the early 1980s the question of mass atrocity was raised primarily as a critique of state repression and the communist regime, by the end of the decade the war crimes debate was retreating to the republican level, and the legitimacy dilemma of the Yugoslav state was reframed in ethno-national terms. Yugoslavia's postwar transition without justice ensured that once the question of mass atrocity entered the public domain, it sparked heated contestation over facts and figures: a sort of discursive zero-sum game in which one set of memories and histories of injustice were validated at the expense of another, which were denied or relativized. In the Croatian context, the war crimes debate increasingly emerged as an arena of struggle over nationalism. Reframing and redefining Croatian nationalism involved pursuing initiatives for national unity and reconciliation, but the revisionist histories and representations of the past on which these nation-building projects relied had little space for the wartime memories and experiences of Croatia's Serbs. Indeed, by the late 1980s and early 1990s, a reinvented Croatian nationalism appeared to become increasingly dependent on suppressing such minority narratives and identities, creating tensions that were further entrenched during the Homeland War.

LAW AND WAR IN THE 1990S

The Homeland War of 1991–1995 raised the question of mass atrocity with a new urgency in Croatia. The formal inception of the war was marked by the offensive of the JNA in the summer of 1991, shortly after Croatia's declaration of independence and the establishment of Serb control over the separatist region of Krajina (the so-called Republika Srpska Krajina). The war was fought by JNA and Serb forces on the one side, and Croatian police and military units on the other, but it also interacted in complex ways with the ongoing conflict in Bosnia and Herzegovina and often exhibited similar patterns of violence, including shelling of urban areas and ethnic cleansing.[5] The town of Vukovar is often invoked to illustrate the brutality of the conflict and the deep scars left in its aftermath. Vukovar was the scene of relentless shelling by JNA forces in 1991, and its fall was accompanied by a major massacre at Ovčara. The town was reintegrated in Croatia after the end of the war, but local Serbs and Croats have remained deeply divided in their memories of the wartime years.

Starting during the conflict and extending into the post-conflict period, the judicial response and the public discussion of war crimes were preoccupied almost exclusively with the responsibility of JNA and Serb forces. From the formal end of the Homeland War in 1995 until the death of Tuđman in 1999, law and public discourse continued to be dominated by nationalist narratives in which questions of sovereignty and mass atrocity were closely intertwined, as Croatia's struggle against aggression provided the framework for interpreting the war crimes issue. Indeed, the memory of wartime suffering emerged as one of the foundations of Croatian national identity and independent statehood, symbolized by the struggle for Vukovar:

> In the new constellation, the battle for Vukovar plays the role of the foundation myth of the Croatian state, and the town of Vukovar, more than any other place in Croatia, became the embodiment of a pure Croatian identity. As a symbol of the sacrifice of the Croatian people and of the birth of the modern Croatian state, Vukovar

---

[5] A detailed analysis of ethnic cleansing in the Yugoslav wars of disintegration is available in Mann (2005: 382–427).

became an imagined place, disengaged from time and space and created at a great distance from its organic surroundings (Kardov 2007: 81–82).

Although the hostilities ended in 1995, for the rest of the decade the public conversation about war crimes and the legal response of the state remained marked by important continuities, calling into question the nature of Croatia's "transition" in that period. On the one hand, representations and interpretations of the Homeland War were shaped by the state and aligned with its nation-building policies and priorities, suppressing dissident histories and minority accounts that may have revealed the complex legacies of abuse inherited from the conflict. On the other hand, Croatian law became increasingly harnessed to validate the official history and national mythology promoted by the state, and often appeared to advance wartime goals by judicial means.

The one-sided public conversation about war crimes in Tuđman's Croatia could be understood as reflecting a broader retreat of the public sphere, precipitated by the war itself but also by the "patriotic" rhetoric and state control of the media that persisted in its aftermath. A number of scholars have highlighted the interplay of nationalism and state repression in that context. Marius Søberg (2007: 37) notes that in the 1990s, the ruling HDZ prioritized the issues of statehood and independence, often at the expense of other transitional goals such as democratization; in that environment, dissidents and opponents of the regime could be labelled "traitors" in the public domain and marginalized with accusations of siding with the enemy. Other scholars direct attention to the variety of methods employed by the HDZ to maintain control of the press and broadcasting, including the role of media ownership and editorial structures, adoption of restrictive legislation, and overt censorship. Stjepan Malović and Gary Selnow (2001: 4–10), for example, emphasize the heavy involvement of the ruling party in the daily *Večernji List* and the HRTV network – the two major sources of news for the Croatian public at that time. Zrinjka Peruško (2007: 233) relates the significance of incorporating the media in the nation- and state-building projects of the state and silencing of critical independent voices:

> Most of the 1990s passed in the division of the media into two categories: "state-building" (*državotvorni*) and independent. Nation-building as state-building was one of the prominent values in Croatian

political discourse in the early 1990s and was seen to be at least as important as freedom in the political and economic spheres. This value assumed such importance (especially in the dominant party rhetoric) that a new word was coined to portray it. "State-building" (državotvorstvo – the exact translation would be state-forming) has become an adjective freely used in such constructions as "state-building journalism," "state-building political parties," etc. The concept has come to signify those "good" Croats who place national interests above all else (for example, above liberalism, or human rights, or freedom of speech). In spite of frequently voiced arguments by the opposition that state-building is necessarily brought about by all activities in an independent nation-state, the "state-building" neologism has stuck as an inclusion/exclusion device.

The Croatian public was rarely confronted with minority accounts and memories of the Homeland War. Only a small number of independent media such as the weekly *Feral Tribune*, and civil society groups such as the Helsinki Committee for Human Rights appeared to be interested in reporting the abuses of Croatia's police and armed forces against Serb civilians. Žarko Puhovski, one of the dissident intellectuals who raised such issues in the public domain during the 1990s, describes the efforts of a handful of individuals to mobilize public opinion and put pressure on the government as "attempts to smuggle certain values from the margins to the mainstream."[6] Such efforts were often frustrated and met with accusations of betrayal. On a few occasions, the weight of the evidence revealed to the public and shocking nature of the crimes involved managed to elicit a response. A rare example is the reporting of *Feral Tribune* on cases of torture and murder of Serb civilians in Pakračka Poljana. A series of articles about these crimes were published in the early and mid-1990s, but had little effect apart from provoking pressures to close down the publication. The authorities took some measures to address the allegations only in 1997, when *Feral Tribune* published the confessions of a member of the implicated special police unit, which shocked the Croatian public.[7]

---

[6] Žarko Puhovski, interviewed by the author at the Faculty of Philosophy, University of Zagreb, 6 May 2008.

[7] See a translation of the interview with Miro Bajramović published in *Feral Tribune*, 1 September 1997, and documents related to the reactions it elicited, retrieved from http://www.ex-yupress.com/feral/feral45.html (accessed 15 January 2012).

Croatian law interacted with public discourse by reinforcing the dominant narratives and representations of the Homeland War, but its role went well beyond simply neglecting the crimes that had been committed on the Croatian side of the conflict. Already at the start of the hostilities, the courts initiated a process of large-scale prosecution of members of the JNA and local Serb forces for war crimes. The majority of these proceedings were conducted in areas heavily affected by the conflict and with little concern for due process. In particular, they often involved summary prosecution of large groups of suspects on the basis of questionable evidence and in the absence of the accused (in absentia); many cases were based on insufficiently established facts and failed to apply the facts to the law; overcharging of low-level offenders for minor crimes was common, and from the mid-1990s this practice also involved charging with genocide.[8]

The work of the Croatian judiciary after the end of the war continued to exhibit ethnic bias in the administration of justice and reinforce narratives of collective guilt and victimhood. Were Croatian courts pursuing wartime goals by other means in the aftermath of the conflict? That impression was taking root among the Serb minority targeted by the problematic war crimes proceedings. Milorad Pupovac, one of the current political leaders of Croatian Serbs, relates their perceptions of the trials this way:

> Most people who live in Croatia and are ethnic Serbs, perceive [war crimes trials] as a tool to prevent people to return, or to create a particular "truth" about the war in Croatia and in Yugoslavia. And, of course, as an additional instrument of a certain type of politics: to prolong the war mentality and war psychology, the "liberation" policy that certain political parties have placed at the heart of their agenda. Also, they see it as a practical instrument of obtaining the property of certain people and preventing them from exercising their rights. And, finally, as a kind of mentality of "our

---

[8] These developments have been documented in great detail by the OSCE in a series of reports on war crimes trials in Croatia, retrieved from http://www.osce.org/zagreb/66067 (accessed 15 January 2012). See also Humanitarian Law Center (Belgrade), Documenta (Zagreb), and Research and Documentation Center (Sarajevo), *Transitional Justice in Post-Yugoslav Countries: Report for 2006*, 30 January 2008, retrieved from http://www.hlc-rdc.org/?p=13184 (accessed 15 January 2012).

five minutes": after the Second World War you accused us of committing war crimes, now it is our turn.[9]

Such interpretations raise a number of unsettling questions about the
role of Croatian law in the post-war period. Rather than facilitating
the transition from war to peace and enabling political transformation,
here the judiciary emerges as an arena that encourages persistent conflict and advances a variety of political and personal interests in keeping alive the idea, if not the enterprise, of war. Although war crimes
trials are usually seen as a step toward reconstructing the rule of law in
the aftermath of mass violence and abuse, the Croatian case suggests
how such judicial processes can also be harnessed in ways that further
reinforce the breakdown of the rule of law. The campaign for prosecuting large numbers of Serbs in absentia on charges of war crimes and
genocide recasts the domestic legal system as an instrument for continuation of the conflict by other means, raising the spectre of vengeance
and ethnic cleansing in the post-war order. Whether the proceedings
involved settling scores and promoting interests at the local level, or
connected to grievances and narratives from the Homeland War, they
were bound to be seen as singling out the Serbs and meting out an
arbitrary collective punishment. Jovan Mirić, one of the few Serb intellectuals in Croatia who has written about the war crimes trials, puts the
issue starkly: "Proceedings before Croatian courts and convictions of
Serbs [for war crimes] often resemble revenge, rather than justly and
legally determined punishment" (2002: 182). On this account, then, in
the post-war order Croatian law became deployed not in the pursuit of
justice but vengeance.

The other argument, which interprets the war crimes proceedings against Croatian Serbs as an attempt to pursue ethnic cleansing
by other means, draws attention to the implications of the trials for
the process of refugee return and reintegration. Croatia established a
framework for normalizing interethnic relations after the war on the
basis of the Erdut Agreement for peaceful reintegration of formerly–
Serb-controlled areas and the adoption of legislation granting a general amnesty for offenses committed between 1990 and 1996, with

---

[9] Milorad Pupovac, interviewed by the author at the Faculty of Philosophy, University
of Zagreb, 6 May 2008.

the exception of war crimes.[10] One of the tenets of the post-war order involved the return and reintegration of Serb refugees, an issue of particular importance given the scale of the Serb exodus in the final stage of the war. By the time these commitments were made, it was already clear that the large number of proceedings and convictions for war crimes in absentia and the arbitrary manner in which many of them were conducted served to obstruct the return of Serb refugees. However, in 1995–1996 a number of war crimes and genocide prosecutions were initiated against the entire Serb population of certain villages, suggesting an attempt to prevent them from returning to their homes.[11] The prosecution offensive peaked in 1996 with 400 indictments and more than 100 convictions, and to many Croatian Serbs it appeared as a continuation of the war by other means.[12] These developments are at the heart of enduring suspicions that Croatia's war crimes trials were used as an instrument of ethnic cleansing.

TRANSITIONAL JUSTICE AFTER TUĐMAN

Croatia entered the twenty-first century with two legacies of abuse inherited from the previous decade: one from the war itself; and the other from the judicial response to war crimes. Since Tuđman's death in 1999 and the arrival shortly thereafter of a moderate government committed to a European future for the country, the war crimes debate has come to the fore once again, and the law's interactions with politics and public discourse have evolved in a new direction. At the heart of these changes has been the challenge to confront the "dark side" of the

[10] See Basic Agreement on the Region of Eastern Slavonia, Baranja, and Western Sirmium, signed by the Croatian government in Zagreb and the local Serbs at Erdut, 12 November 1995; Law on General Amnesty, *Narodne Novine* 80/96, 27 September 1996.

[11] Ivo Josipović, interviewed by the author at the Faculty of Law, University of Zagreb, 7 May 2008.

[12] Statistics for war crimes prosecutions between 1991 and 2010 has been compiled by the State Prosecutor's Office. See Državno Odvjetništvo Republike Hrvatske, *Izvješće o radu državnih odvjetništava u 2010 godini* [State Prosecutor's Office of the Republic of Croatia, *Report on the Work of the State Prosecutor's Office in 2010*], A-468/10, Zagreb, August 2011, retrieved from http://www.dorh.hr/IzvjesceORadu (accessed 15 January 2012). For a detailed account of Operation Storm, see *Prosecutor v. Ante Gotovina, Ivan Čermak, Mladen Markač*, Case No. IT-06–90-T, Trial Judgment, 15 April 2011.

Homeland War, in particular the responsibility of Croatia's police and armed forces for ethnic cleansing and war crimes against Serb civilians. Transitional justice in the post-Tuđman era has shifted the focus of public deliberation about war crimes, raising broader questions about national identity and state legitimacy in the aftermath of mass atrocity and casting a shadow over key political and military figures celebrated as founders and state-builders of independent Croatia.

Despite the fact that several transitional justice processes have been initiated in the past decade and some progress has been made, the process of judicial reckoning with the legacy of the Homeland War has been agonizing, and its overall direction remains uncertain. Important developments in the field of transitional justice include an effort to address the problematic proceedings from the 1990s and stem the tide of war crimes trials of Serbs in absentia; initiation of a small number of war crimes proceedings against members of the Croatian police and armed forces; and the state's reluctant but increasingly forthcoming cooperation with the ICTY in The Hague. I approach these developments through the lens of *deliberative transitional justice*, which conceives of trials as a vehicle for public deliberation that may help expose and manage the "dark side" of nationalism in the aftermath of mass violence and atrocity. The Croatian case affords an opportunity to examine in greater detail the role of judicial processes in encouraging a public conversation that interrogates prevalent nationalist narratives and representations of the past. It also raises intriguing questions about such processes as a form of reckoning that involves public contestation over issues of national identity and state legitimacy, illuminating both their promise and limits.

The opening up of Croatian politics in the wake of Tuđman's rule has reflected a series of political shifts and the emergence of membership in the EU as a key foreign-policy priority in the new dispensation. The victory of the Social Democratic Party and the moderate Stipe Mesić in the 2000 parliamentary and presidential elections signaled the end of an era in which centrist and leftist political forces had been marginalized. The government of Ivica Račan, while remaining careful not to agitate nationalist circles and sensibilities, offered a new direction for the state, reflecting its more democratic and pro-European orientation. This overall orientation has remained in place since HDZ's return to power in 2003, under the governments of Ivo Sanader and Jadranka Kosor. Sanader, in particular, has played an intriguing role in Croatia's post-Tuđman transition. Once in power, his leadership was marked by much more moderate political rhetoric than expected, whereas his impeccable nationalist credentials allowed him to gradually sideline radicals in the ranks of the HDZ. Observers have noted Sanader's tendency to play the nationalist card at the grassroots even as he was promoting a pro-European agenda for the state (Søberg 2007: 51–52). Nevertheless, his firm commitment to Croatia's European future meant that much of the rhetoric and policies of his government were aligned with that overall objective.

In the new dispensation, domestic political pressures on the judiciary started to subside, whereas international scrutiny and supervision increased dramatically, most notably by the EU in the context of the accession process, but also by other international actors such as the OSCE and ICTY. In the domain of war crimes prosecutions, these developments seemed to encourage a process of disaggregation of the Croatian judiciary: although the upper tiers were becoming more responsive to international requirements and standards, many lower courts continued to dispense "local justice" reminiscent of the 1990s. The State Prosecutor's Office, Supreme Court, and Ministry of Justice have made an effort to mitigate some of the outstanding problems in the war crimes proceedings against Serbs, and four special war crimes chambers have been established in the county courts of Osijek, Rijeka, Split, and Zagreb endowed with extraterritorial jurisdiction. In 2008, for example, the State Prosecutor's Office issued instructions intended to address the issue of ethnic bias in the administration of justice and initiated a process of reviewing the problematic war crimes caseload, in particular in absentia proceedings and cases lacking proper evidence.[13] A few war crimes cases that raise concerns about impartiality and intimidation of witnesses have been transferred to the four special war crimes chambers. The Supreme Court

---

[13] See Amnesty International, Croatia: *Briefing to the European Commission and Member States of the European Union (EU) on the Progress Made by the Republic of Croatia in Prosecution of War Crimes*, EUR 64/002/2010, 23 April 2010, retrieved from http://www.amnesty.org/en/library/asset/EUR64/002/2010/en/9e5234fb-9f6c-47bc-b279-bf56f599ac89/eur640022010en.pdf (accessed 15 January 2012).

has reversed a number of decisions of lower courts and returned cases for retrial, and more requests have been filed for reviewing in absentia proceedings.[14]

The task of addressing the problems with the war crimes case-load has proved to be daunting for the judiciary, but the political will required for its completion has also been difficult to muster. By 2008, Croatia was seeking more than 1,000 war crimes suspects, many of them convicted in absentia, and had issued more than 600 international arrest warrants. According to official statistics, as of May 2011, the total number of individuals prosecuted for war crimes was 3,422, of which 2,990 were prosecuted in absentia. Moreover, so far less than 3 percent of all war crimes proceedings have involved cases against members of Croatia's police and armed forces. The majority of war crimes trials have continued to be conducted by lower courts, where ethnic bias in the administration of justice persists. The problem of bias has been evident in prosecuting Serbs for a wide spectrum of crimes but charging Croats only with serious offenses such as murder, and in significant discrepancies in the sentencing practices of the courts. Participation of the accused in the Homeland War as a member of the Croatian army or police has been routinely invoked as a mitigating circumstance; this practice was upheld by the Supreme Court in the high-profile case of Mirko Norac and Rahim Ademi, where the court highlighted Norac's contribution to the legitimate goal of defending his country against aggression. Some courts have even been tempted to dispense historical justice, as illustrated by the judgment in the *Karan* case. The county court in Gospić held the defendant responsible not only for the offenses listed in the indictment but also for 500 years of Serbian crimes against Croatia, and criticized the Croatian government for assisting Serb returnees.[15]

---

[14] See OSCE war crimes trials reports, *supra* note 8.

[15] Sources for this passage include OSCE, *Report of the Head of OSCE Office in Zagreb Ambassador Jorge Fuentes to the OSCE Permanent Council*, Zagreb, 6 March 2008, retrieved from http://www.osce.org/zagreb/66067 (accessed 15 January 2012); Državno Odvjetništvo Republike Hrvatske, *Izvješće o radu državnih odvjetništava u 2010 godini*; Amnesty International, *Croatia: Briefing to the European Commission on the Progress Made by the Republic of Croatia in Prosecution of War Crimes*, EUR

The vast majority of these war crimes cases and the efforts of the authorities to address the problem of ethnic bias in the administration of justice have attracted little attention in the public domain. Much more controversial has been the prosecution of a handful of high-ranking members of the Croatian army and police by the ICTY and domestic courts. These trials have touched a nerve with the Croatian public and political class on a number of occasions in the past decade, prompting yet another shift in the war crimes debate by focusing attention on the responsibility of Croatian forces for atrocities and ethnic cleansing during the Homeland War. The explosive potential of the proceedings can be glimpsed from the fact that over the years these judicial processes have implicated some of the country's most revered military and political figures, including Janko Bobetko, Ante Gotovina, Mirko Norac, and even the deceased Tuđman himself, effectively depicting national heroes and founding fathers of independent Croatia as war criminals. These trials often strike at the heart of the accepted narratives of Croatian nationalism, invoking highly subversive representations of the country's recent past. In the ensuing public debates and contestations, questions about national identity and state legitimacy have loomed large, sometimes completely supplanting questions about the specific charges in the indictments. Indeed, in the public discussions sparked by the trials, prosecuting the country's defenders has often been recast as an attack on the legitimacy of the Homeland War and the Croatian state itself (Peskin and Boduszynski 2003: 1117–1118).

The position of the Croatian judiciary in the 1990s was that war crimes could not be committed in a defensive war and defenders could not be war criminals, effectively granting immunity from prosecution to members of the Croatian army and police for such offenses (Josipović 2005: 232). The arrival of the Račan government marked a shift in that position, suggesting that the courts were now free to prosecute all war crimes. The opportunity was seized in 2001 by the

64/008/2011, 20 May 2011, retrieved from http://www.amnesty.org/en/library/asset/EUR64/008/2011/en/6a4e7b45–2085–463b-8b3d-38debfe53b11/eur640082011en.pdf (accessed 15 January 2012); OSCE, Mission to Croatia, *Supplementary Report:War Crimes Proceedings in Croatia and Findings from Trial Monitoring*, Zagreb, 22 June 2004, retrieved from http://www.osce.org/zagreb/66067 (accessed 15 January 2012).

county court in Rijeka, which indicted Mirko Norac, a respected general and veteran of the Homeland War, and several other officers on charges of war crimes against Serb civilians committed in the town of Gospić in 1991. Norac's name was already mired in controversy: one of the witnesses in the investigation had been murdered after making statements in the media, and Norac and other senior generals had issued an open letter accusing the government of falsifying the record of the Homeland War and undermining its legitimacy by putting Croatia's defenders on trial. In response, President Mesić had swiftly moved to retire the generals, sending a clear message that there could be no negotiation with the army: "It was not easy to send the generals into retirement when everybody was afraid of a coup. But nothing happened."[16]

When the arrest warrant for Norac was issued, however, the scale of the ensuing public contestation took the government by surprise. Associations of war veterans and other nationalist circles were spearheading the campaign to stop the proceedings, setting up road blocks and holding demonstrations across the country, with some 100,000 people turning up for their biggest rally in Split. The leadership of the HDZ, now in opposition, played a prominent role in the protests, including future Prime Minister Ivo Sanader. For these groupings, the trial of Norac represented an assault on the history and memory of the Homeland War that undermined the foundations of the Croatian state. Their solidarity with the accused general and determination to protect the sanctity of the war was expressed in slogans such as, "We Are all Mirko Norac" and "Hands off Our Holy War." There were other groups in civil society, however, which insisted that the government should uphold the independence of the judiciary and ensure the case could proceed. At a counterdemonstration in Zagreb, a crowd of 10,000 rallied behind the slogan, "Our Voice for the Rule of Law."[17] The Račan government ended up reinforcing the message from Zagreb, framing the issue as a contest over democracy and the rule of law:

---

[16] Stipe Mesić quoted in European Stability Initiative, "Croatia's European Rebirth: A Story of Leadership," ESI Newsletter 1/2012, 25 January 2012, retrieved from http://www.esiweb.org/index.php?lang=en&id=67&newsletter_ID=56 (accessed 10 February 2012). See also Subotić (2009: 112).

[17] Vesna Teršelić, interviewed by the author at Documenta in Zagreb, 5 May 2008.

On 9 February, 2 days after the warrant was issued, Račan told parliament that the government would not give in to pressure from those forces that wanted to undermine the rule of law. To Račan, the crisis was a defining moment and "a test for a democratic and law-abiding Croatia." The opposition to the Rijeka court's investigation of Norac, Račan said, constituted an attack on the state from those forces that were lodging "a serious attack on the democratic legal order of the country." Pressure, he added, would not force the government to interfere with the independence of the judiciary and risk isolating Croatia internationally (Peskin and Boduszynski 2003: 1127).

Even more than Norac, the senior figure of Janko Bobetko, former chief of staff of the Croatian armed forces, was a symbol of the Homeland War. In the fall of 2002, the ICTY indicted Bobetko on charges of crimes against humanity and war crimes committed during Operation Medak Pocket in 1993, including the killing of Serb civilians. Faced with the prospect of another political crisis, the government this time appeared to be aligned with the nationalist opposition, invoking the constitutional and legal order of the Croatian state in an attempt to challenge the request for Bobetko's arrest and extradition to The Hague. At the heart of the government's reasoning in appealing the ICTY request for Bobetko was an idea of the Croatian state as a guardian of the nation's history, which had to protect the legitimacy of the Homeland War:

> [B]ased on the fact that the events referred to in the indictment are part of the defensive Homeland War which is an important part of Croatian history, the Republic of Croatia is interested in the accurate portrayal of the historical facts, particularly owing to the general social and political connotations that may lead to an erroneous portrayal of historical events.[18]

Three different lines of argument framed the public discussion sparked by the indictment. The position of the government struggled to balance its desire to protect "Croatian history" and avoid international isolation at a time when the ICTY had the support of the EU and

---

[18] Quoted in OSCE, Mission to Croatia, *Background Report: The ICTY and General Janko Bobetko*, Zagreb, 10 October 2002, retrieved from http://www.osce.org/zagreb/66067 (accessed 15 January 2012).

other powers. In the statements of the opposition and other nationalist circles, the indictment of Bobetko was reinterpreted in simple terms as an indictment of the Croatian state itself.[19] On the opposite side of the debate was President Mesić, who attacked the rising tide of xenophobic nationalism and paranoia that became apparent during the crisis: "Extreme political circles, which have become vociferous and aggressive lately, are persistently reiterating the theory that the world, which allegedly does not want the Croatian state, wishes to destroy its foundations with the Bobetko indictment."[20]

The ailing Bobetko died in Croatia shortly after the ICTY had declared him unfit to stand trial. But the next controversy precipitated by the trials was transformed into a test for Croatia's European commitments, at a time when accession to the EU had emerged as a consensus project for the main political parties. In early 2004, the ICTY indicted three Croatian generals – Ante Gotovina, one of the most revered heroes of the Homeland War, Ivan Čermak, and Mladen Markač – on charges of crimes against humanity committed in Operation Storm and its aftermath. The indictment implicated senior military commanders and Tuđman himself in a joint criminal enterprise at the highest level, aimed at the "forcible and permanent removal of the Serb population from the Krajina region, including by plunder, damage or outright destruction of the property of the Serb population, so as to discourage or prevent members of that population from returning to their homes and resuming habitation."[21] The indictment recast the final chapter of the Homeland War, which had secured Croatia's victory, as a campaign for ethnic cleansing orchestrated from the very top of the political and military establishment. The stakes were raised in May 2005, when the EU announced that it was postponing membership talks with Croatia because of its failure to apprehend Gotovina.

The ensuing controversy highlighted important changes in Croatia's handling of the war crimes issue. Čermak and Markač surrendered voluntarily to The Hague, and the fugitive Gotovina was arrested in the Canary Islands by the end of the year, after the government had

---

[19] Ibid.

[20] Quoted in Peskin and Boduszynski 2003: 1113.

[21] *Prosecutor v. Ante Gotovina*, Case No. IT-01–45-I, Amended Indictment, 19 February 2004, para. 7.

provided key information leading to the arrest and cleared the path for resuming accession negotiations with Brussels. The HDZ, now back in power, adopted a cautious approach that effectively prioritized the country's European project, even as it mobilized the resources of the state behind the defense of the generals. Sanader's public statements, which came as a surprise to many, suggested his own evolution in a more moderate and reformist direction and the changes he had managed to bring about in the HDZ, steering the party away from extreme nationalism and marginalizing radical elements in its ranks. Only three years earlier, Sanader had been at the forefront of the demonstrations sparked by the trial of Norac. By the time of the controversy over Gotovina, however, his tone and position had shifted dramatically: "It is in Croatia's interest," he argued, "to establish the full truth in the case of General Gotovina, as well as in the cases of Generals Mladen Markač, Ivan Čermak, Rahim Ademi, and the six Bosnian Croats indicted by the Tribunal."[22] The media was unleashed in another heated discussion and the associations of war veterans managed to mobilize some 50,000 people in the largest protest in Split, but in places such as Zagreb only small crowds were turning up to express their solidarity with the accused. Indeed, such elements increasingly appeared as an extremist fringe that attacked the entire mainstream of Croatian politics as "traitors": the president, parliament, government, and Sanader himself.[23]

Were all these developments signaling a shift to deliberative transitional justice in Croatia?[24] On this interpretation of transitional justice, the significance of the judicial process is located in its ability to raise questions in the public domain rather than provide definitive answers, in particular questions that open up for public discussion the narratives and projects of nationalism and the representations of the national past that are invoked to substantiate them. The productive potential of the public deliberation sparked by the trials is located in the multiplicity of interpretations that come to the fore in conversation with the events unfolding

---

[22] Quoted in OSCE, Mission to Croatia, *Spot Report: Reaction in Croatia to the Arrest of Ante Gotovina*, Zagreb, 13 December 2005, retrieved from http://www.osce.org/zagreb/66067 (accessed 15 January 2012).

[23] Ibid.

[24] See Chapter 2, § "Transitional Justice and the Challenge of Nationalism."

in the courtroom. These diverse perspectives are validated in the act of their public articulation, rather than by being accepted or incorporated in "shared narratives"; in this sense, the contribution of the trials is in encouraging more contestation than closure in public discourse. As the public conversation shifts from debates over whether or not atrocities have been committed to debates over their significance and interpretation, it creates opportunities to interrogate the limits of "transition" and "transformation" by exposing salient continuities that are often submerged in such narratives of progressive change, and to open up for public reassessment and renegotiation broader questions about national identity and state legitimacy in the aftermath of mass atrocity.

Some of the elements of a deliberative understanding of transitional justice can be detected in Croatia's reckoning with the legacy of the Homeland War over the past decade. The most significant contribution of the judicial processes initiated in that period may be the shift in the focus of the war crimes debate, from an exclusive preoccupation with atrocities perpetrated by members of the JNA and Serb paramilitaries to the emergence of a new focal point for the discussion, which directs attention to the actions of Croatia's police and armed forces. The ensuing public conversation sparked by the trials has been increasingly dominated not by the question of whether or not Croatian forces committed crimes against Serb civilians, but rather by questions about their significance and the implications of the judicial processes invoked to address them. Can war crimes be committed in a defensive war? Can a war of national liberation also be a campaign for ethnic cleansing? Is protecting Croatian history and memory more important than promoting democracy and the rule of law? Are the courts depicting national heroes as war criminals, casting a shadow over the Homeland War and calling into question the legitimacy of the Croatian state forged in the war?

Such questions have been repeatedly raised in the public discussions provoked by the trials, and the "answers" offered by the courts have often been met with the same public uproar that accompanied the proceedings. However, despite the fact that these judicial processes may have stimulated public discussion of the legacy of mass atrocity and competing assessments of the significance of the trials themselves, the limitations of the war crimes debate in Croatia are palpable. What is missing in the public conversation is the discursive engagement of those most directly affected by the crimes listed in the indictments: Croatian Serbs. These minority voices and presences have been largely absent in the public controversies and contestations sparked by the trials, and their memories and interpretations of the war are yet to enter public discourse, despite the shifted focus of the war crimes debate and the seemingly incessant preoccupation of the Croatian media and public with these questions.

There are many reasons why members of the Serb minority in Croatia may choose to stay out of the war crimes discussions. Their political representation and participation in post-Tuđman Croatia have improved significantly,[25] and politicians such as the former and current presidents, Stipe Mesić and Ivo Josipović, have made sustained efforts to promote interethnic peace and minority integration. Such gains may be seen as more valuable than the opportunity to seek recognition for wartime grievances and experiences of injustice by articulating them publicly, and potentially risk reversing the gains and improvements achieved so far. But there is also the issue of fear and intimidation, especially at the local level, where courts and police forces may continue to inspire suspicion among Serb communities. These problems are particularly apparent in the process of refugee return and reintegration, which has been slow and agonizing, plagued by allegations of hostility and violence toward returning Serbs and reluctance of the local authorities to intervene on their behalf. As one observer put it, "This vulnerable social and political position makes it very hard for victim groups to stake a strong claim for transitional justice" (Subotić 2009: 110).

Moreover, despite the creation of special war crimes chambers and the efforts to address the ethnic bias in the administration of justice, the vast majority of war crimes cases in Croatia are still tried by local courts and involve members of JNA and Serb forces, and the practice of prosecuting Serbs in absentia continues.[26] An intriguing question

---

[25] The most significant development in this respect is the 2003 coalition agreement between the HDZ and the Independent Democratic Serb Party, the main party of Croatian Serbs, which remained in place after the 2007 elections. See Jovic (2009: 19).

[26] Between 2005 and 2009, for example, 83 percent of all war crimes trials involved Serb defendants, and nearly half of them were conducted in absentia. See Amnesty International, *Croatia: Briefing to the European Commission*, 11 May 2011.

for further research is the role of "local justice" as a deterrent for refugee return in Croatia, but what is clear is the role of these judicial processes in encouraging suspicion and distrust of state institutions among Croatian Serbs. Even domestic trials of high-ranking Croat defendants have often been criticized for failing to ensure adequate protection for witnesses and promote confidence in the impartiality of the legal system. For example, the war crimes proceedings against Branimir Glavaš, a strongman from Osijek and long-term member of the Croatian parliament, have been accompanied by sustained intimidation of witnesses, including death threats and disclosure of the identity of protected witnesses on television. The failure of the authorities to investigate and halt the intimidation of witnesses in that case prompted Amnesty International to express concerns that the judiciary was sending "a message to potential witnesses in war crimes cases that they risk not being protected, if they agree to come forward."[27]

Whereas Croatian Serbs have been reluctant to intervene in the war crimes debate, the Croatian media for their part have rendered Serb victims and survivors invisible in the public domain. A glimpse of the explosive potential of confronting the Croatian public with unsettling accounts of atrocities against Serb civilians was provided in 2001, when a documentary about the aftermath of Operation Storm, entitled *Storm over Krajina*, was shown on national television. Jelena Subotić (2009: 110–111) notes that the reaction to the documentary served to discourage similar programs for years to come, as the fallout involved "a series of attacks against the filmmakers, including death threats and public condemnations by all major political parties and political figures such as then prime minister Račan, as well as a debate in the parliament."

Another controversy erupted in the summer of 2005 over the *Supplement to Textbooks of Current Croatian History*, prepared by a group of historians from the University of Zagreb. The supplement was commissioned by the government for schools in Podunavlje, a region reintegrated in Croatia in 1998, after a five-year moratorium on teaching current history in that region had expired. The handbook

---

[27] Amnesty International, *Croatia: Briefing to the European Commission and Member States,* 23 April 2010, 13.

was submitted to a review process and the content of some of the negative reviews was leaked in the media. The authors' discussion of the aftermath of Operation Storm and the inclusion of a photo show-ing the Serb exodus from Krajina triggered accusations of falsifying history and equating responsibility for the war in a debate that con-tinued to reverberate in the public domain for several months.[28] Such images are, of course, readily available on the Internet, but there was something very subversive in showing them on national television or including them in a history textbook. Even more subversive may be the presence of Serb victims and voices in the public domain at a time when the law is invoked to address their grievances and experiences of injustice. The public discussion sparked by the trials, however, has been marked by their absence. Pupovac draws attention to the implica-tions of this absence:

> In the case of the famous general Gotovina, and generals Markaš and Čermak, the main contribution in the news of the Croatian television has come from their defenders. They are the ones report-ing to the public what is happening. No victims. No voices of the victims that could create in the public some empathy, or cathartic experience. Eventually, we have to remove the "black spots" from our glorious victim. But what really happened to the people? How did it happen? Very few spaces and very few voices. It looks like a technicality. From this point of view, I'm rather sceptical that jus-tice is creating conditions for people on both sides to understand the character of the war, the way people have suffered, and how people have been driven to commit crimes. We are still in the field of private language, and that means private truths.[29]

At the current juncture, crossing the public-private divide may be a step too far for the majority of Serbs in Croatia, and confronting Serb memories and accounts of the war may still be intolerable for the Croatian media and public. However, without these minority presences and perspectives entering public discourse and becoming registered in

---

[28] The content of the supplement, media clipping of the debates it sparked, and analysis provided by the authors were compiled and published by Documenta, a Zagreb-based NGO. See Documenta, *Jedna povijest, više historija* [*One History, Many Histories*], Zagreb, 2007.

[29] Pupovac interview.

the discussions, the war crimes debate in Croatia will remain impoverished and the potential of transitional justice processes to interrogate the nationalist projects and narratives inherited from the 1990s will continue to be stifled. When trials provide opportunities to raise the larger questions of national identity and state legitimacy in Croatia, the ensuing debates often appear as a process of contestation and negotiation between Croatian nationalists and moderates, hard-liners and reformers, isolationists and internationalists, or between Croatia and the EU. Croatian Serbs, however, who should be front and center as interlocutors in these discussions, and whose discursive engagements are crucial for any meaningful renegotiation of questions of identity and legitimacy in the post-war order, are largely absent from the public domain.

These limitations of transitional justice in Croatia became apparent in the spring of 2011 in the public reactions to the ICTY judgment in the case of the former generals Gotovona, Čermak, and Markač, charged with crimes against Serb civilians during Operation Storm.[30] Throughout the trial, the media relied heavily on the defense team to inform the Croatian public about the proceedings, failing to report those facts established by the court that didn't fit in their narrative, to discuss the plight of the victims, or to relate accounts of survivors. When the court found two of the accused, Gotovina and Markač, guilty of crimes against humanity and war crimes committed in the context of a "joint criminal enterprise" implicating the very top of Croatia's political and military establishment, the disappointment was palpable in central Zagreb, where thousands had gathered to watch the reading of the judgement on a giant screen. The public uproar provoked by the verdict involved street protests and strong condemnations from the political class, media, and public.[31] But again, the

---

[30] See *Prosecutor v. Ante Gotovina, Ivan Čermak, Mladen Markač*, Case No. IT-06–90-T, Trial Judgment, 15 April 2011.

[31] Prime Minster Kosor described the judgment as "unacceptable" and pledged the government's full support to overturn it on appeal, whereas President Josipović stated: "It is a serious political and judicial act that has shocked even me. We are aware crimes were committed, but I am convinced that there was no joint criminal enterprise in the defense of Croatia." Quoted in Marlies Simons, "UN Court Convicts Two Croatian Generals of War Crimes and Frees a Third," *New York Times*, 15 April 2011, retrieved from http://www.nytimes.com/2011/04/16/world/europe/16hague.html (accessed 15 January 2012).

public discussion sparked by the trial was notable not so much for those who engaged in it and expressed their views and interpretations, but for those who didn't.

CONCLUSION

This chapter has examined the war crimes debate in Croatia over the past three decades as a mirror reflecting the shifting relationship between law and nationalism. The consequences of Yugoslavia's transition without justice in the aftermath of the Second World War became apparent in the 1980s and early 1990s, when the question of mass atrocity exploded in public discourse and provided a platform for nationalist mobilization, attacking the legitimacy of the Yugoslav state and unleashing a verbal civil war that foreshadowed the real war that was about to engulf the region. The war crimes debate emerged as an arena of struggle over Croatian nationalism, as the pursuit of national unity and reconciliation involved revising official histories and contesting legacies of abuse. Uniting and reconciling the Croatian nation in this way, however, could only be achieved at the expense of Croatian Serbs, making a reframed Croatian nationalism dependent on suppressing minority identities and memories.

The initiation of war crimes prosecutions during the Homeland War and their continuation and expansion in the post-war period signaled a shift in the relationship between law and nationalism. Rather than serving the interests of justice, however, the Croatian judiciary appeared to be serving the interests of the regime in advancing

According to one opinion poll conducted immediately after the decision was announced, 95 percent of the Croatian public rejected the ICTY ruling. See Davor Butkovic, "Samo 23% Hrvata za ulazak u EU! Čak 95 smatra presudu nepravednom" [Only 23% for Joining the EU! As Much as 95% Consider the Verdict Unjust], *Jutarnji List*, 16 April 2011, retrieved from http://www.jutarnji.hr/istrazivanje-nakon-presude-gotovini–samo-23–hrvata-za-ulazak-u-eu/939458 (accessed 15 January 2012). For a detailed analysis of the media coverage of the trial and the public reactions to the judgment, see Center for Peace, Nonviolence and Human Rights-Osijek, Documenta, and Civic Committee for Human Rights, *Monitoring War Crimes Trials: Report for 2011*, February 2012, retrieved from http://www.centar-za-mir.hr/uploads/monitoring_war_crime_trials.pdf (accessed 17 April 2012).

nation- and state-building. Prosecuting a large number of ethnic Serbs for war crimes in absentia and, at the same time, granting de facto immunity from prosecution for such offenses to members of the Croatian army and police suggests how Croatian law helped obscure the complex legacies of the war and allocated collective guilt and victimhood. These judicial processes have raised serious concerns about the "transitional" role of the law among Serb communities in Croatia, creating perceptions that the trials were used to pursue not justice but vengeance and promote wartime policies by other means. The pursuit of "local justice" in Croatia during the 1990s suggests how the breakdown of the rule of law, associated with the advent of nationalism and war, may be further reinforced by the work of the judiciary itself, blurring the boundaries between the war and postwar order.

The key challenge for transitional justice in Croatia since the turn of the century has been the need to confront two legacies of abuse: one involving atrocities against Serb civilians and ethnic cleansing during the Homeland War; the other concerning the conduct of war crimes trials in its aftermath. Croatian law, like the political class and public, has struggled to confront these legacies in a meaningful way and come to terms with the past. Nevertheless, Croatia's experience with judicial processes in the past decade is useful in illuminating the potential of deliberative transitional justice to interrogate the "dark side" of nationalism, as well as revealing some of its limitations.

The domestic and international trials of high-ranking officers of the Croatian army and police have encouraged important changes in the war crimes debate, shifting the meaning of "war crimes" in the public domain and the subject of public deliberation from an exclusive preoccupation with war crimes committed by the JNA and local Serbs to a focus on the members of the Croatian police and armed forces. Moreover, the discussions sparked by the trials have involved contesting not so much the crimes themselves but their significance and interpretations, and have provided a platform for debating Croatia's commitments to democracy, the rule of law, and Europe. At the same time, the range of interpretations articulated in public discourse have tended to reflect Croatia's long-standing political and ideological divisions but not its cultural diversity, and far too often the discussion has unfolded in conversation with Europe rather than with Croatian Serbs. Without engaging these key interlocutors and their memories and interpretations of the war, the judicial processes and ensuing public debates may be conducted in vain, missing valuable opportunities to renegotiate important questions of identity and legitimacy and bring the past into a productive dialogue with the present.

6 RESISTANCE, PLURALIZATION, AND INTERNATIONAL JUSTICE IN SERBIA

On the night of 29 April 1999, NATO airstrikes hit the building of the Yugoslav Army Headquarters in central Belgrade. A decade and a half later, the building is still in ruins, preserved as a monument of NATO's aggression against Yugoslavia.[1] The remnants of the Yugoslav Army Headquarters can be seen as a metaphor for the legacies inherited from a decade of war and repressive rule: they are partly destroyed and yet, at the same, they are still there. They persist in a variety of forms, often becoming invoked in Serbia's national mythology as a reminder of past grievances and experiences of injustice, but they also serve to obscure other grievances and experiences of injustice, making it easier to forget them and avoid facing the past. Not too far from the site of the former Army Headquarters is the Belgrade office of the ICTY, which has complicated the precarious balance of remembering and forgetting in Serbia's reckoning with the legacies of the 1990s.

In the first part of the book, I argued that the rise of international criminal justice embodies a constitutive tension between nationalism and the rule of law, and that the pursuit of international justice in the Balkans does not simply dissolve or transcend that tension. Instead, international justice stimulates an ongoing process of pluralization of public discourse, politics, and law in the region, generating new sites where the tensions between nationalism and the rule of law become

[1] The Web site of the City of Belgrade features a chronology of the bombing campaign and a photo of the Yugoslav Army Headquarter in a designated page entitled "NATO Aggression, 1999," retrieved from http://www.beograd.rs/cms/view.php?id=201271 (accessed 13 February 2012).

expressed and negotiated.[2] This chapter examines international justice in Serbia since the fall of Slobodan Milošević in order to illustrate some of these arguments but also takes them further, focusing in particular on the persistence of the intertwined legacies of nationalism, war, and repressive rule from the 1990s, and examining their significance and implications for the rule of law. I start by discussing the role of nationalism in explaining the continuing opposition to international justice in Serbia, then broaden the lens and locate the sources of opposition in the more pervasive politics of resistance to dealing with the past, and conclude by examining the evidence of pluralization and the role of Europe in Serbia, seeking to recover along the way the shifting relationship between nationalism and the rule of law and the ways in which the underlying tensions are managed and negotiated.

NATIONALISM REFRAMED: THE SERBIAN PUBLIC AND THE "ANTI-SERB" COURT

Serbia's opposition to international criminal justice during the 1990s was more of a reflex than grand political strategy. Predictably, the regime of Slobodan Milošević refused to extend genuine cooperation to the ICTY; doing so would have amounted to self-incrimination. At the same time, however, the perceived weakness or irrelevance of the Tribunal allowed for some gesturing toward engagement, when it appeared to further the interests of the regime. International negotiators may have used the ICTY indictments of Radovan Karadžić and Ratko Mladić in 1995 as an opportunity to prevent them from coming to the peace talks at Dayton, but the initiation of the proceedings also coincided with Belgrade's attempt to distance itself from the Bosnian Serb leadership.[3] Milošević signed the Dayton Peace Accords, which included provisions for cooperation with international justice, and the ICTY set up an office in Belgrade. For

[2] See Chapter 3, § "From Crimes against Peace to Crimes against Humanity" and § "After the War: The Role of International Justice in the Balkans."

[3] "Seven Questions: Richard Holbrook on Radovan Karadzic," *Foreign Policy*, 24 July 2008, retrieved from http://www.foreignpolicy.com/articles/2008/07/23/seven_questions_richard_holbrooke_on_radovan_karadzic (accessed 13 February 2012).

most of the 1990s, the anti-Hague discourse in Serbia was dominated by other circles, including some academic lawyers and conservative elements in the opposition. The state itself became more
prominent in mobilizing public opinion against international justice
when Milošević himself was indicted during the Kosovo crisis.[4] On
5 October 2000, however, his regime was overthrown and less than
a year later he was arrested and transferred to The Hague.

The events of 5 October marked the end of an era of repressive rule
in Serbia and atrocious wars throughout the region, but they also heralded the beginning of an agonistic transition that has unfolded in the
thick shadow of the past. Serbia's relationship with international criminal justice in the post-Milošević era can be described as schizophrenic.
However reluctantly, the Serbian state has met the requirements of
cooperation with the ICTY, whereas public discourse in Serbia has
been dominated by narratives of opposition and resistance to international justice. Indeed, cooperation itself has often been framed as
a form of resistance, for example when high-ranking suspects such
as General Vladimir Lazarević surrendered voluntarily (or claimed
to do so) and the prime minister, Vojislav Koštunica, publicly praised
them for acting "in line with a long-standing tradition of the Serbian
army, namely, that our officers fight for the interests of the people and
country until the bitter end."[5] A decade after regime change, Serbia
has arrested or encouraged to surrender all suspects wanted by the
court, including Karadžić and Mladić, but the majority of Serbs continue to perceive international justice as biased, hostile, and politically
motivated. In a public opinion poll conducted in 2009, 70 percent of
the respondents viewed the ICTY as biased against Serb defendants;
another survey showed that 40 percent considered Mladić a "hero" at
the time of his arrest in May 2011.[6]

---

[4] Biljana Kovačević-Vučo, interviewed by the author at the Lawyers Committee on
Human Rights in Belgrade, 30 October 2007.

[5] Quoted in Subotić (2009: 50).

[6] See Strategic Marketing Research/OSCE Mission to Serbia, "Views on War
Crimes, the ICTY, and National War Crimes Judiciary," April 2009, retrieved from
http://www.osce.org/serbia/40751 (accessed 20 January 2012); "Limited Support
for Mladic Arrest, Poll Shows," *Balkan Insight*, 16 May 2011, retrieved from http://
www.balkaninsight.com/en/article/limited-support-for-mladic-arrest-poll-shows
(accessed 20 January 2012).

Public opposition to international justice has remained consistently strong in Serbia throughout the past decade, reflecting the traction of what I have labeled the "nationalist" argument in debates over the ICTY: the claim that the Tribunal is a political institution meting out collective guilt and punishment.[7] The more officials at The Hague insisted that only individuals were put on trial, the more local audiences appeared to espouse collectivist and conspiratorial interpretations of international justice (Rangelov 2004). Analysis of public opinion data suggests how the ICTY becomes integrated in some of the narratives of Serbian nationalism inherited from the Milošević era:

> The prevailing attitude has been that the purpose of the ICTY is not to show that war crimes cannot go unpunished and thus to promote the idea of peace and tolerance among nations (only 22 per cent), as 74 per cent interpret the purpose of the ICTY in accordance with their versions of conspiracy theory: to blame the Serbs for war sufferings and thus to make Serbia dependent on the international community; to exculpate NATO for its 1999 aggression against Yugoslavia; or to establish a New World Order with the United States as its leader.(Dimitrijević 2005: 3)

The proceedings against suspects from different nationalities are often seen as evidence of the ICTY's anti-Serb bias:

> The public in Serbia has consistently perceived the ICTY as biased and hostile towards Serbia (in 2003, 2004 and 2005, 69 per cent of the interviewees consistently expected that accused Serbs will not be tried "impartially and on the basis of established facts"). This opinion was based on the impression that a greater number of Serbs were indicted (between 48 and 55 per cent) and that they held higher ranks than the indictees belonging to other nations (between 12 and 16 per cent) and that the trials of Serbs are less impartial (between 8 and 12 per cent). It is believed that Serbia and Serbs are in the least favourable position before the ICTY (82 per cent) compared to Bosniaks, Croats and Albanians. (Ibid.)

One way of understanding these sentiments is to examine the persistence of nationalism in Serbia after Milošević. Much has been written about the ways in which nationalism became mobilized and entrenched

---

[7] See Chapter 3, § "After the War: The Role of International Justice in the Balkans."

in Serbian politics in the late 1980s and 1990s. Sabrina Ramet (2005a: 138) highlights the role of narratives of national victimization and conspiracies of internal and external enemies as core themes of Serbian propaganda during that period, suggesting that they served to engender "a kind of collective psychosis." Others emphasize the inability of the Serbian opposition to offer an alternative to nationalism, as it "became impossible to realistically offer a political programme that did not address the 'national question', and most challengers to Milošević criticized the SPS [the ruling Socialist Party of Serbia] for failing to achieve the goals of Greater Serbia rather than criticizing the attempt to create it in the first place" (Pavlaković 2005a: 8). The dominance of symbolism over politics had far-reaching implications, precipitating Serbia's failure to build a legitimate democratic order (Thomas 1999).

The dramatic end of the Milošević regime, however, was not accompanied by a decisive ideological shift. When I pressed this point to Vojin Dimitrijević, a leading public intellectual and human rights advocate, he told me that most Serbs blamed Milošević for losing the wars, not for fighting them.[8] Serbia's transitional elites proved to be unwilling and unable to mark a clear break with the legacy of nationalism. As one observer put it, the October revolution "failed to remove the ideology of nationalism from the Serbian body politic, which will continue to hinder the development of liberal values (and a stable political system) in the near future" (Pavlaković 2005b: 30). Seen in this light, the prevalence of anti-Hague rhetoric and sentiment in Serbia appears almost inevitable, a symptom of the continuing grip of nationalism on Serbian politics and society and an expression of deeply entrenched tensions between nationalism and the rule of law.

There is much evidence to support this argument. Serbia's democratic opposition came to power in October 2000, but its ambivalence toward the legacy of the previous regime meant that as in the 1990s, it has often been held hostage by nationalism and struggled to steer politics and public discourse in a new direction. The early post-Milošević period was dominated by two figures from the Democratic Opposition of Serbia (DOS), a coalition of diverse parties that had

---

[8] Vojin Dimitrijević, interviewed by the author in Belgrade, 31 October 2007.

little in common apart from opposing the regime: Vojislav Koštunica from the Democratic Party of Serbia (DSS), who became the new president; and Zoran Đinđić from the Democratic Party (DS), the first transitional prime minister. Đinđić was seen as a reformist who rallied the pro-European forces in Serbia behind him and spearheaded the efforts for Milošević's arrest and transfer to The Hague. Koštunica, on the other hand, was a conservative with impeccable nationalist credentials, not least as an archenemy of the Yugoslav Tribunal already in the 1990s. Jelena Subotić (2009: 72) suggests that Đinđić was ultimately a pragmatist who used international justice as a "wedge issue, a defining difference between the two opposing political groupings" in the ruling coalition. But Đinđić's messages were often mixed, whereas Koštunica's attacks against the ICTY were forceful and consistent.[9]

After Đinđić's assassination in March 2003, Koštunica adopted a policy of "voluntary surrenders" to the ICTY and used every opportunity to stoke nationalist sentiment and galvanize public opinion against the Tribunal: "War crimes indictees who had voluntarily surrendered and left for The Hague were glorified as heroes, honourable men sacrificing for the future of Serbia" (Biserko 2006: 74). The ambivalent messages of the "democratic bloc" – extending cooperation to the ICTY under international pressure and at the same time rejecting international justice on principle – have often played into the hands of extremists from the Serbian Radical Party (SRS), who could plausibly claim the moral high ground by making pledges to terminate all forms of cooperation with the Tribunal. The general elections held in December 2003, for example, featured Vojislav Šešelj as a candidate for the SRS, which took the largest share of the vote, and Milošević for the Socialist Party of Serbia, even though both of them were in ICTY custody during the elections. In the February 2008 presidential elections, Tomislav Nokolić from the SRS lost by a tiny margin to the incumbent Boris Tadić from the DS. The elections were dominated by the issue of Kosovo's final status; nevertheless, the Radicals decided

---

[9] Koštunica once described the ICTY in the following way: "As a man lives with a disease, and in the end manages to overcome it, I think that the ICTY in a way has elements of an illness, and sometimes there is something positive in an illness, a man can end up stronger and harder after overcoming it." Quoted in Subotić (2009: 71–72).

to launch their campaign with a public glorification of Mladić, who at that time was Europe's most wanted man and Serbia's biggest obstacle in the accession negotiations with the European Union.[10]

THE POLITICS OF RESISTANCE TO DEALING WITH THE PAST

The persistence of nationalism provides an important source of opposition to international justice in Serbia. But such opposition could also be understood as an expression of broader and more pervasive resistance to any meaningful form of dealing with the past, which has been a constant in Serbian politics since the October revolution. In the course of the past decade, it has become increasingly apparent how Serbia's reluctance to confront the intertwined ideological, political, and criminal legacies inherited from the Milošević era serves to stifle the initiation of a much-needed process of moral and political regeneration. Nenad Dimitrijević (2008: 14) has examined some of the far-reaching consequences of this continuing failure to come to terms with the past:

> A look at Serbia today shows that political, social and cultural dynamics in this country have been decisively shaped by political and societal silence about the [past] crimes. The silence functions as the refusal to acknowledge the true character of what is known to have happened. As a consequence, since the assassination of Prime Minister Djindjic, the worst legacies of the past have resurfaced, including a denial of any involvement by the Serbian regime in the crimes committed in Bosnia, Croatia and Kosovo; a preservation of the destructive core of tribal nationalism disguised as the affirmation of "genuine traditions" and "true identity"; a promotion of war criminals to the pedestal of national heroes and a rise in xenophobic attitudes amongst the general population. In a word, the refusal to reflect on the past has greatly contributed to political and normative confusion, which has effectively brought transition to a halt. Both citizens and political elites are prisoners of the past.

---

[10] Vera Didanović, "Radikalso predizborno pozicioniranje: S Mladićem na čelu – u kampanju" [The Radicals' Pre-election Positioning: With Mladić at the Helm – in the Campaign], *Vreme*, 31 May 2007.

Dimitrijević's argument is important because it suggests that a central problem of Serbia's transition is the political and societal refusal to confront the crimes committed in the course of the 1990s. Seen in this light, the persistence of nationalism emerges as a product of Serbia's failure to confront these crimes, as much as it offers an explanation of that failure. We need to look elsewhere to fully understand the forces that have shaped the politics of resistance to dealing with the past in Serbia, which runs much deeper than the opposition to international justice may suggest, even if such opposition often expresses it most clearly.

In the remaining part of this section, I draw attention to a range of actors and networks that in various ways became implicated in the political and criminal undertakings of the Milošević regime, and since its fall have spearheaded the crusade against the ICTY and other efforts for a critical examination of the legacy of the 1990s. Any such examination entails exposing their own role in the emergence and sustenance of a highly predatory political and economic order involving endemic abuse of power at home, alongside the wars and atrocities in the region. If the previous regime often depended on nationalism and war for political mobilization and legitimation, in the new dispensation the legacies of war and nationalism perform a similar function for certain actors and networks whose continuing power and influence depends on forgetting and denying the criminal legacies of the past. Seen in this light, resisting any meaningful process of dealing with the past, whether it involves international justice or other forms of reckoning, becomes a question of survival.

Some of these actors emerged from Serbian civil society. In a sense, dissident currents in civil society paved the way for the rise of Milošević by developing an ideological narrative and political program that his regime so successfully harnessed. A prominent example is the Memorandum of the Serbian Academy of Sciences and Arts of 1986 (Ramet 1999: 18–19), prefiguring the crucial role that Serbia's intellectual elites were going to play in the resurgence of nationalism (Dragović-Soso 2002). The Serbian Orthodox Church is not monolithic and free from schisms, but it largely supported the Greater Serbia project and often opposed peace initiatives that threatened to frustrate Serbia's territorial aspirations (Ramet 2005b: 256–260). Although the

Church provided an important source of legitimacy for the regime's military campaigns in the 1990s, its influence also reflected a growing dependence on religion to substantiate Serbian national identity. In the post-Milošević era, some of these actors have been key players in the so-called Patriotic Bloc, comprising sections of the intelligentsia, Serbian Orthodox Church, and nationalist media. The ICTY has been one of their favorite targets; indeed, the issue of cooperation with the Tribunal, alongside the question of Kosovo's final status, has often dominated their public agenda. The sort of anti-Tribunal rhetoric regularly employed by the Patriotic Bloc can be glimpsed from the words of one prominent cleric, Metropolitan Amfilohije Radović: "[T]hose who have covered the Serbian people in black at the end of the twentieth and the beginning of the twenty-first century ... want, like Pontius Pilate, to wash their hand in the blood of the righteous and to cover up their own misdeeds."[11]

Other actors had a more ambivalent relationship with the previous regime, oscillating between opposition and collaboration. Their opposition was often mounted from extremist positions and Milošević became adept at using them domestically and internationally, presenting himself as a moderate and raising the spectre of radical nationalism. At the same time, some of these elements became deeply implicated in the enterprise of war and atrocities committed by Serbian forces in different parts of the region. A good example is the SRS and its former leader, Vojislav Šešelj. The SRS recruited volunteers and established paramilitary units that fought for Greater Serbia, but it was also instrumental in the wartime propaganda that encouraged and justified ethnic cleansing. At the time of writing, Šešelj is still on trial at the ICTY, charged with making "inflammatory speeches in the media, during public events, and during visits to the volunteer [SRS] units and other Serb forces in Croatia and Bosnia and Herzegovina, instigating those forces to commit crimes."[12] His figure embodies the imbrications of political and criminal elements and motivations in the legacy inherited from the 1990s, and exemplifies the range of vested interests in resisting any meaningful examination of that legacy. Šešelj's voluntary

---

[11] Momir Turudić, "Ratnik u mantiji" [Warrior in a Robe], *Vreme*, 22 November 2007.

[12] *Prosecutor v. Vojislav Šešelj*, Case No. IT-03-67-3, Indictment, 7 December 2007, para. 10(b).

surrender to the ICTY and continuing involvement in SRS politics should be understood in this light, as an attempt to use the platform of the Tribunal to defend his role in the war and mobilize the Serbian public with his distinctive brand of obscene identity politics.

These elements in civil society and the political class have often been the public face of the anti-Hague lobby in Serbia, actively seeking to shape the public discourse and representations of the ICTY. The politics of resistance to dealing with the past in Serbia, however, has a more opaque underside, which brings to light the process of state capture and criminalization that is the other dark legacy of the previous regime. A set of interlocking networks with links to the security sector, illicit economy, and organized crime emerged during the Milošević era and served multiple purposes, from suppressing dissent at home and fighting wars abroad to providing patronage and protection for a variety of criminal activities. Some of these networks survived the October revolution largely intact and, in some sense, provided a bridge between the old and new regime. Their survival can be attributed to political leverage and a two-pronged strategy for self-preservation: galvanizing "patriotic" rhetoric in the public domain, often by attacking the Yugoslav Tribunal and local advocates of dealing with the past, and raising the spectre of violence.

The proceedings at the ICTY have revealed the extent to which the Serbian state became captured by such networks and their criminal enterprises in the course of the 1990s. The Kosovo indictment of Milošević, for example, also included a former president of Serbia, a deputy prime minister in charge of Kosovo, a chief of staff of the armed forces, and a minster of internal affairs.[13] Trials at The Hague and more recently in Serbia itself have also shed light on the links between the security structures of the state and various "irregular" police units and paramilitary formations, which became heavily involved in war crimes, extortion, looting and smuggling across the region, but also in assassinations of political opponents of the regime and other "special operations" in Serbia itself. Two chiefs of Serbia's State Security Service (DB), Jovica Stanišić and Franko Simatović (also known as

---

[13] See *Prosecutor v. Slobodan Milošević et al.*, Case No. IT-99–37-PT, "Kosovo" Second Amended Indictment, 16 October 2001.

Frenki), are on trial at the ICTY for their role in setting up and running some of the most notorious irregular units, including Arkan's Tigers, the Red Berets, and the Scorpions. These were "secret units which were not legally authorized and [which were] established by or with the assistance of the Serbian DB for the purpose of undertaking special military actions in the Republic of Croatia and Bosnia and Herzegovina."[14] In forging and sustaining these wartime networks, the formal state structures become increasingly captured and implicated in illicit economic activities and organized crime. The DB, in particular, was used by the regime "as the main instrument for infiltrating and subverting neighbouring countries, for infiltrating and spying on the domestic opposition, for sanctions busting, financial manipulation of inflation, foreign exchange, cigarettes and excise goods; for drug trafficking, for controlling the collaborative relationships in the criminal underworld – and for assassinating political enemies" (Vasić 2005: 60).

The events of 5 October removed Milošević from the political scene, but did little to release the Serbian state from the grip of such powerful networks. Indeed, regime change appeared to have entrenched them even further. As one study notes:

> The same clique of individuals, from the overlapping political and criminal elites, was responsible both for the waging of war and the atrocities involved and for the plunder of Serbia. Yet these individuals were very often the ones whose abandonment of Milošević in the autumn of 2000 had made possible the bloodless October revolution and the regime of President Vojislav Koštunica, who, as heir of the nationalist mantle, remained dependent upon their support.(Miljković and Hoare 2005: 213)

The figure of Milorad Ulemak "Legija" embodies the symbiotic relationship between politics and crime in Serbia and the new roles of the old networks. Legija was a small-scale criminal in the mid-1980s when he left Yugoslavia to avoid prosecution for petty crimes and joined the French Foreign Legion. He left the Legion in the early 1990s and joined the ranks first of Arkan's Tigers, a notorious unit operating in

---

[14] *Prosecutor v. Jovica Stanišić and Franko Simatović*, Case No. IT-03–69-PT, Revised Second Amended Indictment, 15 May 2006, para. 3.

Bosnia and Croatia, and later the Unit for Special Operations, known as the Red Berets, eventually becoming its commander.

The Red Berets served as Milošević's "Praetorian Guard" in the second half of the 1990s: reporting directly to him, providing security to the upper echelons of his regime, and executing the most sensitive special operations on his behalf (Vasić 2005: 65–66). A series of trials at Belgrade's Chamber for Organized Crime have revealed the nature and scale of Legija's involvement in criminal activities in service of the regime. The list includes the assassination of Ivan Stambolić, a former president of Serbia and critic of Milošević, and attempted assassination of the opposition leader Vuk Drašković. In 1998–1999, Legija led the operations of the Red Berets in Kosovo and further strengthened his position in Serbia's criminal underworld. This is how the Belgrade weekly *Vreme* sums up his role during that period: "He was a 'patriot' for the politicians; for the criminals he was a defender and a partner; and for the State Security and its top (Milošević) he was an efficient executor."[15]

Legija was aware that the tide was turning and the only way to survive was to shift allegiances and be seen as indispensable for the new regime – a role he masterfully played in the events of 5 October, abandoning Milošević and pledging the support of the Red Berets for regime change. The ensuing negotiations with the DOS leadership were crucial for Legija and those around him, who were desperate to present themselves as a factor of stability in the new dispensation, but they proved to be fatal for Đinđić, who in some sense paid with his life for entering such alliances and dependencies. At a time when the army had already abandoned Milošević and central Belgrade was occupied by half a million agitated citizens, many of them armed, the support of the Red Berets appeared unnecessary and largely irrelevant to the success of the revolution (Vasić 2005: 28). Instead of using this opportunity to disband the Red Berets and undercut their power and influence, the transitional government effectively gave them a new lease on life.

As soon as the changes in Serbia started to gather pace, Legija and his collaborators in the criminal underworld and the security structures

---

15 Miloš Vasić, "Milorad Ulemak Legija: Prilog za Biografiju" [Milorad Ulemak Legija: Contribution to the Biography], *Vreme*, 24 May 2007.

felt threatened once again, and the problems with these networks serving as a bridge between the old and new regimes became increasingly apparent. The DB was probing Legija's involvement in prominent assassination cases and casting a shadow over the activities of his collaborators in the Zemun Clan, a criminal group with close links to the Red Berets. There was even a proposal to deploy the Red Berets to Afghanistan to take part in operations conducted by the United States and United Nations. Faced with the prospect of his imminent marginalization and possible arrest and prosecution, in November 2001 Legija mobilized his power base in the media and politics, the security establishment and the criminal underworld, and staged a mutiny of the Red Berets. This "counterrevolution" demanded removal of the newly installed chiefs of the DB and termination of all cooperation with the ICTY. It created a rift between the prime minister and president: whereas Đinđić resisted the pressure, Koštunica "supported the mutineers and considered their concerns legitimate, once more indicating his position on war crimes and willingness to address some of the dark legacies of the Milošević regime" (Pavlaković 2005b: 34).

The mutiny demonstrated how these networks were threatening to hijack Serbia's transition. They were using the ICTY as a pretext to stir instability; in fact, their goal was to secure their own survival in the new order and avoid domestic, not international, justice. A subsequently established commission of inquiry put this issue starkly in their report:

> The mutiny of the JSO [Red Berets] from November 2001 is a direct consequence of their assessment that the MUP [Ministry of the Interior] of Serbia was starting to take actions to disclose JSO's links with organized crime. In this sense the mutiny of the JSO, which was incited by its leadership, represented an attempt to protect the activities of the Zemun Clan.[16]

Another opportunity to arrest Legija and disband the Red Berets was missed, and Legija soon found himself employing the strategy rehearsed in the mutiny once again, this time plotting the assassination of the prime minister. Although the ICTY was not investigating

---

[16] *Report of the Commission of Inquiry into the Security System of the Prime Minister Dr Zoran Đinđić* (Korać Commission), cited in Vasić (2005: 67).

members of the Red Berets, Legija raised the spectre of arrests and extraditions to The Hague to enlist some of them in a joint operation with the Zemun Clan, which was dubbed Stop the Hague, and culminated with the assassination of Zoran Đinđić on 12 March 2003 in Belgrade.[17]

The government finally dismantled the Red Berets during Operation Sabre following the assassination, which involved rounding up some 10,000 individuals and represented the first attempt for an overhaul of the networks linked into the security sector, judiciary, criminal underworld, and media in Serbia. Legija was eventually arrested and tried in Belgrade for the assassination of one prime minister and one president, two attempts to kill a leader of the opposition, and other crimes exposing the symbiotic relationship between the structures of the state and organized crime. The prosecution of Legija and the Zemun Clan for the assassination of Đinđić became the "trial of the century" in Serbia, suggesting to the Serbian public what historian Latinka Perović had argued shortly after the assassination: that "the 'patriots' Milošević so often praised were in fact killers, thieves and drug dealers."[18] For such "patriotic" actors and networks, resistance to dealing with any aspect of the criminal legacies of the previous regime became a survival strategy. Using anti-ICTY rhetoric to stir nationalist passions provided one way of pursuing that strategy. Serbia's opposition to international justice has to be understood in this context: as one element of the politics of resistance to dealing with the past, whether that past refers to war crimes committed in Bosnia, Croatia, and Kosovo; assassinations of domestic political opponents; or the predatory capture and criminalization of the Serbian state.

PLURALIZATION AND THE ROLE OF EUROPE

Dramatic events such as the assassination of Đinđić have prompted some observers to conclude that on the whole, international justice has been a destabilizing factor that complicated Serbia's transition to

[17] For a detailed account of the events that led to the assassination, see Vasić (2005).
[18] Latinka Perović, "Serbia Enters New Era," IWPR, TU No. 314, 19–23 May 2003, retrieved from http://www.iwpr.net (accessed 20 January 2012).

democracy (e.g., Snyder and Vinjamuri 2003/2004). The impact of the trials of high-ranking suspects, such as Milošević and Šešelj, has been analyzed along similar lines. Broadcasting the trial of Milošević on Serbian television, for example, offered the former leader a convenient platform from which to address domestic audiences. Milošević seized the opportunity to turn his defense into an attack on international justice and the West by framing the proceedings as a political trial, accusing the Tribunal of anti-Serb bias and exposing the duplicity of Western elites, who had treated him for most of the 1990s as a "peacemaker" and "factor of stability" in the Balkans.[19] Vojin Dimitrijević (2005: 7) has pointed out some of the "public relations" mistakes of the Tribunal in this respect, suggesting that "the general popularity of Milošević, which after the collapse of his regime in October 2000 had reached its nadir, increased after his trial started to be regularly aired on television." Moreover, the ICTY seemed to provide the Patriotic Bloc with a convenient target for their attacks, enabling them to galvanize nationalist sentiment and radicalize the Serbian public.

I have argued that the opposition to international justice in Serbia can be attributed to the persistence of nationalism after the October revolution, but also to a range of actors and networks determined to resist any meaningful form of dealing with the past as a matter of survival. Seen in this light, international justice reveals the extent to which criminalization and radicalization have already affected the Serbian state and society, and exposes the forces that have a vested interest in stirring instability and inhibiting reform. The multiple legacies of the Milošević era have ensured that there is no shortage of other issues on the agenda that could be (and have been) harnessed by such elements for "patriotic" mobilization, from the question of Kosovo's final status to the genocide case of Bosnia and Herzegovina against Serbia

---

[19] When the former peace negotiator, Lord David Owen, testified at the trial in 2003, he confirmed that Western leaders had indeed seen Milošević as the only person able to bring peace to the Balkans, but noted that he had suspected Milošević of "playing the nationalist card." See Adam LeBor, "Comment: Milosevic the Peacemaker," IWPR, TU 332, 7 November 2003, retrieved from http://iwpr.net/report-news/comment-milosevic-%E2%80%9Cpeacemaker%E2%80%9D (accessed 20 January 2012). See also LeBor (2002).

at the International Court of Justice (ICJ).[20] Indeed, the Milošević trial took place in the shadow of the ICJ case, and the Serbian state often appeared to be assisting his defense behind the scenes with information and intelligence.[21] Moreover, the ability of defendants such as Milošević and Šešelj to address the Serbian public from the dock in The Hague may be regrettable, but it is also an indication of their potential to mobilize constituencies and promote radicalization if they had remained in Serbia itself.

As for the assassination of Zoran Đinđić, the threat of arrests and extraditions to The Hague was fabricated by Legija and effectively used as a cover, but it was the changing political climate in Serbia and the tightening net around the Red Berets and Zemun Clan, faced with imminent marginalization and prosecution in Serbia itself, which inspired the attack on the prime minister and led to his tragic death. In fact, if the ICTY had investigating the Red Berets and demanded Legija's arrest and extradition, it could have prevented the assassination. Operation Sabre revealed the impotence of the Red Berets and other similar elements to act as "spoilers" of the transition, once the authorities had decided to confront them head-on:

> Operation Sabre cast its net beyond just mafia thugs: newspapers which had called for the removal of Đinđić were shut down, judges who had taken bribes or released mafia members were fired from their jobs, and the Red Berets were immediately disbanded. Although tragic, the murder of Đinđić did initiate the first significant assault on the remains of the Milošević regime, and brought to light the close-knit connection between criminals, state institutions which represented the repressive arm of the Serbian nationalist system, and right-wing politicians: the degree to which Serbia had become a criminal and dysfunctional state became exposed.(Pavlaković 2005b: 39–40)

The lessons of Operation Sabre suggest that the new regime had the means to confront the illicit networks inherited from the old one, and

---

[20] See *Application of the Convention on the Prevention and Punishment of the Crime of Genocide (Bosnia and Herzegovina v. Serbia and Montenegro)*, Judgment, 26 February 2007, ICJ Reports 2007.

[21] Sonja Biserko, interviewed by the author at the Helsinki Committee for Human Rights in Belgrade, 1 November 2007.

apprehend and put on trial key nodes in these networks such as Legija, but it had chosen not to do so. The feared backlash from elements in the security establishment and criminal underworld did not materialize, and Operation Sabre was able to proceed with large-scale arrests and purges. The crackdown enjoyed broad public support, suggesting that many Serbian citizens had in fact expected a thorough overhaul of the system after the October revolution. With hindsight, the decisive factors in the assassination of Đinđić appear to be the initial tolerance of elements deeply implicated in the criminal legacies of the previous regime and the continuing reign of impunity after 5 October, which meant that "members of the Serbian criminal organizations were able to avoid prosecution in a state where they had influence among both the judiciary and government" (Pavlaković 2005b: 34).

The Serbian case calls into question the tendency to frame debates over the impact of international justice in terms of dichotomies – democracy versus stability, reconciliation versus radicalization, and so forth. The role of the ICTY in Serbia over the past decade could be understood as engendering a process of pluralization, which is still ongoing and inconclusive in normative and practical sense. Nevertheless, pluralization represents a significant development in an environment shaped by powerful forces of homogenization and nationalization, where the politics of resistance to dealing with the past has deep roots and powerful patrons. In Chapter 3, I define pluralization as the emergence of transnational discourse, regional politics, and hybrid legal orders in the Balkans, and interpret them as sites where the tensions between nationalism and the rule of law become expressed and negotiated.[22] As in the rest of the region, in Serbia pluralization is encouraged by the ICTY, but it reflects the pervasive interactions of a range of other actors with the norms and structures of international justice. In a sense, international justice can be seen as opening up discursive, political, and legal space for such actors to pursue diverse and often competing projects and purposes. In the remaining part of the chapter, I trace the dynamics of pluralization in public discourse, politics, and law, highlighting how they express the tensions between nationalism and the rule of law and reveal the ongoing attempts to manage and negotiate them.

---

[22] See Chapter 3, § "After the War: The Role of International Justice in the Balkans."

The dynamics of pluralization may be most visible in the legal domain. A specialized War Crimes Chamber of Belgrade High Court and a War Crimes Prosecutor's Office were established in 2003.[23] These structures were created with significant international assistance and involvement, reflecting the intention to build domestic capacities for the prosecution of war crimes that could be used to take over from the ICTY. As of February 2012, the Chamber had prosecuted a total of 385 persons, in 26 completed and 13 ongoing cases.[24] When I interviewed officials and magistrates in Belgrade about the impact of the Tribunal in Serbia, their instinct was to talk about these structures. Rasim Ljajić, who was the minister in charge of Serbia's cooperation with the Tribunal at the time, suggested that without the existence of the ICTY, domestic war crimes trials in Serbia most probably wouldn't have happened.[25] Serbia's War Crimes Prosecutor, Vladimir Vukčević, argued that international justice had created space and momentum that allowed domestic prosecutions to begin, despite prevailing nationalist sentiments: "We wouldn't have been able to start things from here. It would have all been hidden, everyone would have said: These are heroes!"[26]

The War Crimes Chamber occupies a precarious position between the "international" and the "domestic", and embodies the ongoing struggle to manage the tensions between nationalism and the rule of law. It has already completed its first case transferred from the ICTY, *Zvornik*, and its activities are closely monitored by the OSCE, which reports back to the ICTY and supports the trials with capacity building and outreach projects. Moreover, the Chamber has developed extensive regional cooperation in war crimes proceedings with similar structures in Bosnia, Croatia, Montenegro, and even the EULEX mission in Kosovo. Cooperation with Croatia has been particularly

---

[23] A separate Chamber and Prosecutor for Organized Crime were established at the same time. One of their first cases was the assassination of Zoran Đinđić.

[24] See the Web site of the Republic of Serbia, Office of the War Crimes Prosecutor, Cases (10 February 2012), at http://www.tuzilastvorz.org.rs/html_trz/predmeti_eng.htm (accessed 22 February 2012).

[25] Rasim Ljajić, interviewed by the author at the Ministry of Labour, Employment and Social Affairs in Belgrade, 31 October 2007.

[26] Vladimir Vukčević, interviewed by the author at the War Crimes Prosecutor's Office in Belgrade, 1 November 2007.

effective, and dozens of war crimes cases have been exchanged between prosecutors from the two countries. In Serbia itself, the Chamber has become a favorite target of nationalists in the press and political class; in one parliamentary debate, for example, the leader of the SRS called the war crimes prosecutor "an anti-Serb show-off."[27] These elements often portray the Chamber as an extension of the ICTY, prosecuting Serbs for crimes against non-Serbs. The pressures associated with such attacks in the public domain may have informed the prosecutor's decision to initiate proceedings against several Albanians, which in turn has led to accusations by human rights groups that the trials were politically motivated.[28] Other, more powerful pressures have ensured that the vast majority of trials at the War Crimes Chamber involve direct perpetrators rather than their commanders, effectively shielding the Serbian state from confronting its own complicity in the crimes.

Pluralization is also evident in the growing involvement of non-state actors in domestic war crimes proceedings and the emergence of new forms of hybridity, which has attracted little attention from observers despite the fact that it often plays a crucial role in the trials. Since 2003, the Humanitarian Law Center (HLC) and its executive director, Nataša Kandić, have been involved in many of the war crimes cases at all stages of the proceedings: identifying victims and witnesses from Bosnia, Croatia, and Kosovo, encouraging them to testify, and assisting with their protection while they are in Serbia; representing victims in the proceedings; and facilitating the families of the victims to travel to Serbia in order to monitor the proceedings. In effect, these civil society interventions often serve to compensate for the lack of political will and judicial capacity in Serbia. They also enable the participation of witnesses and survivors from neighboring countries, who are inherently suspicious of Serbian institutions and see them as hostile, but

---

[27] Humanitarian Law Center and Documenta, *Transitional Justice in Post-Yugoslav Countries: Report for 2007*, 33, retrieved from http://www.hlc-rdc.org/?p=13820&lang=de (accessed 20 January 2012).

[28] In one of these cases, *Morina*, the evidence against the accused was particularly weak and prompted the presiding judge to state that it was "sad, regrettable and shameful to take advantage of such an event and to bring charges without corroborating evidence." Ibid., 13.

who often come to Belgrade to take part in the proceedings because they trust and respect the HLC (Rangelov 2013b).

The role of international justice is also palpable in public discourse and politics in Serbia, where pluralization is often mediated through the involvement of the EU and its framework for integrating the region, the SAP for South East Europe, which includes full cooperation with the ICTY as a key condition for applicant countries. The role of the EU in the politics of international justice in Serbia has been criticized for using the war crimes conditionality as a bargaining chip, turning it into an instrument for shaping Serbian politics and advancing the EU's strategic priorities in the region, rather than as a catalyst for social and political transformation. The EU suspended accession talks with Serbia in May 2006 over its failure to cooperate with the Tribunal, but later adopted a series of decisions – first to reopen negotiations for a Stabilization and Association Agreement (SAA), then to initial the SAA without ratifying it, and so forth – that appeared to reward Serbia despite its failure to demonstrate full cooperation with the ICTY. These decisions were used strategically by the EU in order to influence Serbian elections and shape reactions to Kosovo's imminent independence. Subotić (2009: 81) puts the issue starkly: "The earlier trade-off – Europe for The Hague – was now replaced by a new one – Europe for Kosovo. Once again, the issue of justice for crimes against humanity became an issue of the lowest order, a matter of deal making and compromise setting, removed as far as possible from the ideas and norms of dealing with the past."

The "policy of appeasement"[29] toward Serbia has a long pedigree in European foreign policy. It could be argued that since the early 1990s, Europe's engagement with Serbia has been driven by two imperatives: a desire to have a partner in Serbia; and a fear of the extremists on the far right. Obrad Kesić (2005: 99) notes that during the war in Bosnia and Herzegovina, "A vicious cycle developed where Milošević used his credibility as peacemaker before an international community desperate for peace in Bosnia to maintain his legitimacy within Serbia." More recently, the "cohabitation" of nationalists and reformers in the "democratic bloc" that took over on 5 October was legitimated and

[29] Biserko interview.

sustained partly by endless compromises and bargains with the EU, until Kosovo's declaration of independence finally made cohabitation untenable.[30] In this environment, pluralization in Serbia has often taken the form of "pragmatist" rhetoric and politics, which negotiates between the nationalist and liberal positions and often frames international justice as a necessary evil. The pragmatist discourse is inherently ambivalent, oscillating between acceptance and rejection of the process of dealing with the past, and gesturing toward multiple audiences. A typical example is the statement of President Boris Tadić during a visit to Sarajevo: "It is important that we condemn all war crimes and prosecute their perpetrators."[31] Is this statement intended to reassure Bosnian Muslims that the Serbian state is committed to hold its own perpetrators accountable? Or is it addressed to Bosnian Serbs, who often complain that the crimes against them are forgotten, seeking to relativize the atrocities committed by Serb forces?

At the same time, the EU's war crimes conditionality has also opened up discursive and political opportunities for the liberal segments of civil society and political class in Serbia, enabling them to pursue projects and purposes that would have been difficult without the involvement of the EU and ICTY, and without the protection afforded by such international connections. Serbia has a fairly small but vocal liberal elite, comprising human rights organizations, artists, public intellectuals, and independent media, which has managed to raise the issue of dealing with the past repeatedly in the public domain, despite the prevailing atmosphere of hostility and powerful forces of resistance. For example, one of the first serious public discussions about the significance of Serbia's European project – the choice

---

[30] When Kosovo declared independence in February 2008 and a number of EU member states recognized the new state, Koštunica demanded termination of accession talks, but Tadić insisted on staying the European course, and the government collapsed over "irreconcilable differences." See "Kosovo Sparks Early Serb Elections," *BBC News*, 8 March 2008, retrieved from http://news.bbc.co.uk/1/hi/world/europe/7285817.stm (accessed 13 January 2012); Tamara Skrozza, "Intervju – Boris Tadić, Predsednik Srbije: Zloupotreba Kosova" [Interview – Boris Tadić, President of Serbia: The Abuse of Kosovo], *Vreme*, 6 March 2008.

[31] "Serbia's Tadic Wants Trials of all War Criminals," *RNW*, 7 July 2011, retrieved from http://www.rnw.nl/international-justice/article/serbias-tadic-wants-trials-all-war-criminals (accessed 20 January 2012).

between technical compliance with EU standards and promotion of European values – was triggered by a series of open letters from civil society coalitions in 2007. The letters were addressed to Brussels at a time when the EU was considering whether to restart its negotiations with Serbia, which had been suspended over its failure to apprehend fugitives such as Ratko Mladić. One of the letters suggested that the European integration of Serbia was more important than cooperation with the ICTY, and that relaxing the conditionality now would facilitate state cooperation with the Tribunal in the future.[32] Another letter emphasized that compromising the conditionality would undermine Europe's credibility and warned that domestic support for European integration was declining, asking the EU to engage not only with the Serbian state but also with society.[33] A third letter insisted that Mladić's arrest and transfer to The Hague should be a precondition for reopening the negotiations: "We want to live in a Serbia committed to establishing the rule of law and accepting the legacy of the past, so that a repetition of these crimes is prevented, the criminal responsibility of the perpetrators is established and justice is served."[34]

Several political parties have also sought to put the question of dealing with the past on the domestic political agenda, including the Civic Alliance of Serbia and the Social Democratic Union, and more recently the Liberal Democratic Party (LDP), which was created in 2005 by one of Đinđić's closest allies, Čedomir Jovanović. The LDP attracts only a small percentage of the vote (5.24 percent in the 2008 elections), but its parliamentary presence has provided an important counterweight to the nationalist and pragmatist rhetoric in parliamentary discussions.[35] As with the liberal sections of civil society, for the LDP the relationship between international justice and the European

---

[32] European Movement in Serbia, Press Release, Belgrade, 5 April 2007, retrieved from http://www.emins.org/sr/press/saopstenja/2007/07–04–05.pdf (accessed 20 January 2012).

[33] Helsinki Committee for Human Rights in Serbia, Press Release, Belgrade, 30 March 2007, retrieved from http://www.helsinki.org.rs/doc/4NGO-Kosovo.pdf (accessed 20 January 2012).

[34] Humanitarian Law Center, Press Release, Belgrade, 4 April 2007, retrieved from http://www.hlc-rdc.org/?p=12889 (accessed 20 January 2012).

[35] Nenad Prokić, interviewed by the author at the offices of the Liberal Democratic Party in Belgrade, 30 October 2007.

project of Serbia often provides a platform for raising the larger issue of dealing with the political and criminal legacies of the Milošević era. As one activist put it, without such connections "it would have been impossible to discuss war crimes the way we do now."[36]

Finally, it should be recognized that these developments are still unfolding, and it may take another decade or more before their significance can be fully understood. The role of international justice in Serbia is not always direct and apparent; it often reflects "unintended consequences," whose cumulative effects have yet to become legible. A good example is the "Srebrenica tape" released during the trial of Slobodan Milošević, which showed a Serbian Orthodox priest giving his blessing to members of the Scorpions unit before they moved on to execute six Bosnian Muslims, including a sixteen-year-old boy. The tape, which had been secured by Kandić with the assistance of the Tribunal, was played over and over on television and deeply shocked the Serbian public[37]: "There were public condemnations on talk shows, and even human rights activists were given full airtime to describe the crime, identify perpetrators, and illuminate the events that had led to the tape's surfacing at The Hague" (Subotić 2009: 63). The media attention and public debate quickly subsided, but since then other events and revelations have continued to spark controversy and contestation in the public domain: the arrests and extraditions of Karadžić and Mladić; public apologies by senior officials and bodies such as RTS, Serbia's national broadcaster; debates sparked by the civil society initiative for RECOM, which advocates the establishment of a regional truth commission; and a seemingly endless series of news reports about war crimes allegations, arrests, and trials in the region and The Hague.

At the time of completing this book, the debate about war crimes in Serbia is reopened once again, this time by the release of a file

---

[36] Staša Zajović, interviewed by the author at the offices of Women in Black in Belgrade, 1 November 2007.

[37] Kandić was able to obtain the tape from an insider with the help of the ICTY, which provided witness protection. Nataša Kandić, interviewed by at the author at the Humanitarian Law Center in Belgrade, 31 October 2011. For a detailed examination of the public reactions to the broadcasting of the Srebrenica tape, see Subotić (2009: 62–66).

implicating the recently appointed chief of staff of the Serbian Armed Forces, Ljubiša Diković, in war crimes committed by forces under his command in Kosovo in 1999.[38] The government strongly rejected the allegations but had to address them somehow, and referred the Diković File to the Office of the War Crimes Prosecutor for examination. The imprint of international justice is palpable in the file itself, which relies to a great extent on facts established by the Tribunal, but more significant is its role in the emergence of discursive and political openings that are enabling local human rights groups to challenge Serbia's power structures by making such claims in the public domain.

CONCLUSION

The retreat of the rule of law in Serbia during the 1990s occurred in the context of brutal wars, targeting of dissidents and political opponents, and a growing capture and criminalization of the Serbian state. These developments challenge conventional understandings as to how to draw the line between war and repressive rule; political and criminal violence; human rights violations committed on the territory of Bosnia, Croatia, and Kosovo, and endemic abuse of power in Serbia itself. They also suggest how nationalism can play a dual role as a political project and discourse on the one side, and a cover for pursuing a range of criminal activities on the other. The more nationalism served as an instrument for political mobilization and legitimation, the more it became inseparable from criminality and abuse of power.

The tensions between nationalism and the rule of law have been reframed in the aftermath of 5 October, reflecting Serbia's struggle to deal with the interconnected political and criminal legacies of the Milošević era. The politics of resistance to dealing with the past in Serbia cannot be explained simply by pointing to the persistence of nationalism after the October revolution without taking into account the entrenched interests of those actors and networks that are implicated

---

[38] Humanitarian Law Center, "File: Ljubiša Diković," HlcIndexOut: 019–3173–2, Belgrade, 23 January 2012, retrieved from http://www.hlc-rdc.org/wp-content/uploads/2012/01/Januar-23–2012-Dikovic-Ljubisa-Dosije1.pdf (accessed 25 January 2012).

in the dark legacies of the 1990s. For such elements in civil society, the state structures, and the criminal underworld, precluding any effort for a critical examination of Serbia's recent past is often a question of survival in the new order, just as the "patriotic" rhetoric they often employ in the public domain is a way of maintaining their legitimacy and influence. The opposition to international justice in Serbia has to be understood as one expression of the deeply rooted politics of resistance to dealing with the past.

The exercise of international justice has not resolved the tensions between nationalism and the rule of law in Serbia; instead, it has encouraged an ongoing process of pluralization of law, politics, and public discourse, which expresses these tensions in new ways and makes legible the continuing struggle for their negotiation. With all of its suspects finally in custody, the ICTY can complete the remaining trials fairly quickly. It may take much longer before international justice itself can be judged and the implications of resistance and pluralization fully understood.

CONCLUSION: LESSONS FROM THE BALKANS AND BEYOND

In a world of pervasive cultural diversity, there is an inherent tension between nationalism and the rule of law. This tension derives from the contradiction between the bounded character of nations and the assumption of equality before the law. In some historical periods, nationalism has served to reinforce the rule of law because it has provided the basis for the legitimacy of the modern state. In such periods, the inclusive aspects of nationalism, such as the extension of citizenship and incorporation of different classes and ethnic groups within a given territory, have been more significant than its exclusive aspects. At the current juncture, the tensions and contradictions between nationalism and the rule of law have become more apparent. On the one hand, the exclusive aspects of nationalism have increasingly come to the fore, challenging the principles of the rule of law and legitimacy of political and legal orders. On the other hand, the instruments of law, particularly in the context of the growth of human rights and international law, have served to offset and moderate the exclusive character of nationalism.

This book has examined the shifting relationship between nationalism and the rule of law at the beginning of the twenty-first century by drawing attention to the many different ways in which the underlying tensions can be expressed and negotiated. It is a mistake to assume that these tensions are relevant only in the context of the more extreme and radical manifestations of nationalism, or only in environments marked by the absence and breakdown of the rule of law. They are also salient in the everyday forms of discrimination and exclusion through which nationhood is reproduced in the routine practices and attitudes of those who make, interpret, and enforce the law. Nationalism can undermine the rule of law not only by subverting the law but also by shaping it. One of the implications of the book is the need to challenge the complacent assumption that some nationalisms are disruptive for the rule of law and others are not, and that some nation-states – those that are liberal, democratic, and legalistic – are immune to the problems that nations and nationalism raise for the rule of law.

These problems are pervasive because all forms of nationalism involve a process of "othering" that produces national subjects and identities by demarcating boundaries and endowing them with moral and political significance. Nationhood is continuously produced and reproduced in this way in public discourse, politics, and social relations, and its interactions with the rule of law in any particular context depend on how exactly this (re)production takes place: it matters a great deal what claims are made, what means are employed, and what practices are implicated. But the larger point is that the relationship between nationalism and the rule of law cannot be grasped by looking only at the legal arena; instead, it requires understanding how nationalism works as a discursive formation, political project, and set of everyday practices that shape social relations. Approaching the tensions between nationalism and the rule of law in this way is important because it encourages us to think about addressing them in different terms, not only by promoting legal change but also by encouraging discursive engagements, political mobilization, and social practices.

One of the central arguments of the book is that the tensions between nationalism and the rule of law can be harnessed for productive purposes, and that unlocking this productive potential depends on the ability of legal processes to open up for public discussion and contestation those issues that implicate the "dark side" of nationalism. Although there is no shortage of such issues, the evidence suggests that some are more important than others. The examples discussed in the book concern fundamental questions about national identity and state legitimacy that arise in the domains of citizenship, transitional justice, and international justice. These are often the sort of questions that upset the balance of remembering and forgetting, which Ernest Renan placed at the heart of nationalism more than a century ago: "Forgetting, I would even go so far as to say historical error, is a crucial factor in the creation of a nation.... Unity is always effected by means of brutality" (Renan 1990: 11). Most nation-states and nationalist movements have such unifying acts of brutality inscribed in their foundations and more recent histories. Some are tacitly celebrated, most are actively forgotten. Perhaps what has changed since Renan's time is that we no longer think about such brutality only in terms of physical violence. The author's country of origin is a good example. What we call ethnic cleansing today paved the way for the creation of an independent Bulgarian state from the ruins of the Ottoman Empire; one century later it was back on the agenda, just before the end of communism heralded the birth of democratic Bulgaria. The recent revival of an aggressive, ethnocentric Bulgarian nationalism at the beginning of the twenty-first century derives in part from our failure to interrogate such legacies of abuse in the public domain, which makes it easier to keep forgetting them.

For those who believe that nationalism cannot be easily transcended but can be managed and transformed, law offers one instrument for interrogating the "dark side" of nationalism in a public and rule-bound framework. To do that, however, we need to think about the role of law and legal institutions in unconventional ways. The revival of interest in the rule of law ideal in recent decades has been accompanied by the emergence of an entire "industry" that seeks to promote the rule of law in a variety of different contexts. International donors and local authorities tend to approach these important tasks in a technical manner, which often depoliticizes the rule of law and neglects its role in the legitimation of political order. The emphasis has been on developing the infrastructure and capacity of legal systems: building courthouses and introducing new technologies; adopting legislation and training judges and prosecutors; improving public communications and creating outreach programs. Measuring the impact of such programs boils down to counting the number of units built, laws adopted, or staff trained. These efforts are, of course, important, but we shouldn't conflate the issues of building state capacity and promoting the rule of law.

An alternative approach emerging from this investigation emphasizes the deliberative character of legal processes. If nationalism works as a discursive formation that shapes social relations and practices, it is important to consider what role law can play in challenging and trans-forming the discourse of nationalism. In the cases examined in the book, domestic courts were unable to bring about such transformative change simply by passing judgment on the excesses of nationalism; in fact, their readings of national history were often complacent and unsatisfactory, even when the judges adhered strictly to the principles of the rule of law. The significance of the judicial process is located elsewhere: in its ability to encourage critical public discussion of the "dark side" of nationalism and its persistence and continuities, bring-ing the past into a productive dialogue with the present. It is the public conversation, sparked by the legal proceedings, that has the potential to interrogate the accepted narratives and myths of nationalism and invite public scrutiny of its submerged and troubling continuities. A deliberative approach suggests that law can play an important role in managing and transforming nationalism when it serves as a vehicle for public debate, opening up for public discussion critical questions of national identity and state legitimacy and encouraging contestation and debate over such questions in the public sphere.

Another central message of the book is that we need to think more deeply about the relationship between nationalism and the rule of law beyond the state. Nations and nationalism organize much of the inter-national legal order and shape the evolving norms and structures of international law, but they do so in contradictory ways. Nation-states are the basic units of analysis in accepted understandings of the inter-national rule of law, which is premised on the principle of state sov-ereignty and aimed at regulating relations between states. At the same time, the international legal regime increasingly addresses other sub-jects and promotes principles and logics that go beyond the nation-state. The book draws attention to the development of international legal norms and structures as a response to nationalism in areas such as accountability for international crimes and human rights more gen-erally, and highlights the ensuing articulation of an international rule of law aimed at suppressing certain manifestations of nationalism and criminalizing their goals and methods. I interpret in this way the evolu-tion of international justice, which reflects a shift in criminalization at the international level from external expansion in the 1940s to ethnic cleansing in the 1990s. These developments are important analytically because they require a different framework for understanding the relationship between nationalism and the rule of law, one that takes into account the emergence of new sites of tension beyond the nation-state and comprehends the interactions of a multiplicity of actors and sources of legitimacy.

But they also have practical implications. International law is often employed as an instrument to address the breakdown of law and order in situations of ethnic conflict and large-scale human rights violations and promote the reconstruction of the rule of law in their aftermath. Conventional thinking about the role of international law in such environments often focuses on issues of compliance, enforcement, or norm diffusion, but my analysis suggests that such approaches are not always useful. They are premised on a clear demarcation between the "international" and the "domestic" and often reflect a top-down understanding of social change, thus effectively reproducing the state-centric framework and missing other important dynamics. In examining the impact of international justice in the former Yugoslavia, I develop an alternative approach that identifies the role of international law in encouraging pluralization of public discourse, politics, and law in the region. These dynamics emerge from the pervasive interactions of diverse social actors with the norms and structures of international justice, and their significance lies in contradicting and partially reversing the homogenizing logic of the region's wars and nationalisms. In the case of the Balkans, the pluralizing effects of international justice can be detected in the emergence of transnational discourse, regional politics, and hybrid legal orders. These pluralized spaces are important because they become sites where the tensions between nationalism and the rule of law are expressed and negotiated. The pluralization perspective calls for rethinking the role of international legal instruments in promoting the rule of law, especially in environments where nationalism presents serious challenges, moving beyond questions of compliance and enforcement to consider how international law may be harnessed to open up new discursive, political, and legal spaces and opportunities.

Finally, there are important lessons from the Balkans for other regions that are emerging from periods of armed conflict and repressive rule, such as the Middle East. Democratization processes often have their origins in popular demands for addressing rule of law failures: state repression; different forms of abuse of power; violations of individual and collective rights. In the ensuing awakening of civil society, nationalist ideas and movements usually represent only one set of agendas and actors among many. And yet, the impulse for democratization can be hijacked by nationalists and other champions of identity politics, as happened in the Balkans, where social movements seeking a transformation of the relationship between state and society ended up paving the way for the rise of a very different political project: claiming the state for one section of society and seeking to exclude and suppress others. When such projects failed to be effectively pursued through democratic means, they relied on violence to impose their logic and achieve their goals. In fact, the wars in the former Yugoslavia were so brutal because extensive use of force was needed to mobilize nations and nationalism. The post-war settlement further entrenched the nationalist logic by creating an assemblage of ethnic states, entities, and enclaves, where the rule of law still struggles to take root long after the hostilities have ended. In all these ways, the resurgence of nationalism can be seen as an outcome of the failures of the rule of law: a consequence and not just a cause of such failures.

Building the rule of law in the Balkans is a daunting task. It requires creative solutions designed to circumvent the blockage at the level of the nation-state and dissolve the dichotomies entrenched by mutually exclusive nationalisms; for example, by promoting regional approaches and bottom-up initiatives that may offer alternative frameworks and logics. The larger question remains: can the rule of law provide an answer to nationalism, even in such difficult environments? I am inclined to end on an optimistic note. My optimism derives from the belief that there are social actors everywhere who come up with new ideas and experiment with innovative solutions to problems that scholars often see as intractable. The best example discussed in the book is RECOM, the civil society initiative for the creation of a regional truth commission to establish the facts of war crimes and other serious violations of human rights committed in the territory of the former Yugoslavia in the period 1991–2001. At the time of this writing, the initiative is at a critical juncture: it has conducted extensive civil society consultations across the region; drafted a statute; and collected hundreds of thousands of signatures from citizens, but it remains to be seen whether the governments in the region will initiate negotiations to establish a commission. Nevertheless, the RECOM process itself is significant for managing to cross ethnic and national divides in the post–Yugoslav space and engaging in a productive dialogue diverse actors, whose identities and politics are often seen as irreconcilable. In a sense, the RECOM initiative is reviving the spirit of the democratization movement from earlier decades, creating a regional framework of public deliberation that seeks to address the most difficult legacies of the disintegration of Yugoslavia, undoing the work of nationalism and building the rule of law from the ground up.

BIBLIOGRAPHY

af Jochnick, Chris and Roger Normand. 1994. "The Legitimation of Violence: A Critical History of the Laws of War." *Harvard International Law Journal* **35**: 49–95.

Akçam, Taner. 2004. *From Empire to Republic: Turkish Nationalism and the Armenian Genocide*. London: Zed Books.

Akhavan, Payam. 1998. "Justice in The Hague, Peace in the Former Yugoslavia? A Commentary on the United Nations War Crimes Tribunal." *Human Rights Quarterly* **20**.4: 737–916.

Allan, T.R.S. 2001. *Constitutional Justice: A Liberal Theory of the Rule of Law*. Oxford: Oxford University Press.

Allen, Tim. 2006. *Trial Justice: The International Criminal Court and the Lord's Resistance Army*. London: Zed Books.

Alvarez, Jose E. 1996. "Nuremberg Revisited: The *Tadic* Case." *European Journal of International Law* **7**.2: 245–264.

Ambos, Kai, Judith Large, and Marieke Wierda, eds. 2009. *Building a Future on Peace and Justice: Studies on Transitional Justice, Conflict Resolution and Development*. Berlin: Springer.

Anderson, Benedict. 1992. *Long-Distance Nationalism: World Capitalism and the Rise of Identity Politics*. Amsterdam: Centre for Asian Studies Amsterdam.

Antonopoulos, Constantine. 2001. "Whatever Happened to Crimes Against Peace?" *Journal of Conflict and Security Law* **6**.1: 33–62.

Aptel, Cécile. 2011. "International and Hybrid Criminal Tribunals: Reconciling or Stigmatizing?" In *Identities in Transition: Challenges for Transitional Justice in Divided Societies*, ed. Paige Arthur, pp. 149–186. New York: Cambridge University Press.

Arendt, Hannah. 1994. *Eichmann in Jerusalem: A Report on the Banality of Evil*. New York: Penguin Books.

Barrington, Lowell W. 2000. "Understanding Citizenship Policy in the Baltic States." In *From Migrants to Citizens: Membership in a Changing World*, eds. Alexander Aleinikoff and Douglas Klusmeyer, pp. 253–301. Washington, DC: The Brookings Institution Press.

Bass, Gary Jonathan. 2000. *Stay the Hand of Vengeance: The Politics of War Crimes Tribunals*. Princeton and Oxford: Princeton University Press.

Batt, Judy and Jelena Obradovic-Wochnik, eds. 2009. *Chaillot Paper No. 116: War Crimes, Conditionality and EU Integration in the Western Balkans*. Paris: EU Institute for Security Studies.

Bauböck, Rainer and Virginie Guiraudon. 2009. "Introduction: Realignments of Citizenship: Reassessing Rights in the Age of Plural Membership and Multi-Level Governance." *Citizenship Studies* **13**.5: 439–450.

Bauman, Zygmunt. 2001. "Wars of the Globalization Era." *European Journal of Social Theory* **4**.1: 11–28.

Beigbeder, Yves. 2006. *Judging War Crimes and Torture: French Justice and International Criminal Tribunals and Commissions (1940–2005)*. Leiden and Boston: Martinus Nijhoff.

Binder, Guyora. 1989. "Representing Nazism: Advocacy and Identity at the Trial of Klaus Barbie." *Yale Law Journal* **98**: 1321–1383.

Biserko, Sonja. 2006. *Human Security in an Unfinished State*. Belgrade: Helsinki Committee for Human Rights.

Blitz, Brad. 2006. "Statelessness and the Social (De)Construction of Citizenship: Political Restructuring and Ethnic Discrimination in Slovenia." *Journal of Human Rights* **5**.4: 383–404.

Boege, Volker, Anne Brown, and Kevin Clements. 2009. "Hybrid Political Orders, Not Fragile States." *Peace Review* **21**.1: 13–21.

Boister, Neil and Robert Cryer, eds. 2008. *Documents on the Tokyo International Military Tribunal: Charter, Indictment and Judgments*. New York: Oxford University Press.

Bojkov, Victor D. 2004. "Bulgaria's Turks in the 1980s: A Minority Endangered." *Journal of Genocide Research* **6**.3: 343–369.

Boomkens, René. 2010. "Cultural Citizenship and Real Politics." *Citizenship Studies* **14**.3: 307–316.

Bosniak, Linda. 2000. "Citizenship Denationalized. Symposium: The State of Citizenship." *Indiana Journal of Global Legal Studies* **7**.2: 447–510.

Breuilly, John. 1993. *Nationalism and the State*. 2nd ed. Manchester: Manchester University Press.

Brochmann, Grete and Idunn Seland. 2010. "Citizenship Policies and Ideas of Nationhood in Scandinavia." *Citizenship Studies* **14**.4: 429–443.

Brubaker, Rogers. 1992. *Citizenship and Nationhood in France and Germany*. Cambridge, MA: Harvard University Press.

1996. *Nationalism Reframed: Nationhood and the National Question in the New Europe*. Cambridge: Cambridge University Press.

2004a. *Ethnicity without Groups*. Cambridge, MA: Harvard University Press.

2004b. "In the Name of the Nation: Reflections on Nationalism and Patriotism." *Citizenship Studies* **8**.2: 115–127.

Brysk, Alison and Gershon Shafir. 2004. "Introduction: Globalization and the Citizenship Gap." In *People Out of Place: Globalization, Human Rights, and the Citizenship Gap*, eds. Alison Brysk and Gershon Shafir, pp. 3–9. London: Routledge.

Calhoun, Craig. 1997. *Nationalism*. Buckingham: Open University Press.

2002. "Imagining Solidarity: Cosmopolitanism, Constitutional Patriotism, and the Public Sphere." *Public Culture* **14**.1: 147–171.

2007. *Nations Matter: Culture, History, and the Cosmopolitan Dream*. London and New York: Routledge.

Canovan, Margaret. 1996. *Nationhood and Political Theory*. Cheltenham: Edward Elgar.

Chinkin, Christine and Iavor Rangelov. 2011. "A Bottom-Up Approach to Redressing Past Violations of Human Rights." In *Bottom-Up Politics: An Agency-Centred Approach to Globalization*, eds. Denisa Kostovicova and Marlies Glasius, pp. 112–126. Basingstoke: Palgrave Macmillan.

Clammer, John. 2007. "Globalisation and Citizenship in Japan." In *Globalisation and Citizenship: The Transnational Challenge*, eds. Wayne Hudson and Steven Slaughter, pp. 30–42. London and New York: Routledge.

Clark, Roger S. 1997. "Nuremberg and Tokyo in Contemporary Perspective." In *The Law of War Crimes: National and International Approaches*, eds. Timothy McCormack and Gerry Simpson, pp. 171–187. The Hague: Kluwer Law International.

Cobban, Helena. 2007. *Amnesty after Atrocity? Healing Nations after Genocide and War Crimes*. Boulder and London: Paradigm Publishers.

Craig, Paul P. 1997. "Formal and Substantive Conceptions of the Rule of Law: An Analytical Framework." *Public Law* **16**: 467–487.

Curtis, Michael. 2002. *Verdict on Vichy*. London: Weidenfeld & Nicolson.

Dedić, Jasminka. 2003. "Discrimination in Granting Slovenian Citizenship." In *The Erased: Organized Innocence and the Politics of Exclusion*, eds. Jasminka Dedić, Vlasta Jalušić and Jelka Zorn, pp. 25–91. Ljubljana: Peace Institute.

Dedić, Jasminka, Vlasta Jalušić and Jelka Zorn, eds. 2003. *The Erased: Organized Innocence and the Politics of Exclusion.* Ljubljana: Peace Institute.

Delanty, Gerard. 2000. *Citizenship in a Global Age: Society, Culture, Politics.* Buckingham: Open University Press.

Deželan, Tomaž. 2011. "Citizenship in Slovenia: The Regime of a Nationalising or Europeanising State?" CITSEE Working Paper 2011/06, available at http://www.law.ed.ac.uk/citsee/workingpapers/ (accessed February 1, 2012).

Dimitrijević, Nenad. 2008. "Serbia after the Criminal Past: What Went Wrong and What Should Be Done." *International Journal of Transitional Justice* 2: 5–22.

Dimitrijević, Vojin. 2005. "The "Public Relations" Problems of International Criminal Courts: Some Lessons to Be Drawn from the Reception of the ICTY in Serbia and Croatia." Paper presented at the international conference "Achievements of the International Criminal Tribunal for the Former Yugoslavia," Ljubljana, September 23–24, 2005.

Djilas, Aleksa. 1991. *The Contested Country: Yugoslav Unity and Communist Revolution, 1919–1953.* Cambridge, MA: Harvard University Press.

Djokić, Dejan. 2002. "The Second World War II: Discourses of Reconciliation in Serbia in Croatia in the Late 1980s and Early 1990s." *Journal of Southern Europe and the Balkans* 4.2: 127–140.

Dobson, Andrew and Derek Bell, eds. 2006. *Environmental Citizenship.* Cambridge, MA: MIT Press.

Douzinas, Costas. 2000. *The End of Human Rights.* Oxford: Hart Publishing.

Dragović-Soso, Jasna. 2002. *"Saviours of the Nation": Serbia's Intellectual Opposition and the Revival of Nationalism.* London: C. Hurst and Co.

Dresch, Paul. 2005. "Introduction: Societies, Identities and Global Issues." In *Monarchies and Nations: Globalisation and Identity in the Arab States of the Gulf,* eds. Paul Dresch and James Piscatori, pp. 1–34. London: I.B.Tauris.

Dworkin, Ronald M. 1978. "Political Judges and the Rule of Law." *Proceedings of the British Academy* 64: 259–287.

Faist, Thomas. 2006. *Beyond Nationhood: Citizenship Politics in Germany since Unification.* Toronto: Munk Centre for International Studies.

Finkielkraut, Alain. 1992. *Remembering in Vain: The Klaus Barbie Trial and Crimes against Humanity.* New York: Columbia University Press.

Fitzpatrick, Peter, ed. 1995. *Nationalism, Racism, and the Rule of Law*. Brookfield, VT: Dartmouth Publishing Company.

Franke, Katherine M. 2006. "Gendered Subjects of Transitional Justice." *Columbia Journal of Gender and Law* **15**.3: 813–821.

Fraser, David. 2005. *Law after Auschwitz: Towards a Jurisprudence of the Holocaust*. Durham: Carolina Academic Press.

Fuller, Lon L. 1969. *The Morality of Law*. 2nd rev. ed. New Haven: Yale University Press.

Gellner, Ernest. 1983. *Nations and Nationalism*. Oxford: Blackwell.

Golsan, Richard J. 2000a. *Vichy's Afterlife: History and Counterhistory in Postwar France*. Lincoln: University of Nebraska Press.

   2000b: *The Papon Affair: Memory and Justice on Trial*. London: Routledge.

Gow, James and Cathie Carmichael. 2000. *Slovenia and the Slovenes: A Small State and the New Europe*. Bloomington and Indianapolis: Indiana University Press.

Griffin, Roger. 1991. *The Nature of Fascism*. New York: St Martin's Press.

Habermas, Jürgen. 1996. *Between Facts and Norms: Contributions to a Discourse Theory of Law and Democracy*, trans. William Regh. Oxford: Polity.

   1998. *The Inclusion of the Other: Studies in Political Theory*. Edited by Ciaran Cronin and Pablo De Greiff. Cambridge, MA: MIT Press.

Hayden, Robert M. 1992. "Constitutional Nationalism in the Formerly Yugoslav Republics." *Slavic Review* **51**.1: 1–15.

   1994. "Recounting the Dead: The Rediscovery and Redefinition of Wartime Massacres in Late- and Post-Communist Yugoslavia." In *Memory, History and Opposition under State Socialism*, ed. Rubie S. Watson, pp. 167–184. Santa Fe: School of American Research Press.

Hayek, F.A. 1960. *The Constitution of Liberty*. Chicago: University of Chicago Press.

Hilberg, Raul. 2003. *The Destruction of the European Jews*. 3rd ed. New Haven: Yale University Press.

Hobsbawm, Eric. 1990. *Nations and Nationalism since 1780: Programme, Myth, Reality*. Cambridge: Cambridge University Press.

Huntington, Samuel P. 1991. *The Third Wave: Democratization in the Late Twentieth Century*. Norman: University of Oklahoma Press.

Ignatieff, Michael. 1994. *Blood and Belonging: Journeys into the New Nationalism*. London: Vintage.

Independent International Commission on Kosovo. 2000. *The Kosovo Report: Conflict, International Response, Lessons Learned*. Oxford: Oxford University Press.

Jalušič, Vlasta. 1994. "Troubles with Democracy: Women and Slovene Independence." In *Independent Slovenia: Origins, Movements, Prospects*, eds. Jill Benderly and Evan Kraft, pp. 135–157. Basingstoke: Macmillan.

2003. "Organized Innocence." In *The Erased: Organized Innocence and the Politics of Exclusion*, eds. Jasminka Dedić, Vlasta Jalušić, and Jelka Zorn, pp. 7–24. Ljubljana: Peace Institute.

Jalušič, Vlasta and Jasminka Dedić. 2007. "(The) Erasure – Mass Human Rights Violation and Denial of Responsibility: The Case of Independent Slovenia." *Human Rights Review* **9**: 93–108.

Joppke, Christian. 2003. "Citizenship between De- and Re-Ethnicization." Russell Sage Foundation Working Paper # 204, March 2003, available at http://printfu.org/joppke (accessed August 18, 2011).

2007a. "Transformation of Citizenship: Status, Rights, Identity." *Citizenship Studies* **11**.1: 37–48.

2007b. "Transformation of Immigrant Integration: Civic Integration and Antidiscrimination in the Netherlands, France, and Germany." *World Politics* **59**.2: 243–273.

Josipović, Ivo. 2005. "Implementation of International Criminal Law in the National Legal System and the Liability for War Crimes: Example of the Republic of Croatia." In *Responsibility for War Crimes: Croatian Perspective – Selected Issues*, ed. Ivo Josipović, pp. 185–233. Zagreb: University of Zagreb Faculty of Law.

Jovic, Dejan. 2009. "Croatia after Tudjman: The ICTY and Issues of Transitional Justice." In *Chaillot Paper No. 116: War Crimes, Conditionality and EU Integration in Western Balkans*, eds. Judy Batt and Jelena Obradovic-Wochnik, pp. 13–27. Paris: EU Institute for Security Studies.

Kaldor, Mary. 1999. *New and Old Wars: Organized Violence in a Global Era*. Cambridge: Polity Press.

2004. "Nationalism and Globalization." *Nations and Nationalism* **10**.1–2: 161–177.

Kalyvas, Stathis N. 2001. "'New' and 'Old' Civil Wars: A Valid Distinction?" *World Politics* **54**.1: 99–118.

Kardov, Kruno. 2007. "Remember Vukovar: Memory, Sense of Place, and the National Tradition in Croatia." In *Democratic Transition in Croatia: Value Transformation, Education and Media*, eds. Sabrina P. Ramet and Davorka Matić, pp. 63–88. College Station: Texas A&M University Press.

Kastoryano, Riva. 2006. "Redefining German Unity: From Nationality to Citizenship." In *Citizenship and Ethnic Conflict: Challenging the Nation-State*, ed. Haldun Gülalp. London: Routledge.

Keating, Michael. 2009. "Social Citizenship, Solidarity and Welfare in Regionalized and Plurinational States." *Citizenship Studies* **13**.5: 501–513.

Kesić, Obrad. 2005. "An Airplane with Eighteen Pilots: Serbia after Milošević." In *Serbia since 1989: Politics and Society under Milošević and After*, eds. Sabrina P. Ramet and Vjeran Pavlaković. Seattle: University of Washington Press.

Kibe, Takashi. 2006. "Differentiated Citizenship and Ethnocultural Groups: A Japanese Case." *Citizenship Studies* **10**.4: 413–430.

Klinar, Peter. 1994. "Social and Ethnic Stratification: Global Social and Ethnic Relations." In *Small Societies in Transition: The Case of Slovenia*, eds. Frane Adam and Gregor Tomc, pp. 99–116. Ljubljana: Slovene Sociological Association.

Knežević-Hočevar, Duška. 2004. "Vanishing Nation: Discussing Nation's Reproduction in Post-Socialist Slovenia." *Anthropology of East Europe Review* **22**.2: 22–30.

Kohn, Hans. 1944. *The Idea of Nationalism*. New York: Macmillan.

Koller, David S. 2005. "The Moral Imperative: Toward a Human-Rights Based Law of War." *Harvard International Law Journal* **46**.1: 231–264.

Kraft, Evan, Milan Vodopivec, and Milan Cvikl. 1994. "On Its Own: The Economy of Independent Slovenia." In *Independent Slovenia: Origins, Movements, Prospects*, eds. Jill Benderly and Evan Kraft, pp. 201–223. Basingstoke: Macmillan.

Kymlicka, Will. 1995. *Multicultural Citizenship: A Liberal Theory of Minority Rights*. Oxford: Oxford University Press.

2000. "Nation-Building and Minority Rights: Comparing East and West." *Journal of Ethnic and Migration Studies* **26**.2: 183–212.

LeBor, Adam. 2002. *Milošević: A Biography*. London: Bloomsbury.

Levy, Daniel and Yfaat Weiss, eds. 2002. *Challenging Ethnic Citizenship: German and Israeli Perspectives on Immigration*. New York: Berghahn Books.

Longva, Anh Nga. 2005. "Neither Autocracy nor Democracy but Ethnocracy: Citizens, Expatriates, and the Socio-Political Regime in Kuwait." In *Monarchies and Nations: Globalisation and Identity in the Arab States of the Gulf*, eds. Paul Dresch and James Piscatori, pp. 114–135. London: I.B. Tauris.

MacLean, Sandra J., David R. Black, and Timothy M. Shaw, eds. 2006. *A Decade of Human Security: Global Governance and New Multilateralisms*. Aldershot: Ashgate.

MacMaster, Neil. 2002. "The Torture Controversy (1998–2002): Towards a "New History" of the Algerian War?" *Modern & Contemporary France* **10**.4: 449–459.

Malović, Stjepan and Gary W. Selnow. 2001. *The People, Press, and Politics of Croatia.* Westport: Praeger.

Mamdani, Mahmood. 1996. *Citizen and Subject: Contemporary Africa and the Legacy of Late Colonialism.* Princeton: Princeton University Press.

Mann, Michael. 2005. *The Dark Side of Democracy: Explaining Ethnic Cleansing.* Cambridge: Cambridge University Press.

Marshall, T.H. 1992 [1950]. *Citizenship and Social Class.* London: Pluto Press.

Mastnak, Tomaž. 1994. "From Social Movements to National Sovereignty." In *Independent Slovenia: Origins, Movements, Prospects*, eds. Jill Benderly and Evan Kraft, pp. 93–111. Basingstoke: Macmillan.

McCormack, Timothy. 1997. "From Sun Tzu to the Sixth Committee: The Evolution of an International Criminal Law Regime." In *The Law of War Crimes: National and International Approaches*, eds. Timothy McCormack and Gerry Simpson, pp. 31–63. The Hague: Kluwer Law International.

McMahon, Patrice C. and David P. Forsythe. 2008. "The ICTY's Impact on Serbia: Judicial Romanticism Meets Network Politics." *Human Rights Quarterly* **30**.2: 412–435.

Mégret, Frédéric. 2011. "The Lagacy of the ICTY as Seen through Some of Its Actors and Observers." *Goettingen Journal of International Law* **3**.3: 1011–1052.

Mello, Patrick A. 2010. "In Search of New Wars: The Debate about a Transformation of War." *European Journal of International Relations* **16**.2: 297–309.

Midlarsky, Manus I. 2011. *Origins of Political Extremism: Mass Violence in the Twentieth Century and Beyond.* Cambridge: Cambridge University Press.

Miljković, Maja and Marko Attila Hoare. 2005. "Crime and the Economy under Milošević and His Successors." In *Serbia since 1989: Politics and Society under Milošević and After*, eds. Sabrina P. Ramet and Vjeran Pavlaković, pp. 192–226. Seattle: University of Washington Press.

Miller, David. 1995. *On Nationality.* Oxford: Clarendon.

Miller, Richard Lawrence. 1995. *Nazi Justiz: Law of the Holocaust.* Westport: Praeger.

Mirić, Jovan. 2002. *Zlocin i kazna: Politološko-pravni ogedi o ratu, zločini, krivinji i oprosti* [*Crime and Punishment: Politico-Legal Perspectives on*

War, Crimes, Responsibility and Forgiveness]. Zagreb: Srpsko kulturno
   društvo "Prosvjeta."

Myerson, Moses Hyman. 1944. *Germany's War Crimes and Punishment: The
   Problem of Individual and Collective Criminality*. Toronto: Macmillan
   Co. of Canada.

Nedelsky, Nadya. 2003. "Constitutional Nationalism's Implications for
   Minority Rights and Democratization: The Case of Slovakia." *Ethnic
   and Racial Studies* **26**.1: 102–128.

Norrie, Alan. 1993. *Crime, Reason and History: A Critical Introduction to
   Criminal Law*. London: Weidenfeld & Nicolson.

Okey, Robin. 1999. "The Legacy of Massacre: The 'Jasenovac Myth' and
   the Breakdown of Communist Yugoslavia." In *The Massacre in History*,
   eds. Mark Levene and Penny Roberts, pp. 263–282. New York: Berghahn
   Books.

Orentlicher, Diane F. 1998. "Citizenship and National Identity." In
   International Law and Ethnic Conflict, ed. David Wippman, pp. 296–325.
   Ithaca and London: Cornell University Press.

Osiel, Mark. 1997. *Mass Atrocity, Collective Memory, and the Law*. New
   Brunswick: Transaction.

Özkirimli, Umut. 2000. *Theories of Nationalism: A Critical Introduction*.
   Basingstoke: Macmillan.

Parekh, Bhikhu. 2000. *Rethinking Multiculturalism: Cultural Diversity and
   Political Theory*. Basingstoke: Macmillan.

Pavlaković, Vjeran. 2005a. "Introduction: Serbia as a Dysfunctional State."
   In *Serbia since 1989: Politics and Society under Milošević and After*, eds.
   Sabrina P. Ramet and Vjeran Pavlaković, pp. 3–10. Seattle: University
   of Washington Press.

   2005b. "Serbia Transformed? Political Dynamics in the Milošević Era
   and After." In *Serbia since 1989: Politics and Society under Milošević
   and After*, eds. Sabrina P. Ramet and Vjeran Pavlaković, pp. 13–54.
   Seattle: University of Washington Press.

Paxton, Robert O. 2004. *The Anatomy of Fascism*. New York: Knopf.

Payne, Stanley G. 1995. *A History of Fascism, 1914–1945*. Madison:
   University of Wisconsin Press.

Peled, Yoav. 2005. "Restoring Ethnic Democracy: The Or Commission and
   Palestinian Citizenship in Israel." *Citizenship Studies* **9**.1: 89–105.

   2008. "The Evolution of Israeli Citizenship: An Overview." *Citizenship
   Studies* **12**.3: 335–345.

Peruško, Zrinjka. 2007. "Media and Civic Values." In *Democratic Transition
   in Croatia: Value Transformation, Education and Media*, eds. Sabrina

P. Ramet and Davorka Matić, pp. 224–244. College Station: Texas A&M University Press.

Peskin, Victor and Mieczyslaw P. Boduszynski. 2003. "International Justice and Domestic Politics: Post-Tudjman Croatia and the International Criminal Tribunal for the Former Yugoslavia." *Europe-Asia Studies* **55**.7: 1117–1142.

Petrovic, Drazen. 1994. "Ethnic Cleansing – An Attempt at Methodology." *European Journal of International Law* **5**.1: 342–359.

Popovski, Vesna. 1996. "Citizenship and Ethno-politics in Lithuania." *International Politics* **33**.1: 45–55.

Ramet, Sabrina P. 1999. *Balkan Babel: The Disintegration of Yugoslavia from the Death of Tito to the War for Kosovo*. 3rd ed. Boulder: Westview Press.

2005a. "Under the Holy Lime Tree: The Inculcation of Neurotic and Psychotic Syndromes as a Serbian Wartime Strategy, 1986–95." In *Serbia since 1989: Politics and Society under Milošević and After*, eds. Sabrina P. Ramet and Vjeran Pavlaković, pp. 125–142. Seattle: University of Washington Press.

2005b. "The Politics of the Serbian Orthodox Church." In *Serbia since 1989: Politics and Society under Milošević and After*, eds. Sabrina P. Ramet and Vjeran Pavlaković, pp. 255–285. Seattle: University of Washington Press.

Rangelov, Iavor. 2004. "International Law and Local Ideology in Serbia." *Peace Review* **14**.3: 331–337.

2013a. "The Role of Transnational Civil Society." In *Responding to Genocide: The Politics of International Action*, eds. Adam Lupel and Ernesto Verdeja, pp. 203–233. Boulder, CO: Lynne Rienner Publishers.

2013b. "Contesting the Rule of Law: Civil Society and Legal Institutions." In *Civil Society and Transitions in the Western Balkans*, eds. Vesna Bojicic-Dzelilovic, James Ker-Lindsay, and Denisa Kostovicova, pp. 71–84. Basingstoke: Palgrave Macmillan.

Rangelov, Iavor and Ruti Teitel. 2011. "Global Civil Society and Transitional Justice." In *Global Civil Society 2011: Globality and the Absence of Justice*, eds. Martin Albrow and Hakan Seckinlegin, pp. 162–177. Basingstoke: Palgrave Macmillan.

Ratner, Steven S. 1998. "The Schizophrenias of International Criminal Law." *Texas International Law Journal* **33**.1: 237–256.

Raz, Joseph. 1979. *The Authority of Law*. Oxford: Clarendon.

Renan, Ernest. 1990 [1882]. "What Is a Nation?" In *Nation and Narration*, ed. Homi Bhabha. London and New York: Routledge.

Rousso, Henry. 1991. *The Vichy Syndrome: History and Memory in France since 1944*. Cambridge, MA: Harvard University Press.

Rupel, Dmitrij. 1987. "Odgovor na Slovensko Narodno Vprašanje." *Nova Revija* **4**(57): 57–74.

  1994. "Slovenia's Shift from the Balkans to Central Europe." In *Independent Slovenia: Origins, Movements, Prospects*, eds. Jill Benderly and Evan Kraft. Basingstoke: Macmillan.

Sassen, Saskia. 2006. *Territory, Authority, Rights: From Medieval to Global Assemblages*. Princeton: Princeton University Press.

Scott, Joan Wallach. 2007. *The Politics of the Veil*. Princeton: Princeton University Press.

Segesser, Daniel Marc and Myriam Gessler. 2005. "Raphael Lemkin and the International Debate on the Punishment of War Crimes (1919–1948)." *Journal of Genocide Research* 7.4: 453–468.

Shachar, Ayelet. 2002. "The Thin Line between Imposition and Consent: A Critique of Birthright Membership Regimes and Their Implications." In *Breaking the Cycles of Hatred: Memory, Law and Repair*, ed. Martha Minow. Princeton: Princeton University Press.

Shaw, Jo. 2010. "The Constitutional Mosaic across the Boundaries of the European Union: Citizenship Regimes in the New States of South Eastern Europe." CITSEE Working Paper 2010/07, available at http://www.law.ed.ac.uk/citsee/workingpapers/ (accessed 1 February 2011).

Shepard, Todd. 2006. *The Invention of Decolonization: The Algerian War and the Remaking of France*. Ithaca: Cornell University Press.

Shklar, Judith N. 1986. *Legalism: Law, Morals and Political Trials*, 2nd ed. Cambridge, MA: Harvard University Press.

Siddle, Richard. 2003. "The Limits to Citizenship in Japan: Multiculturalism, Indigenous Rights, and the Ainu." *Citizenship Studies* 7.4: 447–462.

Simpson, Gerry J. 2007. *Law, War and Crime: War Crimes Trials and the Reinvention of International Law*. Cambridge: Polity.

Slaughter, Anne-Marie. 1998. "Pushing the Limits of the Liberal Peace: Ethnic Conflict and the 'Ideal Polity'." In *International Law and Ethnic Conflict*, ed. David Wippman, pp. 128–144. Ithaca and London: Cornell University Press.

Smith, Anthony D. 1986. *The Ethnic Origins of Nations*. Oxford: Blackwell.

1991. *National Identity.* London: Penguin.

1995. *Nations and Nationalism in a Global Era.* Cambridge: Polity.

1998. *Nationalism and Modernism: A Critical Survey of Recent Theories of Nations and Nationalism.* New York: Routledge.

2001. *Nationalism: Theory, Ideology, History.* Cambridge: Polity.

Smith, Graham. 1996. "When Nations Challenge and Nations Rule: Estonia and Latvia as Ethnic Democracies." *International Politics* **33**.1: 25–41.

Smith, Graham, Vivien Law, Andrew Wilson, Annette Bohr, and Edward Allworth. 1998. *Nation-Building in the Post-Soviet Borderlands: The Politics of National Identities.* London: Routledge.

Smooha, Sammy. 1997. "Ethnic Democracy: Israel as an Archetype." *Israel Studies* **2**.2: 198–241.

Snyder, Jack and Leslie Vinjamuri. 2003/2004. "Trials and Errors: Principle and Pragmatism in Strategies of International Justice." *International Security* **28**.3: 5–44.

Søberg, Marius. 2007. "Croatia since 1989: The HDZ and the Politics of Transition." In *Democratic Transition in Croatia: Value Transformation, Education and Media*, eds. Sabrina P. Ramet and Davorka Matić, pp. 31–62. College Station: Texas A&M University Press.

Soysal, Yasemin. 1994. *Limits of Citizenship: Migrants and Postnational Membership in Europe.* Chicago: University of Chicago Press.

Štiks, Igor. 2010. "A Laboratory of Citizenship: Shifting Conceptions of Citizenship in Yugoslavia and Its Successor States." CITSEE Working Paper 2010/02, available at http://www.law.ed.ac.uk/citsee/working-papers/ (accessed 1 February 2011).

Subotić, Jelena. 2009. *Hijacked Justice: Dealing with the Past in the Balkans.* Ithaca: Cornell University Press.

Šumi, Irena. 2004. "Postsocialism, or What? Domestication of Power and Ideology in Slovenia." *Anthropology of East Europe Review* **22**.2: 76–83.

Tamanaha, Brian Z. 2004. *On the Rule of Law: History, Politics, Theory.* Cambridge: Cambridge University Press.

Tamir, Yael. 1993. *Liberal Nationalism.* Princeton: Princeton University Press.

Teitel, Ruti. 2000. *Transitional Justice.* New York: Oxford University Press.

2003. "Transitional Justice Genealogy." *Harvard Human Rights Journal* **16**: 69–94.

2011. *Humanity's Law*. New York: Oxford University Press.

Thomas, Robert. 1999. *The Politics of Serbia in the 1990s*. New York: Columbia University Press.

Trahan, Jennifer. 2011. "The Rome Statute's Amendment on the Crime of Aggression: Negotiations at the Kampala Review Conference." *International Criminal Law Review* **11**.1: 49–104.

Tully, James. 1995. *Strange Multiplicity: Constitutionalism in an Age of Diversity*. Cambridge and New York: Cambridge University Press.

United Nations War Crimes Commission (UNWCC). 1948. *History of the United Nations War Crimes Commission and the Development of the Law of War*. London: H.M.S.O.

Vasić, Miloš. 2005. *Atentat na Zorana Đinđića* [*The Assassination of Zoran Đinđić*]. Belgrade: Politika.

Vega, Judith and Pieter Boele van Hensbroek. 2010. "The Agendas of Cultural Citizenship: A Political-Theoretical Exercise." *Citizenship Studies* **14**.3: 245–257.

Weber, Eugène. 1979. *Peasants into Frenchmen: The Modernisation of Rural France, 1870–1914*. London: Chatto and Windus.

Weisberg, Richard. 1996. *Vichy Law and the Holocaust in France*. New York: New York University Press.

Wilke, Christiane. 2011. "Staging Violence, Staging Identities: Identity Politics in Domestic Prosecutions." In *Identities in Transition: Challenges for Transitional Justice in Divided Societies*, ed. Paige Arthur, pp. 118–148. New York: Cambridge University Press.

Yamanaka, Keiko. 2004. "Citizenship, Immigration and Ethnic Hegemony in Japan." In *Rethinking Ethnicity: Majority Groups and Dominant Minorities*, ed. Eric P. Kaufmann. London: Routledge.

Young, Iris Marion. 1990. *Justice and the Politics of Difference*. Princeton: Princeton University Press.

Yuval-Davis, Nira. 1997. *Gender and Nation*. London: SAGE.

Zorn, Jelka. 2009. "A Case for Slovene Nationalism: Initial Citizenship Rules and the Erasure." *Nations and Nationalism* **15**.2: 280–298.

INDEX